INDIVIDUALS IN THUCYDIDES

INDIVIDUALS
IN THUCYDIDES

BY

H. D. WESTLAKE

Professor of Greek
University of Manchester

CAMBRIDGE

AT THE UNIVERSITY PRESS

1968

Published by the Syndics of the Cambridge University Press
Bentley House, 200 Euston Road, London, N.W.1
American Branch: 32 East 57th Street, New York, N.Y.10022

© Cambridge University Press 1968

Library of Congress Catalogue Card Number: 68–23918

Standard Book Number: 521 07246 8

Printed in Great Britain
at the University Printing House, Cambridge
(Brooke Crutchley, University Printer)

CONTENTS

PREFACE

IT has long been my conviction that the art of historical writing as practised by Thucydides did not remain static but underwent appreciable modifications as his *History* progressed. It was still a young and relatively undeveloped art when he wrote, and there was plenty of scope for new ideas. One aspect of his work in which some change of approach seems to me to be traceable is his presentation of leading individuals, and this is the subject of my book.

I have, I hope, made due acknowledgement in footnotes to modern works from which I have profited. Because I have, for a variety of reasons, been slow to complete this book, it has been impossible to take account of some recent publications. It will be very clear that I am much indebted to work on Thucydides by A. W. Gomme and by J. de Romilly, especially to the second and third volumes of his *Historical Commentary on Thucydides* and to her *Histoire et raison chez Thucydide*. Among works by scholars of an earlier period I have found most stimulating those of Eduard Meyer and Eduard Schwartz, even when, as has often been the case, I have found myself disagreeing with their conclusions. The work from which I have learned most, however, is the *History* of Thucydides. I have endeavoured to make his *History*, rather than what modern scholars have written about it, the starting point of my investigations.

The spelling of Greek proper names in this book is doubtless inconsistent. I have been unashamedly wayward and have adopted the form to which I have myself become most accustomed. In another respect also I have not tried to avoid inconsistency. When discussing what is written in works which are still very much alive by authors who died many centuries ago, it is sometimes difficult to decide whether to use the past tense or the present. I have used whichever seemed to be the more natural in the context.

PREFACE

I am very grateful to two colleagues and friends, D. M. Leahy and D. M. MacDowell, who read most of this work in draft and have given me the benefit of their advice on many aspects of it, both general and detailed. They have helped me to remove inaccuracies, inconsistencies and infelicities. For those remaining I alone am responsible. My thanks are also due to A. G. Woodhead for valuable suggestions and to T. J. Quinn, who has read the proofs. I owe a special debt to Miss Joan Sutcliffe, who has typed the manuscript not only of this book but of all my published work over a period of nearly twenty years.

H.D.W.

University of Manchester

ABBREVIATIONS

Books and articles cited by the name of the author only are listed below. Elsewhere the customary abbreviations have been used.

Adcock	F. E. Adcock, *Thucydides and his History*, Cambridge, 1963.
Brunt	P. A. Brunt, 'Thucydides and Alcibiades', *Revue des études grecques*, LXV (1952), 59–96.
Busolt	G. Busolt, *Griechische Geschichte*, III, 2, Gotha, 1904.
Delebecque	E. Delebecque, *Thucydide et Alcibiade*, Aix-en-Provence, 1965.
de Romilly (1)	Jacqueline de Romilly, *Thucydides and Athenian Imperialism* (Eng. trans.), Oxford, 1963.
de Romilly (2)	Jacqueline de Romilly, *Histoire et raison chez Thucydide*, Paris, 1956.
de Romilly (Budé)	Jacqueline de Romilly, *Thucydide, La guerre du Péloponnèse*, Collection des universités de France, Paris, Livres I (1953), II (1962), VI–VII (1955, in collaboration with L. Bodin).
Dover	K. J. Dover, *Thucydides, Books vi–vii* (2 vols.), Oxford, 1965.
Finley	John H. Finley, Jr., *Thucydides*, Cambridge (Mass.), 1942.
Freeman	E. A. Freeman, *History of Sicily*, III, Oxford, 1892.
Gomme (1)	A. W. Gomme, *A Historical Commentary on Thucydides*, Oxford, I (1945), II–III (1956).
Gomme (2)	A. W. Gomme, *The Greek Attitude to Poetry and History*, Berkeley, 1954.
Gomme (3)	A. W. Gomme, *More Essays in Greek History and Literature*, Oxford, 1962.
Grundy	G. B. Grundy, *Thucydides and the History of his Age*, I–II (2nd ed.), Oxford, 1948.
Hatzfeld	J. Hatzfeld, *Alcibiade*, Paris, 1940 (reprinted 1951).
Luschnat	O. Luschnat, *Die Feldherrnreden im Geschichtswerk des Thukydides*, Philologus, Supplbd. XXXIV, 2, 1942.

ix

Schwartz   E. Schwartz, *Das Geschichtswerk des Thukydides*, Bonn, 1929.

Sealey   R. Sealey, 'Athens and the Archidamian War', *Proceedings of the African Classical Associations*, I (1958), 61–87.

Steup   *Thukydides*, erklärt von J. Classen, bearbeitet von J. Steup (8 vols.), Berlin, 1963 (reprint).

Woodhead   A. G. Woodhead, 'Thucydides' Portrait of Cleon', *Mnemosyne*, XIII (1960), 289–317.

References in which the name of the author is not stated are to the *History* of Thucydides. Where two or more consecutive references are to the same book of the *History*, the book number is not normally repeated.

CHAPTER I

INTRODUCTION

THE *History* of Thucydides falls into two parts. These two parts, which consist of 1. 1 to 5. 24 and 5. 25 to 8. 109, are very roughly equal in length, and it will be convenient, even though some slight sacrifice of mathematical accuracy is involved, to refer to them throughout this work as 'the first half' and 'the second half'.[1] The first half is an account of the Archidamian war (431–421 B.C.) and its causes. The second half is unfinished: it was demonstrably intended to cover the period from the Peace of Nicias in 421 to the fall of Athens in 404 (cf. 5. 26. 1), but it breaks off abruptly when it has reached the autumn of 411. Thucydides insists, in a tone reserved for expressions of opinion on controversial topics, that the whole period of twenty-seven years from 431 to 404 must be regarded as a single war, because the Peace of Nicias produced only an ὕποπτος ἀνοκωχή (5. 26. 2–4, cf. 25. 3). He does, however, mark a division in his *History* at the Peace of Nicias by making a fresh start at this point (26. 1, γέγραφε δὲ καὶ ταῦτα ὁ αὐτὸς Θουκυδίδης Ἀθηναῖος)[2] and inserting a passage commonly known as the second introduction (26. 1–6). Besides discussing the length and unity of the war, Thucydides here dwells upon his own special qualifications to write a history of it, particularly the advantage given to him by his banishment in being in a position to obtain information from both sides (26. 5). This second introduction has attracted attention mainly

---

[1] The first half amounts to approximately four-sevenths of the whole; but so far as the present work is concerned, this disparity is more than counterbalanced by the fact that the first book of the *History*, dealing with the causes of the war, does not contribute much to the subject under discussion.

[2] This phrase may be compared with the opening words of the *History*, Θουκυδίδης Ἀθηναῖος ξυνέγραψε τὸν πόλεμον τῶν Πελοποννησίων καὶ Ἀθηναίων (1. 1. 1).

because it has figured prominently in the controversy, now more than a century old, about the composition of the *History*. Since it is applicable, or at least partly applicable, to the whole *History*, it would, in the opinion of many scholars, have been more appropriately prefixed to the first half than to the second. It is therefore thought to provide evidence that Thucydides completed, or almost completed, the first half when the Peace of Nicias appeared to have brought the war to an end, and that he subsequently added a continuation only when this view proved to be an illusion. No work on the *History* can ignore the problem of its composition, which is by no means without relevance to the present investigation. Here, however, the crucial point about the division into two halves relates to structure rather than to date of composition. Whether a long interval, or a short interval, or no interval at all, is believed to have elapsed between the composition of the first half and that of the second, the existence of a structural division between the two halves can hardly be disputed, since it is made by Thucydides himself.

The purpose of this book is to examine the treatment of leading individuals in the *History* and to try to show that in this single aspect of the work divergences may be observed between the first half and the second. Such divergences, if they exist, might be attributable to the distinctive characteristics of the leading individuals whose achievements are recorded. It would, for example, be almost impossible for any historian to deal with the careers of Pericles and Alcibiades in exactly the same way. Other extraneous factors, such as basic differences in the subject-matter to be treated or in the sources of information available to Thucydides, might well have exerted some influence. On the other hand, divergences not readily explained by considerations of this kind must surely owe their origin to changes in his own general outlook and interests, in his interpretation of his duty as a historian, in his selection and presentation of historical material. They may therefore help to show that his technique did not remain static and even to shed a little light upon his intellectual development, which is a very difficult subject.[1] The present investigation cannot be expected to make a very substantial contribution to the controversy about the composition of the *History*, since any modifications in the methods of Thucydides in treating individuals could have developed in a relatively short time. Nevertheless, if such modifications proved to be extensive, the case for believing that the first half was virtually completed before the second half was even envisaged, which on other grounds has much to recommend it, would be somewhat strengthened.

This work will attempt a broad and fairly comprehensive enquiry into Thucydidean methods of presenting leading individuals, which will not be confined to consideration of the question whether or not these methods remain the same in both halves of the *History*. To have focused attention exclusively upon features suggesting that divergences do exist would have involved risks of producing a distorted picture and even of prejudging the outcome of the discussion. Thucydides seldom expresses his own views on any subject in explicit terms: he chooses rather to convey them to the reader indirectly in various subtle ways, and he does this very frequently, since it is his aim to provide not only information but also instruction. How he applies this technique to the presentation of individuals will be examined here. Suggestions also will be offered to explain why on some points he makes his opinion absolutely clear while on others he gives only a hint or seems to withhold judgement entirely; why he deals with certain actions or topics in detail, with others briefly or not at all. Consideration of such matters may or may not be relevant to the question whether there are differences between the first half of the *History* and the second. It is therefore hoped that this work may make

---

[1] W. Schadewaldt, *Die Geschichtschreibung des Thukydides* (1929), 35–40, attempts in a few brilliantly written pages to trace the intellectual development of Thucydides. He admits, however, that this part of his work depends on factors which are not really demonstrable. His conclusions are based upon the stratification theory, now rejected by most scholars, namely that Thucydides undertook a fundamental revision of his first draft when he realised the unity of the whole Peloponnesian war, adding large sections of what is here called the first half of the *History*.

some broader contribution to the study of Thucydides by noting his working methods and habits of mind. Although its aim is not primarily historical, it may even throw some light upon the individuals whose part in the *History* is examined. The treatment of each individual chosen for study will be investigated separately. Because in many cases their careers overlapped, a certain amount of reiteration is inevitable, but its extent will, so far as possible, be limited by the use of cross-references. A substantial amount of narrative has been included: without it the presentation of each individual by Thucydides could not have been adequately examined. The choice of leaders may well be thought to be arbitrary. The most celebrated of them choose themselves, but there is much to be learned by studying the presentation of some who played relatively minor roles. In deciding whether or not to include such lesser figures the yardstick adopted here is the prominence given to them by Thucydides rather than their importance as historical characters.[1] Twelve leaders have been selected for study: six of them are Athenians—Pericles, Phormio, Cleon, Nicias, Demosthenes, Alcibiades—and six are Spartans—Archidamus, Cnemus, Alcidas, Brasidas, Gylippus, Astyochus.[2]

[1] Among those who might seem to have claims to be included are Hermocrates, Agis and Tissaphernes. Hermocrates has been excluded mainly because I have already published in *Ryl. Bull.* XLI (1958), 239–68, a study of his career, which is to a considerable extent concerned with the treatment of him by Thucydides. Agis is an unsatisfactory figure in the *History*: Thucydides presents him unsympathetically and seems to have been unable to obtain trustworthy information about Spartan military planning during the summer of 418, when the battle of Mantinea was fought. Tissaphernes is a prominent character in the eighth book, and his diplomatic skill evidently impressed Thucydides, but he remains a mystery, and on some important issues his feelings and motives could only be inferred (8. 46. 5; 56. 3; 87. 1–5). Themistocles and Pausanias have been excluded because they died many years before the Peloponnesian war began and appear only in digressions, where Thucydides presents them in a different way from contemporary personalities.

[2] It is a coincidence that there are six of each: the selection has not been influenced by any desire for symmetry. It would be a false symmetry, since most of the Athenians play a much larger part in the *History* than most of the Spartans.

CHAPTER II

EXPLICIT JUDGEMENTS ON ABILITY AND CHARACTER

BEFORE examining how Thucydides presents each of the twelve leaders chosen for separate study, a preliminary investigation will be conducted which may throw some light upon his treatment of individuals. In this chapter passages in the *History* containing explicit judgements on ability and character will be collected and discussed. The purpose of this survey, which is not confined to the twelve selected leaders, is twofold. In the first place, it will show that in all parts of the *History* such explicit judgements are few and mostly brief.[1] Thucydides is evidently chary of expressing his own views about leading individuals, and where he does so, there is often some special reason. It is abundantly clear that he is not content to accept public opinion uncritically, though he sometimes reports it, or merely to echo the views of his informants; that, unless he has convincing evidence and is very confident that he is right, he is unwilling to commit himself. He differs in this respect from other ancient historians, who show a much greater readiness to include explicit verdicts on ability and character.[2] He adopts his normal practice, mentioned in the previous chapter, of implanting judgements in the mind of the reader by indirect means. Accordingly, if one wishes to discover what he feels about the ability or character of any individual—or indeed how far he is prepared, or is conscious of any obligation, to commit himself even by implication—it is

---

[1] Several consist only of ἀνήρ followed by a brief definitive phrase.

[2] As will be pointed out in an appendix to this chapter (see below, 16–19).

necessary to examine thoroughly all the relevant narrative and speeches. Even when he does express personal views, these do not in many cases amount to a general, comprehensive assessment. The second aim of this chapter is to examine how the passages on ability and character are distributed in the *History* and to see what pattern, if any, emerges. Although these passages make only a small contribution to the general presentation of individuals, a study of their distribution may provide the basis of a preliminary test on a small scale, which could be a useful prelude to the much wider investigation to be conducted in the following chapters. Before any conclusions are drawn, the passages must be listed and their distribution noted.

Not all the descriptive phrases attached to the names of individuals[1] are relevant to this discussion but only those relating to ability or character, where Thucydides is voicing personal opinions not necessarily acceptable to others. Little exercise of judgement is involved in describing a person as powerful; provided that the facts are accurately recorded, there cannot be much scope for disagreement. For example, the power enjoyed by Eurymachus at Thebes in 431 (2. 2. 3, ἀνδρὸς Θηβαίων δυνατωτά-του) can hardly have been in doubt.[2] For the same reason passages defining the political affiliations or sympathies of individuals will not be considered here.[3] Another type of passage to be excluded consists of those in which Thucydides reports the reputation enjoyed by an individual among contemporaries without stating whether or not he subscribes to it. In a phrase sometimes misinterpreted as a personal judgement by Thucydides,[4] the reputa-

---

[1] G. T. Griffith, *Proc. Camb. Phil. Soc.* VII (1961), 21–33, has collected and studied these phrases, and his paper has been of great value to me in the present chapter. His aim is rather different from mine because he expressly excludes consideration of judgements made by Thucydides (27).

[2] Cf. 7. 1. 4 (on the Sicel Archonides) and 8. 5. 3 (on Agis at Decelea in 413, which is more complex).

[3] Cf. 8. 90. 1 on Aristarchus, a member of the Four Hundred (ἀνὴρ ἐν τοῖς μάλιστα καὶ ἐκ πλείστου ἐναντίος τῷ δήμῳ).

[4] Cf. P. Cloché, *Ét. class.* XII (1943), 83, cf. 86, 89; W. Mueri, *Mus. Helv.* IV (1947), 259–60.

tion of the Spartan king Archidamus for intelligence and integrity is mentioned (1. 79. 2, ἀνὴρ καὶ ξυνετὸς δοκῶν εἶναι καὶ σώφρων).[1] Finally, passages will not be considered relating to persons whose careers were over before the Peloponnesian war began. Simple examples are his brief references to the intelligence of Theseus (2. 15. 2) and to the uprightness and intelligence of the Peisistratidae (6. 54. 5). More complex is the celebrated passage in which he analyses the genius of Themistocles in considerable detail (1. 138. 3).

Of the passages relating to persons active during the Peloponnesian war there are, as is natural, more expressing opinions on ability than on character, though a few are concerned with both. Thucydides takes care to impress upon his readers that the character of a leading figure might influence events very profoundly, as is seen most clearly in a well-known passage on Alcibiades (6. 15. 3–4). On the other hand, the moral behaviour of individuals is not in itself important to him, and, unlike Plutarch, he does not use ethical standards as his yardstick in assessing them. He is looking rather for military and political capacity or incapacity, because these qualities had most effect upon the course of the war, and it is to intellectual ability, which for him is crucial for the planning and direction of great enterprises, that he gives most weight.[2] The relevant passages will most conveniently be listed in the order in which they appear in his *History*.

1. Pericles (three passages)

Of the three relevant passages two are brief and similar to one another: 1. 127. 3, ὢν γὰρ δυνατώτατος τῶν καθ᾽ ἑαυτὸν καὶ ἄγων τὴν πολιτείαν, and 1. 139. 4, ἀνὴρ κατ᾽ ἐκεῖνον τὸν χρόνον πρῶτος Ἀθηναίων, λέγειν τε καὶ πράσσειν δυνατώτατος. The relevance of the first passage to the present discussion is questionable: it might

---

[1] See below, 123.
[2] Cf. J. de Romilly, *Entretiens Fondation Hardt*, IV (1958), 42–8, who suggests that to be able to predict the future is to Thucydides a vitally important element in the intellectual make-up of great leaders.

be excluded on the ground that it refers only to the power of Pericles and not to his ability. On the other hand, the wording of the second passage, which seems to be deliberately designed to reinforce the first,[1] suggests that δυνατώτατος in the first passage may refer partly to ability. At the point where the first passage occurs Pericles has not been mentioned in the account of the events immediately preceding the outbreak of war, and because he is to play a predominant role, some description of him is essential here.[2] The third passage, which is much more complex, is the celebrated vindication of Periclean policy in which Thucydides states his own views on the reasons why the Athenians lost the war (2. 65. 5–13). Though not a general assessment of Pericles, as will be seen in the next chapter,[3] it does dwell upon the quality of his war leadership, in which, according to Thucydides, he showed himself to be immeasurably superior to his successors. The opinions about him expressed here by Thucydides were certainly not acceptable to all contemporaries.

2. Cleon (two passages)

Two passages on Cleon, like the first two on Pericles, are very similar: 3. 36. 6, ὢν καὶ ἐς τὰ ἄλλα βιαιότατος τῶν πολιτῶν τῷ τε δήμῳ παρὰ πολὺ ἐν τῷ τότε πιθανώτατος and 4. 21. 3, ἀνὴρ δημαγωγὸς κατ᾽ ἐκεῖνον τὸν χρόνον ὢν καὶ τῷ πλήθει πιθανώτατος. Thucydides is not content to allow the words and deeds of Cleon to speak for themselves. Although δημαγωγός has not yet become a term of disparagement, βιαιότατος is a very strong word not used by Thucydides of any other contemporary,[4] while πιθανώτατος acknowledges the ability of Cleon as an orator but is not by any means complimentary.[5] It carries with it a tinge of unscrupulous-

---

[1] Griffith, Proc. Camb. Phil. Soc. vii, 28–9.
[2] See below, 26, where this point is more fully considered.
[3] See below, 41–2.   [4] He uses βίαιος of Pausanias (1. 95. 1).
[5] Woodhead, 298, who cites Dem. 37. 48, where it is coupled with πονηρός. Cleon is pictured by the Sausage-seller as abusing the Knights ξυνωμότας λέγων πιθανώτατα (Knights 628–9).

ness and dishonesty, suggesting not the leadership practised by Pericles but the methods of his successors. In other passages Thucydides shows strong disapproval of Cleon, including some attributing dishonourable motives to him, but none is an explicit statement of opinion.

3. Brasidas (one passage)

An expression of opinion about the character and ability of Brasidas occurs in a passage explaining how his mission to the northern Aegean had the effect of creating among allies of Athens a favourable impression of Spartan leaders, which continued even into the years after the Sicilian expedition (4. 81. 1–3). The discussion is concerned mainly with the reputation of Brasidas, both at Sparta (1, δοκοῦντα δραστήριον εἶναι ἐς τὰ πάντα) and abroad (3, δόξας εἶναι κατὰ πάντα ἀγαθός), and not with the opinions of Thucydides about him. Nevertheless, integrity and intelligence (2, ἀρετὴ καὶ ξύνεσις) are attributed to him as though his possession of them was indisputable, so that the passage does convey an assessment of him if a slightly indirect one.[1]

4. Alcibiades (one passage)

The famous sketch of Alcibiades (6. 15. 3–4), which has some remarkable features, includes judgements both on character and on ability. Nowhere else does Thucydides provide nearly so much information about the behaviour of a contemporary personality in private life. His reason for referring to the personal extravagance and licentiousness of Alcibiades is that they influenced the course of history:[2] he expresses the conviction that they ultimately

---

[1] ἑαυτὸν παρασχὼν δίκαιον καὶ μέτριον (2) is noteworthy: it was doubtless the intention of the Spartan government that officers sent overseas should behave justly and moderately, but very few of them did. I have not included 4. 84. 2, ἦν δὲ οὐδὲ ἀδύνατος, ὡς Λακεδαιμόνιος, εἰπεῖν. Because of the qualification ὡς Λακεδαιμόνιος this backhanded compliment, which is expressed in a somewhat casual parenthesis, hardly amounts to a judgement on the ability of Brasidas.

[2] Griffith, Proc. Camb. Phil. Soc. VII, 28.

had a disastrous effect upon the fortunes of Athens (*ibid.* 3). At the same time he pays an unusually warm tribute to the military leadership of Alcibiades (*ibid.* 4, δημοσίᾳ κράτιστα διαθέντι τὰ τοῦ πολέμου).[1] An earlier passage in which Alcibiades is mentioned for the first time (5. 43. 2) strikes an exceptionally personal note but does not include any assessment of his character or ability.

5. *Athenagoras* (*one passage*)

This demagogue is described in terms evidently designed to mark him out as the Syracusan counterpart of Cleon: 6. 35. 2, δήμου τε προστάτης ἦν καὶ ἐν τῷ παρόντι πιθανώτατος τοῖς πολλοῖς. Thucydides uses πιθανός only here and in the two passages on Cleon quoted above. The derogatory tone of this introductory description is abundantly confirmed by the violent and misguided speech of Athenagoras which follows it (6. 36–40).

6. *Hermocrates* (*one passage*)

The assessment of Hermocrates, whom Thucydides probably admired more than any contemporary leader except Pericles, is remarkably compressed, embracing intellectual qualities, military competence and personal bravery: 6. 72. 2, ἀνὴρ καὶ ἐς τἄλλα ξύνεσιν οὐδενὸς λειπόμενος καὶ κατὰ τὸν πόλεμον ἐμπειρίᾳ τε ἱκανὸς γενόμενος καὶ ἀνδρείᾳ ἐπιφανής. Although Thucydides makes very clear in narrative and speeches his belief that Hermocrates was endowed with these qualities, he attributes them to him explicitly here. He has chosen to do so at the point where all the qualities to which he refers began to show themselves most prominently.[2] He could have chosen the first appearance of Hermocrates, which was as the principal speaker at the Congress

---

[1] On the date of composition see below, 15. The passage will be further discussed in the chapter on Alcibiades (see below, 219–20).

[2] Griffith, *Proc. Camb. Phil. Soc.* VII, 30–1.

of Gela in 424; there only his name and patronymic are given (4. 58).[1]

7. Nicias (two passages)

Two passages on Nicias are concerned with character and not with ability. Both belong to the end of his life, though he was a prominent figure in the Archidamian war from 427 onwards. In a parenthesis attention is drawn to one aspect of his character which had a disastrous effect upon the fortunes of the Athenians in Sicily: 7. 50. 4, ἦν γάρ τι καὶ ἄγαν θειασμῷ τε καὶ τῷ τοιούτῳ προσκείμενος.[2] In the other passage Thucydides, after recording the execution of Nicias, pays an unexpected and uncharacteristic tribute to his personal virtues: 7. 86. 5, ἥκιστα δὴ ἄξιος ὢν τῶν γε ἐπ᾽ ἐμοῦ Ἑλλήνων ἐς τοῦτο δυστυχίας ἀφικέσθαι διὰ τὴν πᾶσαν ἐς ἀρετὴν νενομισμένην ἐπιτήδευσιν. This passage can best be considered in its context, and discussion of it must accordingly be postponed to a later chapter.[3]

8. Antiphon (one passage)

The ability of Antiphon is rated very highly: 8. 68. 1, ἀνὴρ Ἀθηναίων τῶν καθ᾽ ἑαυτὸν ἀρετῇ τε οὐδενὸς ὕστερος καὶ κράτιστος ἐνθυμηθῆναι γενόμενος καὶ ἃ γνοίη εἰπεῖν. Thucydides goes on to note the value of his advice on political and legal matters and the outstanding quality of the speech delivered by him in his own defence when he was put on trial after the fall of the Four Hundred (ibid. 1–2). This passage is exceptionally detailed. The principal reason doubtless is that, as Thucydides here states, Antiphon shunned the limelight owing to popular distrust of his reputation for cleverness; hence he appears very little in the

---

[1] It is true that his speech (4. 59–64) is full of Thucydidean sentiments and arguments, but he is not a mere mouthpiece, cf. Ryl. Bull. XLI (1958), 242–4.

[2] Plutarch, Mor. (De Mal. Herod.) 855b points out that Thucydides might have referred to this characteristic of Nicias in less gentle terms. If the second slave in the opening scene of the Knights is to be identified with Nicias, a passage in this scene (32–4) shows that he had in 424 already acquired the reputation of being superstitious.

[3] See below, 209–11.

narrative,[1] and his great ability cannot be brought to the notice of the reader by the normal method of indirect implication. Nevertheless, both the warmth and the personal tone of this judgement are remarkable, especially as Thucydides certainly did not share the political convictions of Antiphon, who seems always to have favoured the narrowest form of oligarchy.[2]

9. Phrynichus (one passage)

Immediately after the passage on Antiphon, Thucydides reports the motives of Phrynichus in supporting the oligarchical revolution and adds a comment on his fortitude: 8. 68. 3, πολύ τε πρὸς τὰ δεινά, ἐπειδήπερ ὑπέστη, φερεγγυώτατος ἐφάνη. The general picture of Phrynichus presented by Thucydides gives prominence mainly to intellectual qualities such as shrewdness and inventiveness.[3] Here, in referring to his trustiness when facing dangerous situations, Thucydides touches on another side of his personality which is less obviously deducible from the narrative.

10. Theramenes (one passage)

In the next sentence after his comment on Phrynichus, Thucydides expresses his opinion on the ability of Theramenes, who is mentioned here for the first time: 8. 68. 4, ἀνὴρ οὔτε εἰπεῖν οὔτε γνῶναι ἀδύνατος. Unlike Antiphon and Phrynichus, Theramenes survived the fall of the Four Hundred, and this assessment would

---

[1] Apart from this passage he is mentioned only in 8. 90. 1–2.

[2] The widely accepted belief that Thucydides was the pupil and friend of Antiphon rests on very shaky evidence, as is shown by J. S. Morrison, *Proc. Camb. Phil. Soc.* VII (1961), 53 and 56. It is probably no more than an over-bold inference by Caecilius of Caleacte, or some predecessor, from the presentation of him by Thucydides.

[3] Cf. 8. 27. 5 (ἔδοξεν ... οὐκ ἀξύνετος εἶναι), where Thucydides certainly subscribed to the general belief in the intelligence of Phrynichus; 48. 4–7, where it is clear that Thucydides approved of the views of Phrynichus expressed in a speech reported in *oratio obliqua*; and 50–1, describing the extraordinary episode in which Phrynichus communicated with the Spartan Astyochus (see below, 243–7).

have been more easily compared with the treatment of him in the narrative if the work of Thucydides had been completed and had included the last years of the war. Theramenes is, however, prominent in the account of the intrigues designed to overthrow the Four Hundred (8. 89–94). Although his motives and those of his associates are expressly condemned (89. 2–3), he is seen to have shown good judgement throughout, as well as much skill in stirring up popular feeling against his opponents.

11. *Hyperbolus* (one passage)

When reporting the murder of Hyperbolus at Samos shortly before the establishment of the Four Hundred, Thucydides describes him in language worthy of, and perhaps even influenced by, Aristophanes:[1] 8. 73. 3, μοχθηρὸν ἄνθρωπον, ὠστρακισμένον οὐ διὰ δυνάμεως καὶ ἀξιώματος φόβον, ἀλλὰ διὰ πονηρίαν καὶ αἰσχύνην τῆς πόλεως. No mention has been made of Hyperbolus while he was active in Athenian political life before his ostracism. Hence it is necessary to explain here who he was; but the context does not demand more than a statement that he was a demagogue and had been ostracised. Thucydides has chosen to pass judgement upon him in terms even harsher than those used of Cleon.[2]

This survey of explicit judgements on ability and character shows that the practice of Thucydides in this respect underwent an appreciable change as his work proceeded. It is true that the number of passages is not much larger in the second half of his work than in the first, but the number of individuals on whom he comments is substantially larger in the second half; and from

---

[1] Aristophanes uses μοχθηρός (*Knights* 1304) and πονηρία (*Clouds* 1066; cf. *Peace* 684) of Hyperbolus. Thucydides uses μοχθηρός in this passage only.

[2] A passage about the Corinthian Ariston, 7. 39. 2, ἄριστος ὢν κυβερνήτης τῶν μετὰ Συρακοσίων (cf. Griffith, *Proc. Camb. Phil. Soc.* VII, 26), might have been included in the list. I have excluded it not so much because Ariston is a minor figure but rather because Thucydides is here, one imagines, merely repeating what some informant has told him about the professional skill of Ariston and is not expressing his own judgement.

other factors the change will be seen to be much more marked than it appears to be at first sight. The lengthy discussion about Pericles (2. 65. 5–13) was demonstrably written after the fall of Athens, and the passage in which Brasidas is credited with integrity and intelligence (4. 81. 1–3) cannot have been written much earlier, since it refers to the period after the Sicilian expedition. Each of these passages shows some discrepancies with the narrative in which it is set; accordingly both are believed, with good reason, to be later additions to the narrative, which may therefore be presumed to have been written relatively early.[1] Thus the only passages belonging to the main narrative of the Archidamian war and its antecedents are two relating to Pericles (1. 127. 3 and 139. 4) and two relating to Cleon (3. 36. 6; 4. 21. 3). As has already been pointed out, it is questionable whether the first of the passages on Pericles should be included.[2] Anyone writing a history of the Peloponnesian war would be obliged to rank Pericles and Cleon as persons of very great importance whose influence, for good or ill, on the course of events was profound. They are the two contemporary leaders about whom Thucydides felt most strongly; for Pericles he felt greater admiration than for anyone else, for Cleon greater distaste. It is easy to believe that in each of these two cases, being particularly desirous of giving his readers the clearest possible guidance, he was not content to adopt his usual technique of implied assessment, but chose—a choice unparalleled in this part of his work—to include an explicit statement of his own opinion. The foregoing survey suggests

---

[1] Gomme (3), 92–101. Griffith, *Proc. Camb. Phil. Soc.* VII, 29–30, drawing attention to a syntactical awkwardness in the first sentence of the passage on Brasidas (4. 81. 1), suggests that here was the point at which the later addition was joined to the original text. If this suggestion is accepted, Thucydides originally reported only the reputation of Brasidas for energy without expressing any opinion of his own; the passage would then be parallel to that on the reputation of Archidamus (1. 79. 2), which, as pointed out above (6–7), is not a personal judgement. 2. 100. 2 on Archelaus of Macedon, another passage believed to be a later addition, could be regarded as an estimate of ability, though in form it is rather a record of achievement.

[2] See above, 7–8. It will be suggested below (60) that the treatment of Cleon is in many respects altogether exceptional.

that, though continuing to pass judgement on the ability and character of individuals mainly by indirect methods, he became less reluctant to express his own views. He also began to include persons who, though not unimportant, were much less famous than Pericles and Cleon. This development may have been the outcome of increased confidence in his own judgement or of a feeling that he had not provided his less discerning readers with sufficiently definite guidance. It could also have been influenced by his increasing conviction, to which attention will be drawn in other chapters, that the course of history was largely determined by the personality of its leading figures and their relations with one another. Whatever the origin of this change, it undoubtedly took place.

There is reason to believe that this tendency on the part of Thucydides to become more disposed to include his own judgements on ability and character is not only a late development but a very late development. It is true that several of the passages cited from the second half of his work belong to his account of the Sicilian expedition, which was very probably composed soon after it ended.[1] The sketch of Alcibiades, however, which is the fullest and most significant of these (6. 15. 3–4), almost certainly refers to the end of the war and is therefore believed to have been added long after the main narrative of the sixth and seventh books was completed.[2] It has already been seen that the long discussion on Pericles and the passage on Brasidas must have been written towards the end of the war or after its close. Hence a disproportionately large number of the passages listed above either belong to the eighth book or are late additions to other books.

---

[1] To the works cited in C.Q. VIII (1958), 109 n. 1, on this topic, may now be added A. Andrewes, *Historia*, X (1961), 7–14.

[2] de Romilly (1), 214 and 223; Andrewes, *ibid.* 9–10; Adcock, 132–5.

APPENDIX TO CHAPTER II

THE HABITS OF OTHER HISTORIANS

Other Greek historians commit themselves more readily than Thucydides, even in the latest parts of his work, to expressions of opinion about the ability and character of individuals. If they use indirect methods of suggesting judgements to their readers, they do so much less freely than he does, and they tend to be much less wary of accepting mere hearsay. It is not their practice when assessing individuals to weigh merit and demerit against one another so scrupulously as he does. A brief survey, not designed to be at all exhaustive, will show how wide the differences are.

The *History* of Herodotus is a very personal work, in which he expresses his own views very freely on all manner of subjects, including the ability and character of individuals. He mentions a vast number of persons, of whom many appear only in a single episode, and often he attaches to their names short descriptions evaluating their qualities. The phrase ἀνὴρ δόκιμος, which is so common as to be almost a mannerism (cf. 1. 158. 2; 3. 75. 3; 4. 155. 1; 7. 141. 1), is too vague to be of much significance.[1] Bravery is the quality most commonly attributed to individuals, either in the simple phrase ἀνὴρ ἀγαθός (6. 114 and 117, 2; 9. 75, cf. 71. 2) or in other ways (1. 123. 1, Κύρῳ...ἐόντι τῶν ἡλίκων ἀνδρηιοτάτῳ, cf. 7. 99. 1 and 107. 1). In contrast to these, Aristagoras is described as ψυχὴν οὐκ ἄκρος (5. 124. 1). Phanes of Halicarnassus and Onesilus a Carian are credited with military virtues evidently not confined to personal bravery (3. 4. 1; 5. 111. 1). Intellectual shrewdness is another quality ascribed by Herodotus to a number of persons. Of some he merely uses σοφός (cf. 1. 96. 1; 2. 49. 2; 3. 85. 1; 5. 50. 2); the wisdom of others is somewhat more fully defined (6. 70. 3 on Demaratus; 8. 110. 1, ἐφάνη ἐὼν ἀληθέως σοφός τε καὶ εὔβουλος, on Themistocles).[2] Herodotus also passes moral judgements: Aristeides is highly praised (8. 79. 1, τὸν ἐγὼ νενόμικα...ἄριστον ἄνδρα γενέσθαι ἐν Ἀθήνῃσι καὶ δικαιότατον), while Artaÿctes is condemned as a Persian who failed to live up to Persian standards (9. 116. 1, ἀνὴρ μὲν Πέρσης, δεινὸς δὲ καὶ ἀτάσθαλος). Actions planned by Oroetes (3. 120. 1)

---

[1] Similarly λόγιμος (cf. 9. 16. 1 and 37. 1) and τῶν ἡλίκων πρῶτος (1. 34. 2; 5. 42. 1).

[2] In its context this phrase is less complimentary than it appears to be. Another passage on Themistocles (8. 124. 1) refers only to his reputation for wisdom.

and by Etearchus a Cretan (4. 154. 2) are described as impious (οὐκ ὅσιον).[1]

Some of the differences between the methods of Herodotus and Thucydides arise from differences in subject-matter. Herodotus was writing not about contemporaries but, for the most part, about persons long dead and in many cases evidently known to him only from some local tale picked up in the course of his travels. Sometimes, in the manner of the fairy story, he merely ascribes to a person the qualities displayed in the episode which he is about to relate, assuming that these qualities are typical. His whole attitude towards the treatment of individuals, which differs widely from that of Thucydides, is influenced by his belief that, as part of his duty as a historian, he is in some degree under an obligation to record what he has been told (cf. 7. 152. 3, ὀφείλω λέγειν τὰ λεγόμενα). It is largely because of his punctiliousness in this respect that the process of sifting and evaluating conflicting evidence derived from prejudiced sources has often been left incomplete. Consequently he sometimes fails to provide his readers with a clear and coherent picture of a leading personality; apparently he has not formed such a picture in his own mind. A notable example is his presentation of Cleomenes.[2]

The treatment of individuals by Xenophon in the Hellenica bears some superficial resemblance to that of Thucydides, but fundamentally the affinity is not at all close. The Hellenica is mainly a somewhat mechanical record of events interspersed with lively descriptions of selected episodes, which are notable for their literary and dramatic qualities. This method of writing history leaves little scope for the exercise of judgement, except in the choice of these episodes. Unlike Thucydides, Xenophon gives hardly any guidance to the reader trying to understand the course of history, and his attitude towards events and the persons involved in them is determined largely by his unconcealed prejudices as well as by his quest for dramatic episodes. He is much interested in personality and likes to introduce personal touches, but the limitations of his approach to history make him a poor judge of ability. He admires most the virtues which he claims for himself in the Anabasis when describing his own experience of military command, especially the capacity to win the devotion of men on active

---

[1] I have excluded passages paying tribute to the professional skill of an individual, such as 1. 23 (Arion), 3. 125. 1 (Democedes) and 8. 8. 1 (Scyllies).

[2] I am here particularly indebted to suggestions by D. M. Leahy.

17

service. He tends to rate minor figures who seemed to him to have exhibited these virtues above much greater men for whom he feels less sympathy.[1] He shows no disinclination to attribute distinctive qualities, good and bad, to persons about whom he writes. In some cases he merely reports the reputation of an individual, using δοκῶν or ἐδόκει (cf. *Hell.* 1. 1. 31 on Hermocrates; 3. 1. 8 on Dercylidas; 4. 8. 31 on Thrasybulus; 5. 2. 28 on Phoebidas); but this is not due to a cautious reluctance to commit himself to a personal opinion, since his narrative fully substantiates the verdict which he cites. He does, however, explicitly state his own opinion, in some instances uncomplimentary, about a number of individuals, most of them being of secondary importance. The most striking examples are the following: Satyrus (2. 3. 54, θρασυτάτου τε καὶ ἀναιδεστάτου); Cinadon (3. 3. 5); Peisander (3. 4. 29); Diphridas (4. 8. 22, εὔχαρίς τε οὐκ ἧττον τοῦ Θίβρωνος, μᾶλλον τε συντεταγμένος καὶ ἐγχειρητικώτερος στρατηγός); Nicolochus (5. 4. 65); Callias (6. 3. 3); Alexander of Pherae (6. 4. 35).

Theopompus was notorious for the violence of his emotional judgements about individuals. Many fragments censure leading personalities for profligacy in private life. A typical example describes Apollocrates, the son of the younger Dionysius: ἀκόλαστος ἦν καὶ φιλοπότης (*F. Gr. Hist.* 115 F 185). Other persons castigated on moral grounds include Chabrias (F 105), Hegesilochus of Rhodes (F 121), Charidemus (F 143), Pharax (F 192), Timolaus of Thebes (F 210), Chares (F 213), Archidamus (F 232), and the younger Dionysius (F 283). He was fond of exposing the licentiousness of persons to whom he attributed great ability in public life: the best-known example is Philip of Macedon (F 27 and elsewhere), but others were similarly presented (cf. F 97 on Callicrates). Intellectual qualities also came in for criticism, as in a fragment describing Thrasydaeus, a Thessalian supporter of Philip: μικρὸν μὲν ὄντα τὴν γνώμην, κόλακα δὲ μέγιστον (F 209). Fragments show that Theopompus did pass some favourable judgements, for in addition to Philip persons praised by him included Lysander (F 20, cf. F 333), Antisthenes (F 295) and Agesilaus (F 321). Because many fragments of Theopompus happen to have been preserved by writers like Athenaeus with a taste for scandal, his habit of expressing violent opinions about individuals is in some danger of being exaggerated in modern times. It did, however, make a deep impression upon ancient critics, notably

---

[1] I have discussed the shortcomings of his criteria in regard to individuals in *Ryl. Bull.* XLIX (1966), 246–69.

Dionysius of Halicarnassus (T20a) and Plutarch (F333), who were able to read his works in full. In his treatment of individuals Theopompus was evidently almost the antithesis of Thucydides: he judged them emotionally rather than logically, and to him the personal element in history, including the private lives of its characters, seems to have been more important than any other.

The treatment of individuals by other historians of the fifth and fourth centuries cannot be determined with any confidence; but the author of the *Hellenica Oxyrhynchia* (14. 2 and 20. 6, Bartoletti) and Ephorus (*F. Gr. Hist.* 70F71 and F207) were prepared to state explicitly their opinions about certain leading personalities.

In the aspect of his technique examined in this chapter Thucydides shows a characteristic individuality of outlook. He adopted methods dissimilar from those of other historians, because his aims and principles in writing history differed from theirs. As in many other respects, he broke away from his predecessors and was not imitated by his successors, who through imperfect understanding of his methods learned very little from him.

FIRST HALF

(1. 1–5. 24)

FIRST HALF

CHAPTER III

PERICLES

IT was a basic belief of Thucydides that of all the leading figures in the Peloponnesian war Pericles was by far the greatest. To persuade his readers to accept his assessment of Pericles and of Periclean war policy was among his major aims. He does not, however, provide them with a complete and sharply drawn portrait. Other characters in the *History* whose qualities of leadership and whose influence upon the course of the war are not comparable with those of Pericles make a far livelier impact upon the reader, largely because light is thrown upon their feelings and motives and upon their personal contacts with other leading figures. It is true that the career of Pericles belongs mainly to the period before the war began and that he survived its outbreak by only two and a half years (2. 65. 6). It is also true that he was notoriously reserved and aloof, as is attested by other contemporary authorities. Nevertheless, Thucydides seems to have deliberately chosen to direct the attention of his readers only to certain characteristics of Pericles: the far-sighted creator of a strategy which could and should have won the war, the persuasive orator who was almost always able to sway the assembly, the resolute leader of an irresolute populace, the idealist who championed the Athenian way of life.[1] This choice has certainly been influenced by the criterion of relevance to the war;[2] throughout his work Thucydides has interpreted very narrowly his duty as a historian of the war, and he normally excludes purely biographical detail and anecdote. There is, however, abundant, if not always wholly reliable, evidence from other sources to show that in his treatment

---

[1] These qualities correspond roughly with those claimed by Pericles for himself in his last speech (2. 60. 5).
[2] The relevance of the Funeral Speech will be discussed below, 34–5.

of Pericles he has omitted much that must have been known to him and is by no means entirely irrelevant to the history of the war.[1] His purpose is not so much to provide a general account of the part played by Pericles in the first stages of the war and its antecedents and to show how influential he was; it is rather to select, for the instruction of the reader, the principal issues of this period and to demonstrate the wisdom of Pericles in dealing with each of them. An examination of narrative and speeches will indicate whether this interpretation has any validity. It will be an examination with a limited aim and will not, it may be noted, be concerned at all with some problems much discussed in recent years, namely whether he has given an accurate and complete account of Periclean strategy, and whether that strategy was in the circumstances preferable to any other.[2]

Pericles is first mentioned by Thucydides in the sketch of the Pentecontaetia, where the references to him relate solely to military operations. There are very brief reports on his expedition to the Corinthian Gulf (I. III. 2-3) and his campaign in Euboea, which after being interrupted by the revolt of Megara and the Peloponnesian invasion of Attica was subsequently resumed (114. 1-3). His part in the suppression of the Samian revolt is somewhat more fully described (115. 2-117. 3), and there is perhaps an implication that, unofficially at least, he had a greater share than his colleagues in the direction of the Athenian operations.[3] Nowhere,

---

[1] The brilliant sketch of Pericles by E. Meyer, *G.d.A.* IV, I (1944), 697–702 (which naturally applies to his whole career) owes less to Thucydides than to other authorities, especially Plutarch, and yet is not biography but history.

[2] J. Vogt, *Hist. Zeit.* CLXXXII (1956), 249–66, criticised by H. Strasburger, *Hermes*, LXXXVI (1958), 29 n. 5; M. Chambers, *Harv. Stud.* LXII (1957), 79–92; Sealey, 78–9.

[3] K. J. Dover, *J.H.S.* LXXX (1960), 61–77, argues, rightly, in my opinion, that the phrase δέκατος αὐτός used here (116. 1) and in 2. 13. 1 of Pericles as strategos does not mean that he had any constitutional authority superior to that of his colleagues. I doubt, however, whether Thucydides intends the phrase to be a reminder that Pericles 'was not an autocrat but a member of a board of *ten* generals' (Dover, *ibid.* 76—his italics). It seems rather to imply that, though he had nine colleagues whose authority was legally equal to his own, his personal prestige enabled him to exert a predominant influence over the decisions of the board.

however, is there any suggestion that even towards the end of the Pentecontaetia he exerted a dominating influence upon Athenian foreign or domestic policy; but the excursus was written for a special and very limited purpose, and information about the parts played by individuals, particularly Athenians, is sparse.[1] In the circumstances the absence of any reference to his political ascendancy is not surprising.

It is, on the other hand, remarkable that in the earlier part of the first book, which describes in detail the series of events leading to the breach between Athens and Sparta and which precedes the excursus on the Pentecontaetia, there is no mention of Pericles. The two αἰτίαι involving the Athenians in military action at Corcyra and Potidaea and bringing them to the brink of war with the Peloponnesian League called for momentous decisions upon which Pericles must have made his views known in the assembly. Plutarch declares categorically that Pericles persuaded the Athenians to ally with Corcyra and to send a squadron there (*Per.* 29. 1). This statement may originate from some authority other than Thucydides, but it could equally well be a rather bold inference from Thucydides himself,[2] who, when he does eventually introduce Pericles into his account of the dispute with the Peloponnesians, certainly suggests that Pericles had long advocated resistance to Peloponnesian demands, believing war to be inevitable (127. 1–3; 140. 1; 144. 3).

It is necessary to consider why Thucydides postpones so long the entry of Pericles. In his accounts of the Corcyra and Potidaea αἰτίαι and the two congresses at Sparta he focuses attention mainly upon the relations between the states involved and hardly at all upon the personal contributions of individuals, with the noteworthy exception of the Corinthian Aristeus at Potidaea.[3] Not only in describing the antecedents of the war but also in his narrative of its first five years he is preoccupied mainly with

---

[1] *C.Q.* V (1955), 56.
[2] Cf. G. De Sanctis, *Pericle* (1944), 224.
[3] *C.Q.* XLI (1947), 25–30. The part played by Archidamus before the outbreak of war is discussed below, 123–5.

political and moral problems arising from inter-state relations.[1] This preoccupation, however, does not cause him to banish individuals altogether. When he does allow Pericles to appear, towards the end of the first book, as a leading figure in the negotiations with Sparta, he makes him completely dominate the narrative and enjoy almost a monopoly of the speeches from this point to the crisis resulting in his dismissal from office in the second summer of the war. A probable explanation is as follows. Thucydides, being interested rather in the war strategy of Pericles than in his personality, postpones his entry until that strategy is about to be brought into operation and until Pericles is on the verge of success in convincing a substantial majority of his fellow-countrymen that war is inevitable and will bring victory. Hitherto his policy appears to have won acceptance by a small margin only. If, as has been seen above to be very probable, he advocated the alliance with Corcyra, he was almost defeated in this issue; Thucydides states that the Athenians accepted the alliance only after changing their minds on the second day of the debate (44. 1). Hereafter his control of Athenian policy, though not unchallenged, became much firmer.

The first mention of Pericles in the account of the events leading to the war occurs in connexion with the diplomatic manœuvre whereby the Spartans tried to cause his banishment, or at least to bring him into disrepute, by demanding that the Athenians should drive out 'the curse of the goddess' (126. 2; 127. 1-2). In reporting this almost trivial incident Thucydides attributes to the Spartans the belief that, if Pericles were removed, they would have a better prospect of obtaining satisfaction from the Athenians (127. 1); and because the reader has not yet been informed of his importance, a brief definition of his position and policy is added (127. 3).[2] The narrative is then interrupted by the major digression on Pausanias and Themistocles (128-38), and when it is

---

[1] I have drawn attention, C.Q. XLI (1947), 28, to the sparsity of references to the personal motives and plans before the latter part of the third book.
[2] See above, 8.

resumed, the further course of the negotiations is described, culminating in the delivery of an ultimatum by a last embassy from Sparta (139. 1–3). At a meeting of the assembly held to decide what answer should be given some speakers were in favour of going to war, while others wished to preserve peace by yielding to the Spartan demands (139. 4). Thucydides does not name any of these speakers nor does he give even the briefest summary of any arguments put forward, being content to report only the speech of Pericles. His silence could be, and indeed has been,[1] interpreted as evidence that the opposition to Pericles was at this time almost negligible. It may have been, but the silence of Thucydides does not provide any indication that it was. When Pericles was challenged on two subsequent occasions, which will be discussed below, namely in 431 and in 430, Thucydides does not state who his opponents were, though in 431 they caused him much anxiety and in 430 secured his dismissal.

Attacks were made on the friends of Pericles at some stage with the purpose of undermining his position. Thucydides does not refer to these attacks, and one consequence of this omission is that their date has been much disputed by modern scholars, some accepting the tradition of Ephorus[2] that they occurred before the war and others linking them with the prosecution of Pericles in 430, which Thucydides does mention. It would be inappropriate to discuss this problem fully here, but some consideration of it is necessary because of its relevance to the treatment of Pericles by Thucydides. Most scholars believe that the decree of Dracontides, which Plutarch dates before the war (*Per.* 32. 3–4), really belongs to 430 and was a preliminary to the successful prosecution of Pericles for embezzlement in that year.[3] The date of the attacks

---

[1] Gomme (1), I, 464.

[2] F. *Gr. Hist.* 70 F 196 (from Diodorus). This tradition is reflected in the account of Plutarch (*Per.* 31. 2–32. 6; he found the subject puzzling, as his final remark shows) and elsewhere.

[3] F. E. Adcock, *C.A.H.* v (1927), 478; Gomme (1), II, 187; F. Jacoby, *F. Gr. Hist.* IIIb, Komm. (1955), 88 (n. on 338 F 9). F. J. Frost, *J.H.S.* LXXXIV (1964), 69–72, has recently challenged this view and argued that the dating by Plutarch

on Pheidias, Anaxagoras and Aspasia, if indeed they all took place at the same time, is much more controversial. It does, however, seem reasonable to separate the attacks on the friends of Pericles from the prosecution of Pericles himself. As has been seen above, there was apparently strong opposition to the policy of Pericles when the appeal from Corcyra was debated, but it would doubtless have been unrealistic at any time in the last few years before-the war to have attempted to secure his dismissal from office by indicting him personally,[1] whereas indirect attacks upon him through prosecutions of his friends may have appeared to offer some prospect of weakening his position. In 430, on the other hand, the sufferings of the Athenians from the plague and the war rendered him so much more vulnerable that direct attack might well, and in fact did, prove successful. It is true that Ephorus in his account of the attacks on the friends of Pericles evidently fell into the common error of taking the evidence of comedy too seriously. He accepted as a statement of fact a passage of Aristophanes (*Peace* 605–18) in which Pericles is accused of having issued the Megarian decree and started the war in order to avoid sharing the fate of Pheidias.[2] Rejection of this fanciful explanation does not necessarily involve rejection of its implication that Pheidias was in trouble of some sort before the outbreak of war; the explanation would indeed be more characteristically Aristophanic, and more effectively comic, if its setting were real. There is little substance in the argument that to assign the attacks on the friends of Pericles to a date before the war is the equivalent of preferring the evidence of Ephorus to that of Thucydides.[3] The

is correct. The childish story of the advice given to Pericles by Alcibiades when the former was in danger of prosecution is dated before the war by Diodorus (12. 38), though apparently not by Plutarch (*Alcib.* 7. 3), but it is an obvious fabrication (Hatzfeld, 62), founded perhaps on some fictitious dialogue (comparable with that between Alcibiades and Pericles in Xen. *Mem.* 1. 2. 40–6).

[1] The account of the Spartan attempt to discredit him through the 'curse of the goddess' (127. 1–2) provides some confirmation of this view.

[2] It may be noted that the next few lines of the *Peace* draw a fantastic picture of the Athenian allies bribing the Spartans to go to war.

[3] As Gomme (1), II, 184–5, argues.

latter does not refer to attacks on the friends of Pericles at any time, and his silence about them is no more easily explained if they occurred in 430 than if they occurred before the outbreak of war.

The adversaries of Pericles at this time were apparently not at all strong,[1] perhaps through lack of unity, and certainly their opposition was ineffective. They included, however, the speakers at the debate in the assembly who advocated concessions to the Spartans (139. 4) and probably those responsible for the attacks on his friends. To have been given some information about them and their tactics would have been instructive to the reader.[2] The reason why Thucydides omits to provide it is not that prejudice has led him to suppress the case against Pericles. It is rather that at this early stage of his work he has not yet developed the technique whereby the influence exerted by leading characters is seen by showing them in contact with other leading characters.

It was at the meeting of the assembly called to consider the Spartan ultimatum that Pericles delivered the first of his speeches reported by Thucydides (140–4). The Thucydidean version is probably an amalgam of several speeches made during these lengthy negotiations.[3] Its first section briefly urges the Athenians to stand firm because any concession will evoke further Spartan demands; they must be prepared to fight if they are to avoid enslavement (140. 2–141. 1). The second and longest section argues that the Athenians are stronger than the Peloponnesians and will win if they follow the advice of Pericles. This conclusion is based upon the principle, already familiar to readers of the discussion on early Greek history known as the Archaeology, that financial strength and control of the sea, both possessed by Athens,

---

[1] Cf. Sealey, 64–5, though he relies partly on the silence of Thucydides.

[2] Jacoby, F. Gr. Hist. II c (1926), 93 (n. on 70 F 196) and III b, Suppl. I (1954), 489–90 (n. on 328 F 121) with II, 397 (n. 32), is critical of Thucydides for omitting the attacks on the friends of Pericles.

[3] The opening words, τῆς μὲν γνώμης, ὦ Ἀθηναῖοι, αἰεὶ τῆς αὐτῆς ἔχομαι (140. 1), show that Pericles had advocated the same policy in earlier speeches (cf. also the second sentence).

are the only really secure foundations upon which to build the power of a state (141. 2-143. 4).[1] Pericles then outlines his strategic plan, laying great emphasis on his conviction that the Athenians must not risk a land battle to save Attica from devastation (143. 5-144. 1). After suggesting how they ought to reply to the Spartan ultimatum, he urges them to be worthy of their fathers' achievement in defeating the Persians and winning the Athenian empire (144. 2-4). This final exhortation is his only concession to the conventions of patriotic rhetoric.

This speech performs admirably an important function, perhaps the principal function, of Thucydidean speeches, namely to point out to the reader the salient factors of the situation described in the narrative and to help him to understand them. It is concerned mainly with the resources of war, and it foreshadows and explains the uses to which these resources were put during the next few years. It is a speech about power, not about persons; it outlines the basis of a policy and, unlike some later Thucydidean speeches, throws little light on the personality of the speaker. It does not contain any personal touches such as are prominent in the self-revealing speech of Alcibiades at Sparta (6. 89-92). The arguments of Pericles are coldly intellectual and logical, so that they are consistent with what is known of his character from other sources; but arguments of this type pervade Thucydidean speeches, including some where they are conspicuously inappropriate to the speaker. That Pericles had complete confidence in the policy which he advocated may legitimately be inferred by readers of this speech. Its essence, however, lies in its logical analysis of a logical plan of action.

The assembly accepted the recommendations of Pericles without reservation (1. 145), and Thucydides implies that after the outbreak of war his authority became even more complete by

---

[1] Many points in this section are virtually replies to the speech of the Corinthians at the second congress at Sparta (especially 121. 2-122. 1); in almost every instance the Archidamian war proved Pericles to have been right and the Corinthians wrong. Cf. J. de Romilly, *Entretiens Fondation Hardt*, IV (1958), 44-6.

assuming that his policy and Athenian policy were identical, except during the two major crises when opposition flared up. Two small incidents, however, suggest that from the outset his knowledge of Athenian instability caused him considerable anxiety. When the Peloponnesians after mobilising their forces at the Isthmus sent an envoy to Athens, the Athenians declined to receive him because Pericles had earlier persuaded them to agree that, when once the enemy were in the field, they would conduct no further negotiations (2. 12. 1–2). He also formally presented his property in Attica to the state, believing that Archidamus might spare it from devastation either because of the ties of friendship between them or by order of the Spartan government, who might hope thereby to stir up ill-feeling against him (13. 1). He may, however, have made this gesture solely because of its value as propaganda in support of his policy. It is only here that Thucydides refers to the private interests of Pericles, and they are mentioned because the incident was politically of some importance.

There follows a summary in *oratio obliqua* of a speech delivered by Pericles in the assembly when the Peloponnesians were on the point of invading Attica (13. 2–9). It begins with a brief restatement of his defensive strategy (13. 2), but the bulk of it consists of a catalogue of Athenian resources in finance and manpower designed to convince his audience that these, if used in conjunction with his strategic plan which was based upon them, were sufficiently powerful to ensure victory.[1] The content of the speech, which has in modern times provided a battleground for historians, is largely factual, and it is doubtless for this reason that Thucydides has chosen to reproduce it in *oratio obliqua*.[2] It has the air of

[1] Gomme (1), II, 43–4, complains that Thucydides gives no corresponding figures of enemy resources with which these Athenian figures may be compared. The reason surely is that he is not at all likely to have been able to obtain trustworthy information about Peloponnesian resources, at any rate for this period of the war, and that rather than give untrustworthy information he has preferred to give none at all.

[2] Passages of some length in *oratio obliqua* become more frequent in later books.

a Government White Paper. It tells the reader hardly anything about Pericles himself, apart from illustrating how carefully he had worked out his strategic plan.

The first outbreak of popular feeling against him occurred when the Peloponnesians reached Acharnae and began to devastate an area not very far from the city (21. 2–3). The reaction of most Athenians, which Thucydides regards as perfectly natural (ὡς εἰκός), was to demand that they should march out and engage the enemy in defence of their property; they vented their anger on Pericles, whom they accused of cowardice (ἐκάκιζον) and held responsible for all their troubles. He stood firm and resisted their demands, convinced that he was right in advocating the abandonment of the Attic countryside to devastation (22. 1). Thucydides pictures this conflict of opinion as one between a majority of the Athenians, who were governed by emotion, and Pericles, who was governed by reason.[1] He does not attribute the movement against Pericles to the instigation of political opponents but sees its origin in spontaneous and informal discussions between Athenians gathering in groups (21. 3, κατὰ ξυστάσεις γιγνόμενοι).[2] Leading politicians must have played some part in the development of this reaction, and there is no reason to reject the statement of Plutarch (*Per.* 33. 7–8), who, quoting the contemporary comic poet Hermippus (fr. 46), names Cleon as one of them. It is characteristic of Thucydides at this early stage of his work that he here describes the feelings of the Athenian populace generally and the swing of public opinion against the strategy of Pericles but gives no information about positive measures adopted by Pericles to rally his supporters and to frustrate his political opponents. Such information would have helped the reader to understand the course of events.

One negative measure taken by Pericles to avert the danger

---

[1] de Romilly (Budé), II, *Notice* xviii–xix, shows how careful Thucydides has been to mark this contrast by his choice of words.

[2] Cf. the use of ξυνιστάμενοι in 88. 1 (the nervous sailors of Phormio) and in 8. 83. 3 (the mutinous sailors of Astyochus).

that the public reaction against his strategy might lead to hasty and unwise decisions does receive mention. He somehow contrived that no public meetings were held during the crisis (22. 1). How he prevented the convening of the assembly is not altogether clear, since he had no authority to overrule a majority decision by the board of strategoi. The phrase used by Thucydides here, ἐκκλησίαν τε οὐκ ἐποίει αὐτῶν οὐδὲ ξύλλογον οὐδένα, seems to mean that Pericles was successful in persuading a majority of his colleagues to support a resolution that no meeting should be convened.[1] If this interpretation is correct, the following words, τοῦ μὴ ὀργῇ τι μᾶλλον ἢ γνώμῃ ξυνελθόντας ἐξαμαρτεῖν, do not record an undisclosed motive of Pericles[2]—which Thucydides does nowhere else—but rather a point made when urging the other strategoi to agree to his recommendation. It is regrettable that more light is not thrown upon his relations with his colleagues on this occasion and on many others.[3] At all events, his tactics were effective in easing the tension, and the Athenians did not allow themselves to be provoked into risking a hoplite battle to protect Attica from devastation.

As soon as the Peloponnesian army withdrew from Attica, he seems to have regained the complete confidence of the Athenians. Various military and financial measures taken at this time bear the stamp of his influence although not expressly attributed to him (24. 1–2). Significant among these is the decision to safeguard a special reserve fund, now established for the first time, by imposing the death penalty upon anyone proposing that it should be

[1] Dover, *J.H.S.* LXXX (1960), 74–5, cf. P. A. Brunt, *Phoenix*, XIX (1965), 265 n. 37. In the next sentence (22. 2, ἐξέπεμπεν) the sending out of cavalry to defend cultivated districts near the city is attributed to Pericles alone, though the decisions must have been taken by the board of strategoi on his recommendation.

[2] As I wrongly stated in *C.Q.* XLI (1947), 28.

[3] It would also have been instructive, and by no means irrelevant to the history of the war, to have been given information about his activities as the leader and organiser of a political group. He was evidently successful in securing the election of his supporters to the board of strategoi, cf. V. Ehrenberg, *Sophocles and Pericles* (1954), 78–83.

3   33

used except in specified circumstances of grave emergency (24. 1). This measure reflects his lack of confidence in the stability of the Athenians, which had been strikingly confirmed by recent events. The invasion of the Megarid led by Pericles in the first autumn of the war was notable for the size of the army engaged in it, which included the entire force of hoplites apart from those at Potidaea (31. 1–2). An invasion on such a scale can hardly have been entrusted to a single strategos,[1] though only he is named. Doubtless he had a personal reason for wishing to lead this expedition himself, namely to belie the charge of cowardice brought against him during the invasion of Attica (21. 3). The expedition was short, amounting to little more than a raid, and nothing more ambitious than extensive plundering was attempted, doubtless in retaliation for the plundering of Attica. Nevertheless, its results must have been deemed at least satisfactory, since it was repeated in each succeeding year (31. 3).[2] This offensive operation, like other offensive operations conducted or planned by Pericles,[3] is described by Thucydides in a few cold and strictly factual sentences. This bleakness may cause surprise, but it is consistent with the practice of Thucydides in directing the attention of his readers towards the essential factor, as he sees it, of any situation. To him the offensive element in Periclean strategy was relatively unimportant by comparison with the defensive element, which could have won the war for Athens.

The Funeral Speech (35–46) provides Thucydides with an opportunity to present a side of Pericles of which there is hardly any trace in the other speeches or in the narrative. It may, however, be doubted whether a desire to present this side of Pericles, and to show that he was a master of another kind of oratory, influenced to any great extent the decision of Thucydides to include a report

[1] Dover, *J.H.S.* LXXX (1960), 64.
[2] Cumulatively this series of raids caused a considerable amount of distress to the Megarians; cf. 4. 66. 1 and Aristoph. *Ach.* 761–3.
[3] Including the seaborne raids of this summer (17. 4; 23. 2; 25; 30), which, though not conducted by Pericles himself, were certainly planned by him.

of the speech.[1] To give a picture of the Athenian democratic system and way of life at the moment when Athenian power was at its zenith (cf. 31. 2) was surely his principal aim, though it was convenient to him that the picture of Athenian greatness could be drawn by the greatest of Athenians, who could be shown to have been an idealist as well as a realist. The dramatic effect of the contrast between the speech and the account of the plague, which immediately follows it (47. 3–54), has often been noted.[2] The speech appears at first sight to be totally irrelevant to a history of the war,[3] but it is not, though its relevance does not lie in its contribution to the Thucydidean portrait of Pericles. The institutions and outlook of the Athenians are contrasted with those of others, especially the Spartans, though they are named only once (39. 2). The fundamental differences between the Athenians and the Spartans help to explain why the war took place at all and why it assumed the pattern which emerges from the narrative of its first year. Thucydides is following his normal practice of seeking to explain and to instruct.

During the second invasion of Attica in 430 Pericles again insisted that the Athenian army should not engage the Peloponnesians in the field (55. 2). On this occasion, though the devastation was more widespread and severe than in the previous summer (55. 1; 57. 2; 3. 26. 3), his advice was accepted without demur, presumably because of the outbreak of the plague. It was perhaps because he felt himself no longer needed to restrain the Athenians from challenging the enemy in Attica that he took command, doubtless with other strategoi, of a strong expeditionary force sent to attack coastal districts of the Peloponnese. This expedition was on a greater scale and more ambitious than that of the

---

[1] According to Gomme (1), II, 143 (n. on 45. 2), the coldness of the personal consolation to the relatives of the dead is consistent with the reserved character of Pericles. I doubt very much whether Thucydides deliberately produces this effect. It is rather that to Thucydides, and probably to Pericles also, the general lessons of the speech were more important than the occasion which gave rise to it.

[2] Cf. Finley, 150. [3] Cf. de Romilly (Budé), II, Notice xxv.

previous year: the hoplite army was much larger, and a cavalry squadron was transported by sea for the first time (2. 56. 1–2, cf. 6. 31. 2). Again, however, Thucydides records very briefly offensive operations undertaken by the Athenians and gives few details even of a raid on Epidaurian territory, which seems to have nearly brought about the fall of Epidaurus itself (2. 56. 4–6).

It was after the withdrawal of the Peloponnesians from Attica and his own return from this raiding expedition that the storm broke which was to sweep Pericles from office (59. 1–2). The Athenians again allowed their sufferings, now enormously increased by the plague, to sway their judgement, and, as he had foreseen (59. 3; 60. 1), they angrily turned against him. This outburst of popular feeling resembled that of the previous summer[1] but was far more serious, since the issue at stake was no longer how the war should be fought but whether it should be fought at all. Reversing the policy to which they had committed themselves, the Athenians were now eager to make peace and even sent envoys to Sparta to negotiate a settlement. Thucydides has not chosen to state who were responsible for instigating these overtures,[2] what terms the envoys were empowered to offer or what arguments they used in trying to convince the Spartans, if indeed they were granted a hearing. He mentions only that the negotiations failed (59. 2). Their failure intensified the bitterness against Pericles, who now arranged for the assembly to be convened. He then delivered the last of his speeches reported by Thucydides (59. 3).

He begins by criticising the Athenians for two reasons: first for their unreasonable anger against him in blaming him for their misfortunes for which they are themselves jointly responsible

---

[1] de Romilly (Budé), II, Notice xix–xxi, shows how Thucydides marks the similarity between the two episodes by describing them in similar language: the emotion of the Athenians is again contrasted with the reason of Pericles.

[2] They must have been, or at least have included, the unspecified ἀπράγμονες to whom Pericles refers (63. 2–64. 1), but there is no means of identifying them precisely. See Gomme (3), 109–10, with (1), II, 177–8, though I would not include Nicias, who despite his pacifism was not one to yield to adversity. For other identifications see A. Andrewes, Proc. Camb. Phil. Soc. VI (1960), 8 with n. 1.

because they accepted his advice to go to war (60); and secondly for their irresolution and lack of patriotism in being overwhelmed by their personal sufferings and allowing these to outweigh the security of the state (61). He then argues that their undisputed command of the sea offers them opportunities for expansion far beyond the limits of their existing empire. This empire, which their fathers won, must be preserved by their efforts; it has come to resemble a tyranny, and to abandon it now would be perilous because of the enmity which their possession of it has engendered (62–3). After returning to the point that they are unjustified in holding him responsible for their sufferings, particularly those arising from the plague, he urges them not to yield but to defend the power and glory of Athens, which will be remembered for all time (64).

This is the speech of a brave man. Only a brave man would have refused to appease the assembly, and indeed have adopted a most unconciliatory attitude, when he well knew that, in theory at least, he might have been condemned to death.[1] No one could accuse Pericles of the failing with which he charged the Athenians, that of neglecting public security through preoccupation with private misfortunes.[2] It is not surprising to learn that the speech was more effective in rekindling in the Athenians the will to resist than in softening their anger against him (65. 2–3). It is also the speech of an enlightened man, a master of political psychology, who in formulating his strategy had accurately predicted the course of events, apart from the plague which was an unpredictable visitation from heaven (64. 1–2). Abundant evidence that Pericles was endowed with these qualities has been given earlier, and this speech, though among the greatest of Thucydidean speeches, does not add very much, other than confirmation, to the picture of him already presented. Its most

---

[1] According to Plato, Gorgias 516a, the Athenians very nearly did impose the death penalty. Dodds, n. *ad loc.* is inclined to regard this statement as an exaggeration.

[2] That his private misfortunes were many and grievous is attested by Plut. *Per.* 36.

valuable contribution, if judged from this standpoint alone, is to stress the extent to which he possessed, and strove to arouse in others, a type of patriotism more strictly practical than that of the Funeral Speech.

Thucydides explains why the Athenians, both rich and poor, refused to relent in their attitude towards Pericles (65. 2), but he devotes only a single sentence to the results of their continued displeasure: οὐ μέντοι πρότερόν γε οἱ ξύμπαντες ἐπαύσαντο ἐν ὀργῇ ἔχοντες αὐτὸν πρὶν ἐζημίωσαν χρήμασιν (65. 3). He gives no further details about this *cause célèbre*, mentioning neither the nature of the charge nor the name of the prosecutor nor the reactions of Pericles himself nor the size of the fine.[1] Only from a reference in the next sentence to his reelection is it learned for certain that the conviction involved his dismissal from the board of strategoi. The passage illustrates, perhaps more strikingly than any other, the principles of Thucydides in the earlier parts of his work in regard to the presentation of individuals. It is in marked contrast to his treatment of another *cause célèbre* in the sixth book, where he gives a very full account of the circumstances leading to the condemnation of Alcibiades in 415.[2] It may be that in choosing to exclude any details about the trial of Pericles he was influenced in some degree by a desire to justify him.[3] If, however, he believed Pericles to be the victim of injustice, as he assuredly did (cf. 65. 8), another method, and a more effective method, of justifying him would have been to have exposed the falsity of the charges against him, and of the arguments upon which they were based, by reporting them fully instead of suppressing them.[4] The principal

[1] Plato, *Gorgias* 516a, states that he was convicted of embezzlement; Diod. 12. 45. 4 that the charges were trifling. According to Plutarch (*Per.* 35. 5) Idomeneus, Theophrastus and Heracleides Ponticus each named a different prosecutor, one of these being Cleon.

[2] See below, 221–2. It is true that Androcles, the principal accuser of Alcibiades, is not mentioned till 8. 65. 2.

[3] Cf. de Romilly (Budé), II, *Notice* xxiii.

[4] Cf. the wild and palpably false accusations thrown out by the Syracusan demagogue Athenagoras (6. 36–40), which serve to strengthen the confidence of the reader in the integrity and wisdom of Hermocrates.

reason for this silence on the part of Thucydides is to be sought in his determination, which is so conspicuous in the earlier books, to banish from his record of contemporary history any material that could be classed as biography or personal detail. In this part of his work his conviction that it is his duty to instruct his readers by pointing out the general lessons deducible from events, rather than to entertain them with trivialities, is almost an obsession (cf. 1. 22. 4). This conception of his duty is doubtless a reaction partly against Herodotus, who loves to introduce entertaining stories about the private lives of great men and is ever seeking personal motives to account for great events. It is perhaps to a greater extent a reaction against such writers as Ion of Chios and Stesimbrotus of Thasos, who reported gossip and scandal about leading personalities including contemporaries. In this instance Thucydides appears to have felt obliged to omit all information about the trial of Pericles except its result:[1] he has already drawn attention to the contrast between the calm wisdom of Pericles and the emotional folly of the Athenians, and to do so again would be superfluous. This conclusion is consistent with his interpretation of his duty as seen in the earlier parts of his work. Nevertheless, some information about the trial could have been extremely valuable to anyone seeking further enlightenment on the state of public opinion at this moment of crisis or wishing to understand how it was that the personal authority of Pericles, though seemingly so securely based, proved to be so vulnerable. There is little doubt that, had this episode belonged to the period covered by the later books, Thucydides would have treated it very differently.

The fickleness for which Pericles had censured the Athenians now benefited him. They soon relented and reinstated him in office (65. 4, ὅπερ φιλεῖ ὅμιλος ποιεῖν), perhaps after only a few weeks.[2] Thucydides does not refer to any decisions regarding the

---

[1] E. Meyer, *G.d.A.* IV, 2 (1956), 45 n. 2, approves the view that only the result was relevant.
[2] Gomme (1), II, 183.

direction of the war instigated by others while he was out of office,[1] or indeed to any action initiated by him in the interval, amounting probably to at least nine months, between his reinstatement and his death. This apparent inactivity cannot be interpreted as an indication that he never fully regained his former influence, since Thucydides expressly states that he did (65. 4). At this time the Athenians were so severely weakened by the plague that they were incapable of much offensive action,[2] and Pericles himself, who according to Plutarch (*Per.* 38. 1) died a lingering death, may have been totally incapacitated for several months.[3] He died in the autumn of 429, two and a half years after the outbreak of the war (65. 6).

The previous chapter referred briefly to the famous passage (65. 5–13) in which Thucydides expounds his considered opinion that the Athenians lost the war because they abandoned the policy of Pericles after his death and because no leader of his outstanding ability emerged to succeed him.[4] Some further consideration of this passage is necessary here. It has often been described as an obituary of Pericles,[5] but this term is a misnomer. It would be more accurately described as an obituary of Periclean strategy. It does not review his entire career but is concerned mainly, though not exclusively,[6] with his leadership during the war; it deals only with his military strategy and his influence over the populace; its primary aim is not to assess his ability but to establish that the Athenians could have been victorious if they had continued to follow his advice. It is concerned almost as much with their folly as with his wisdom.

---

[1] The statement of Plutarch (*Per.* 37. 1) that the Athenians were dissatisfied with their advisers during the period is probably an inference from the impression created by Thucydides (65. 4) and not derived from an independent source.

[2] The disastrous attack on Spartolus (79. 1–7) was evidently a sequel to the fall of Potidaea (70. 1–4): the same generals were in command.

[3] F. Miltner, *R.E.* XIX, I (1937), 787.   [4] See above, 8.

[5] Cf. Jacoby, *F. Gr. Hist.* IIIb, Suppl. 1 (1954), 135.

[6] 65. 5 refers to his leadership in time of peace, presumably from 445 to 431, and the account of his relations with the Athenian populace (65. 8–9) is applicable to the whole period of his ascendancy.

While there is no certainty that the whole passage (5–13) was written at or after the end of the war, as the last part of it undoubtedly was (12),[1] the sequence of thought develops continuously and coherently throughout. The entire discussion seems to be a unity and a detachable unity. The preceding narrative has been chronological (65. 1–4), but at the beginning of this passage the chronological sequence is broken (5) and the discussion ranges over a period of some years. It is not necessarily to be assumed that Thucydides merely inserted the passage at the appropriate point in his work without making any alterations to the surrounding narrative. In this instance, as in others where he is believed to have made later additions,[2] he doubtless revised his original text to some extent in order to avoid any awkwardness or repetition.[3] Unless, however, his whole work is believed to have been written after the end of the war, a substantial part of this passage, and probably the whole of it, is a later addition.[4]

Although the passage is not, as has been pointed out above, a general assessment of Pericles, it does furnish a more clearly defined picture of him than is supplied by the foregoing narrative and speeches. The qualities here attributed to him could for the most part have been inferred by a discerning reader from the record of what he did and said, but Thucydides now commits himself to a categorical expression of opinion that he possessed them. They are no longer implicit but explicit. References to his moderation (5), his vigilance in safeguarding the public interest (5), his foresight (5, 6, 13), his intellectual eminence (8), his integrity (8), his strength of character which enabled him without

---

[1] A general statement in the first part (7) seems to refer mainly to the Sicilian expedition.

[2] See below, 219, on 6. 15. 3–4.

[3] It is impossible to be sure whether or not the original text contained any reference to the death of Pericles either at this point or in its chronological setting near the end of the second book.

[4] Adcock, 127–31, who believes that the whole of 65. 1–9 was written at the same time as the speech preceding it, suggests that the rest of the chapter was added in stages as the situations and actions occurred to which Thucydides refers.

flattery to control the populace and to exercise a virtual ἀρχή (8–9)—all these help to clarify the picture. It seems reasonable to conclude that towards the end of the war, when Thucydides had, as will be suggested below, modified his attitude towards leading personalities and his method of presenting them, he felt dissatisfied with his presentation of Pericles, which had an austerely archaic look; accordingly, when adding his own assessment of the reasons why the Athenians lost the war, he seized the opportunity to add also some touches to his sketch of Pericles, making it somewhat clearer and less incomplete. It is very much to the benefit of posterity that he did.

CHAPTER IV

PHORMIO

W HEN at the end of 430 Phormio was sent with a squadron of twenty ships to Naupactus (2. 69. 1), he already had a long record of service in command of Athenian forces overseas, though not, it seems, an exceptionally distinguished one. In 440 he was one of three strategoi sent with a naval reinforcement to aid Pericles during the final stages of the Samian revolt (1. 117. 2). At some unspecified date, which may well be 437,[1] he was in sole command of thirty ships sent to north-western Greece in response to an appeal by the Acarnanians and Amphilochians, and he helped them to recover Amphilochian Argos from the Ambraciots (2. 68. 7). In 432 he led a force of hoplites to Chalcidice with orders to complete the circumvallation of Potidaea. After accomplishing this task without opposition, he ravaged hostile territory in the neighbourhood and captured a few insignificant towns (1. 64. 2-65. 2). He was still in Chalcidice in the following summer (2. 29. 6), but how long he and his troops remained there is unknown. Thucydides mentions only that they had been withdrawn before a force under Hagnon reached Potidaea in the summer of 430 (2. 58. 2). This mission to Potidaea perhaps offered Phormio few opportunities to show his merits, but he does not appear to have made any substantial contribution towards hastening the end of the costly siege. Had he not fought his two celebrated naval battles near the mouth of the Corinthian Gulf in 429, he would have ranked among the host of nonentities whose names Thucydides so punctiliously preserves as leaders of unimportant missions. These two battles, though they were not on a large scale and did not produce immediate results of any great consequence, interested Thucydides because

---

[1] Busolt, 763 n. 6, whose dating seems more convincing than any other.

they illustrated basic differences between the Athenians and the Spartans. As he is fond of showing elsewhere, one of these differences was in military leadership. While the personality of Phormio evidently proved attractive to Thucydides, he is presented mainly as an exemplar of Athenian dash and enterprise, which are contrasted with the slowness and caution of Spartan leaders in the Archidamian war with the exception of Brasidas.

During the period from their arrival at Naupactus in the winter of 430/29 until the following midsummer Phormio and his squadron were engaged in patrol duty to prevent shipping from sailing out of or into the Corinthian Gulf (2. 69. 1). He then had to face a dangerous situation created by a Peloponnesian offensive directed mainly against Acarnania. The Spartan *nauarchos* Cnemus was to transport a Peloponnesian force to Leucas and thence to invade Acarnania, while a fleet from Corinth and other cities was to sail out of the Corinthian Gulf and operate against the Acarnanian coast (80. 1–3; 83. 1). The part played by Cnemus in this campaign will be studied elsewhere.[1] Here it is necessary only to note that Phormio, because his forces were too small to be divided, could do nothing to hinder the Peloponnesians under Cnemus from reaching Leucas. Their transports crossed from the western Peloponnese unobserved by him (80. 4), and he had to refuse Acarnanian requests for help on the grounds that he could not leave Naupactus unguarded when an enemy fleet was on the point of sailing from Corinth (81. 1).[2] It was against this fleet, which consisted of forty-seven ships, that he fought the first of his naval battles.

He first sighted the enemy ships sailing westwards and hugging the Peloponnesian shore. Keeping them under observation as they passed through the narrows at the mouth of the Gulf and into the

[1] See below, 137–9.

[2] Although the Ambraciots, when suggesting this offensive to the Spartans, had included the prospect of taking Naupactus eventually (80. 1), the fleet from Corinth was under orders to sail direct to Acarnania (83. 1); but Phormio could at this stage only guess the strategic intentions of the enemy. It was certainly to the advantage of the Athenians that he should remain where he was.

relatively open waters beyond, he did not attack them but waited until they attempted to cross during the night from Patrae in the direction of the Aetolian coast. Soon after daybreak he succeeded in engaging them far from either shore, where his squadron had ample room for manœuvre. They at once ranged their ships in a large circle with bows facing outwards, a defensive formation designed to deny Phormio the opportunity to put into operation the skilled movement known as διέκπλους used by the Athenians in single line ahead to break through enemy fleets in the conventional formation of line abreast. The Athenians were under orders not to attack until Phormio gave the signal but to sail round the circle contracting it further and further. As he had anticipated, the Peloponnesian triremes with their inexperienced crews collided with one another and with the small transports which were in the middle of the circle. The confusion was increased when an easterly wind began to make the sea choppy: Phormio was relying on the effects of this wind, which normally sprang up early each morning. He then gave the signal, and the Athenians routed the enemy, who lost several ships and were now in such disorder that they made little resistance. The remainder scattered in flight towards the Achaean coast, and in the pursuit twelve of them were lost with most of their crews (83. 1–84. 4). In consequence of this debacle the Peloponnesian fleet was unable to make the contribution expected of it in the Acarnanian campaign.

The technique of Thucydides in describing battles is admirably illustrated by his account of this engagement. He follows his normal practice of underlining the factors responsible for victory and defeat, pointing out how the aims and expectations of the leaders on the winning side were fulfilled while those of the leaders on the losing side were disappointed.[1] Phormio succeeded in bringing the Peloponnesians to battle against their will, and in open waters where they were at a disadvantage: in his plan of

---

[1] As is shown by de Romilly (2), 125–8, who gives an excellent analysis of this account, choosing it as a relatively simple example of a Thucydidean battle narrative.

attack he exploited most effectively the superior seamanship of the Athenians and his own knowledge of local weather conditions. His masterly handling of the situation is seen to have depended largely upon intelligent foresight, whereas the Peloponnesian commanders are shown to have been mistaken in their predictions. On the other hand, Thucydides nowhere suggests that the Peloponnesians were guilty of indefensible miscalculations. It was reasonable to expect that the Athenian fleet of twenty ships would shrink from an engagement with their fleet of forty-seven. Accordingly they were justified in having equipped themselves not for a naval battle but for operations on land in Acarnania, where specified duties had already been assigned to them (83. 3, cf. 87. 2 and 5). It was also reasonable in the circumstances that, when Phormio was seen to be shadowing them, they should have sought to avoid a battle; and in trying to steal across by night from Patrae they were adopting a sensible if somewhat obvious expedient (83. 3). Their decision, which must have been provisionally agreed in advance, to form a defensive circle, as soon as a battle in open waters was seen to be inescapable, seems to have been prudent in view of the universally acknowledged superiority of the Athenians in naval technique. The critical moment of the battle came (84. 3, κατὰ τὸν καιρὸν τοῦτον) when through lack of experience (ἄνθρωποι ἄπειροι) the seamanship of the Peloponnesian crews proved unequal to the demands made upon it.[1] That Thucydides believed the inexperience of the Peloponnesian crews to have been the decisive factor may be seen both in his account of the battle and also in subsequent references to it,[2] though he does not underestimate the contribution made by the intelligence and enterprise of Phormio. He finds

---

[1] Cf. the graphic touch βοῇ τε χρώμενοι καὶ πρὸς ἀλλήλους ἀντιφυλακῇ τε καὶ λοιδορίᾳ. Thucydides tends to introduce such graphic touches at critical points in battle narratives, cf. 91. 2 (the second battle) and 4. 34. 2 (the first phase of the battle on Sphacteria).

[2] 85. 2 (the mistaken views of the Spartans on receiving news of the battle; here Thucydides makes his own opinion very clear); 87. 2–5 (the speech of the Peloponnesian leaders before the second battle); 89. 2–3 and 7–8 (the speech of

in the outcome of this naval battle, the first of the war (85. 2), a lesson of great importance for the enlightenment of his readers: that because the Athenians were so much more experienced at sea, their fleets enjoyed an advantage in quality which could more than outweigh a substantial superiority in numbers on the Peloponnesian side. This lesson is reinforced by the account of the second naval battle.

The Spartans appear to have been more disturbed by this defeat than by the failure of their operations on land in Acarnania (85. 1). Cnemus and his advisers prepared for another naval battle by refitting their remaining ships and summoning more from allied states, while Phormio sent to Athens a report of their preparations and an urgent request for reinforcements to meet the impending threat (85. 3–4). It may be noted here, since the point will be seen later to be important, that according to Thucydides the plans of the Peloponnesians were directed wholly towards fighting a naval battle to retrieve their defeat, and that Phormio was aware of their intentions and was expecting daily to have to fight at sea.[1] The Athenians sent twenty more ships but ordered them to sail by way of Crete and to engage in operations there, an unwise decision involving the loss of valuable time, as Thucydides very clearly implies (85. 5–6; 92. 7).

The Peloponnesians succeeded in mustering seventy-seven ships and so enjoyed an overwhelming superiority in numbers. They stationed their fleet just inside the mouth of the Corinthian Gulf, while Phormio stationed his off the opposite shore just

Phormio). The question whether or not Thucydides was right is irrelevant to the present discussion, which is not concerned with establishing the true cause of the Peloponnesian defeat. A. Köster, *Studien zur Geschichte des antiken Seewesens* (*Klio*, Beiheft XXXII, 1934), 83–7, maintains that the Peloponnesian leaders were to blame; that in reporting the defeat they tried to lay the responsibility for it upon their crews; that their attempt to avoid discredit by inculpating others coloured the information derived by Thucydides from Peloponnesian sources. I doubt whether he can have allowed himself to be misled to this extent by prejudiced sources, especially as his account is certainly derived mainly from the Athenian side.

[1] 85. 1 and 3–4; 86. 6; 87. 1; 90. 1.

outside it. For about a week the two fleets watched each other across the straits, the Peloponnesians being as reluctant to fight in the relatively open waters outside the Gulf as the Athenians were to fight in the narrows just inside it. The crews of both fleets were lacking in confidence (86. 5–6; 88), and it was for this reason that speeches of encouragement were delivered on both sides, of which Thucydides gives reports (87; 89). The speech to the Peloponnesians is attributed to 'Cnemus and Brasidas and the other generals of the Peloponnesians' (86. 6), and that of Phormio is to a large extent an attempt to refute their arguments, so that the two speeches form an antilogy.[1] Both speeches consist almost wholly of general exhortation based on somewhat unrealistically intellectual reasoning about bravery and experience. Thucydides doubtless had information about their real content, but he seems to have improvised rather freely through a desire to reinforce the principal lesson of his narrative, namely that the two battles illustrate differences between Athenians and Peloponnesians. He often uses such speeches delivered before battles as a means of explaining the military situation by including information about the tactical plan of the speaker.[2] If the Peloponnesian leaders outlined their tactical plan, this part of their speech has not been reported by Thucydides. Nor does Phormio mention his tactics except to declare that he will not, if he can avoid doing so, fight in the Gulf or sail into it; and he adds his reasons (89. 8). This negative statement is valuable in helping to show how completely he was outmanœuvred in the opening phase of the battle.

The Peloponnesians, wishing to fight before the Athenian reinforcement arrived (86. 6), eventually took the initiative and put into operation a skilfully conceived plan.[3] To lure the Athenians into the Gulf they moved further into it themselves in a north-

[1] As is shown very clearly in the analysis by de Romilly (2), 140–50.
[2] Cf. Luschnat, 107–13.
[3] Modern scholars have suggested that Brasidas was responsible for it, cf. Busolt, 980 and Gomme (1), II, 229; but, if Thucydides had possessed information that this was so, he would probably have made use of it. Elsewhere he is careful to note early signs of distinction in Brasidas (see below, 149).

easterly direction in four columns line ahead, with their best ships leading; they skirted the Achaean shore but gave the impression that they were making for Naupactus. Phormio, apparently not anticipating that the enemy would attempt anything so bold or imaginative, had left Naupactus unguarded because he needed its Messenian troops to support his fleet by occupying the northern coast of the Gulf near its mouth. He was now forced to do precisely what he had tried to avoid, and he made for Naupactus with all possible speed, evidently hoping to arrive there before the enemy, who had a somewhat shorter distance to cover but might be expected to move less rapidly. His Messenian allies hurried along the coast to support him. At a prearranged signal the Peloponnesians turned sharply so as to face the northern shore in line abreast four ships deep and bore down upon the Athenians with the intention of forcing them aground. Eleven of the Athenian ships escaped from this movement; the remaining nine were caught and their crews killed or captured except for those who swam ashore. Some of these ships were towed away by the enemy, but others were saved by the Messenians plunging into the shallow water (90).

The eleven Athenian ships continued on their course, and ten of them reached Naupactus, easily outstripping the twenty enemy ships pursuing them. The eleventh was being chased by a Leucadian ship as it approached the harbour. Rounding a merchantman which was riding at anchor, it rammed and sank the Leucadian vessel. At this point the inferior seamanship of the Peloponnesians again had disastrous consequences. Already in some disorder because of their hasty pursuit, they were thrown into complete confusion by this sudden setback at a moment when they believed themselves to be victorious. Many stopped rowing, a fatal error which illustrates their inexperience. The Athenians attacked and after a brief struggle routed them. It was now the turn of the Peloponnesians to be pursued as they made for the Achaean coast, and they lost six ships together with the crews. The Athenians also recovered almost all their ships captured by the enemy in the first stage of the action. So discouraged were the Peloponnesians by this engagement and by the prospect of the Athenian reinforcements arriving that, although they would still have enjoyed a substantial superiority in numbers, they decided to discontinue naval operations in this area. Accordingly their fleet dispersed, most of it stealing away by night in the direction of Corinth (91–2).

Despite this brilliant recovery against heavy odds the victory of the Athenians was not by any means decisive if judged in terms of the losses sustained by each side. They had lost a considerable number of highly skilled men (90. 5), and some of their ships had been reduced to wrecks (92. 4),[1] while the losses inflicted on the enemy were not heavy in relation to the size of the Peloponnesian fleet (92. 2).[2] Thucydides makes very clear that the balance of material advantage gained by the Athenians was slight.[3] Strategically their gains were much greater: they had foiled the Peloponnesian attempt to destroy their control over the mouth of the Corinthian Gulf, and they continued to benefit from their possession of a western base at Naupactus. Still more important were the effects of this episode on morale.[4] The Athenians are seen, even when weakened by the plague, to have maintained an enormous superiority in naval technique which profoundly influenced the course of the war. This is the principal lesson of both their victories.

The second victory, even more than the first, was the achievement of the Athenians collectively. Phormio is not prominent in the account of Thucydides: after he took the decision to make his dash for Naupactus (90. 3) he is not mentioned again. The engagement was fought throughout by 'the Athenians', and Thucydides

[1] The one ship captured with its crew (90. 6) was not recovered (92. 5).

[2] The Peloponnesians justifiably set up a trophy to mark their success in the first phase of the battle (92. 5).

[3] According to Diodorus (12. 48. 3) Phormio ἀμφίδοξον ἔσχε τὴν νίκην, which probably reflects the conclusion drawn by Ephorus from the narrative of Thucydides.

[4] F. E. Adcock, C.A.H. v (1927), 210.

does not state who was responsible for issuing the crucial order
when the Athenian trireme turned and rammed its Leucadian
pursuer outside the harbour of Naupactus (91. 2–3).[1] The only
aspect of the part played by Phormio to which any attention is
directed is that he wished to fight outside the Gulf, where there
was room for manœuvre, and not in its narrow waters, where his
fleet would be at a disadvantage, and that he signally failed to
achieve this aim. Frequent references to this aim, and to the fact
that he was forced by the successful tactics of the Peloponnesians
to do precisely what he most wished to avoid,[2] emphasise the
extent to which he was outmanœuvred. Thucydides makes
abundantly clear that the Athenian victory was not the outcome
of his foresight.

A more complex issue, on which Thucydides does not express
any judgement, is whether Phormio was wise to station his small
fleet outside the mouth of the Gulf when he could, at least until
the expected reinforcement arrived, have taken up a defensive
position off Naupactus, where his fleet could have been more
effectively covered by the Messenians. By choosing the mouth of
the Gulf he was not necessarily ensuring that he would be able to
fight in open waters but only that he might from there contrive
some means of securing this end. The enemy, as he must have
known, were most unwilling to fight outside the Gulf because
of their recent defeat (86. 5). He had caught their ships in the open
on that occasion because their aim was not to engage his fleet but
to reach Acarnania with the least possible delay. It might be suggested that Phormio believed the intention of the Peloponnesians
on this occasion also to be to cross to Acarnania rather than to
engage his fleet in battle,[3] but this explanation is unconvincing.
Had their destination been Acarnania, their best prospect of
evading him would have been to have made a wide detour,
starting perhaps from Cyllene, and to have kept far to the west of

[1] Gomme (1), II, 232, draws attention to this omission.
[2] 86. 5; 89. 8–9; 90. 1–4, cf. de Romilly (2), 145–6.
[3] Cf. Gomme (1), II, 222 and 229–30.

the straits, as Cnemus apparently did when he avoided interception earlier in the summer (80. 4). Thucydides gives not the smallest hint that the Peloponnesians had any intention of reopening their offensive in Acarnania, which seems to have been entirely abandoned after the defeat at Stratus (82; 84. 5). Narrative and speeches alike presuppose that their sole aim was to wipe out the disgrace of their defeat by crushing the fleet of Phormio in a second naval battle and that he was fully aware of their intentions.[1]

Another suggestion is that he stationed his fleet outside the entrance of the Gulf because it would there be in the best position to make contact with the reinforcement from Athens, which might otherwise have been caught and destroyed by the enemy before it could join him.[2] That danger could, however, have been averted by sending out a single ship to meet this squadron and to give information of the enemy's whereabouts; if necessary, the squadron could have passed through the narrows in darkness, hugging the northern shore. A more probable explanation may perhaps be found in the sentence describing how Phormio used to assure his sailors that they were capable of successfully challenging enemy fleets of any size and how they had long come to accept this estimate of their capabilities (88. 2). He may well have found his hand forced by the very success of his past efforts to inspire his men with confidence. If he had now belied what he had been in the habit of telling them by taking up a defensive position off Naupactus and seeking to avoid a battle, their morale might have been broken instead of being only shaken, as it was when he chose to anchor near the mouth of the Gulf (88. 1 and 3). There is some difference in tone between his speech delivered just before the battle and his exhortations in the past. Thucydides may intend to suggest that the latter had been over-optimistic and even unwise.[3]

Whatever the reasons may have been for the decision of

---

[1] Cf. 85. 1 and 3–4; 86. 6; 87. 1; 90. 1.   [2] Adcock, *C.A.H.* v (1927), 209.

[3] Yet another explanation is suggested by the statement of Diodorus (12. 48. 3) that Phormio τῇ προγεγενημένῃ νίκῃ φρονηματισθεὶς ἐτόλμησεν ἐπιθέσθαι

Phormio to station his fleet outside the mouth of the Gulf, it appears to have evoked criticism at Athens that he had taken an unjustifiable risk which very nearly led to a serious defeat. Before considering the problem of the consequences believed to have arisen from this criticism, it will be convenient to mention the last operation of his mission to north-western Greece, which was also, so far as is known, the last of his career. This was an expedition made in the following winter (429/28) to Acarnania, where he carried out what were evidently security measures designed to ensure that the principal towns were controlled by leaders whose loyalty to Athens was beyond suspicion (102. 1). He did not attack Oeniadae, the only town hostile to Athens, because flooding from the Achelous made military action impracticable there in winter (102. 2).[1] Such were his contacts with Acarnania (cf. 68. 7) that this phenomenon can hardly have been unknown to him when he started; and the reference to the fact that he did not attack Oeniadae, together with the explanation of it, may reflect dissatisfaction expressed by ill-informed Athenians at home who thought that he ought to have exploited more effectively the advantage gained by the Athenians in this area. At all events, his expedition achieved very little. Early in the spring of 428 he and his ships returned to Athens (103. 1): there was no longer any need, for the present at least, to maintain a strong fleet at Naupactus.

It was not long before the Acarnanians were again asking for an Athenian to lead them. During the summer of the same year Asopius, the son of Phormio, was sent with a small fleet[2] to the west κελευσάντων ᾿Ακαρνάνων τοῦ Φορμίωνός τινα σφίσι πέμψαι ἢ υἱὸν ἢ

τοῖς πολεμίαις ναυσὶν οὔσαις πολλαπλασίαις. Although it is not true that he attacked the enemy, his previous victory may have made him overconfident, and to form this opinion after reading the narrative of Thucydides would not be unreasonable.

[1] Thucydides here inserts a geographical and mythological digression (102. 2–6), which is much longer than his account of the expedition.

[2] Asopius had only twelve ships with him in the west. Of the thirty which he used to raid coastal districts in Laconia the majority returned home (3. 7. 2–3), doubtless because of the strain on Athenian resources imposed by the revolt of Mytilene.

ξυγγενῆ ἄρχοντα (3. 7. 1). Phormio himself evidently could not be sent for some reason. It is a natural assumption from the highly condensed account of Thucydides that the Acarnanians first asked for Phormio and only after learning that he was not available suggested a son or relative.[1] Thucydides could have explained in a few words why Phormio was not available; he must have known the reason but has chosen, rather surprisingly, not to give it. Phormio could have died or fallen ill soon after returning from Naupactus in the spring. He could also have been deemed too old to serve again, though this explanation is not at all satisfactory: only a few months had passed since his last command, and his great experience of warfare in the peculiar conditions of western Greece, combined with his popularity with the Acarnanians, would surely have outweighed any objections to his appointment on the grounds of his age.[2] A more convincing explanation links the fact that he was not available with a tradition, which seems to be perfectly authentic though the circumstances are obscure, that he was prosecuted after one of his terms of service as strategos. A scholiast on Aristophanes *Peace* 347, who cites Androtion as his authority, states that Phormio was fined at his εὔθυνα and being unable to pay the fine suffered ἀτιμία; that, when the Acarnanians asked for his services as general, a subterfuge was found whereby the fine was paid from public funds and his ἀτιμία cancelled.[3] Unfortunately the scholiast does not supply the date, which, if not actually stated by Androtion, must have been deducible from the context. Phormio could well have been criticised for having accomplished very little during his mission to Potidaea,[4] and this

---

[1] V. Ehrenberg, *A.J.P.* LXVI (1945), 124, who thus links the passage in Thucydides with the fragment of Androtion which will be discussed below.

[2] There is in fact no clear evidence that he was elderly at this time. His first attested tenure of office on the board of strategoi was in 440/39 (1. 117. 2).

[3] *F. Gr. Hist.* 324 F 8, which Jacoby discusses exhaustively in a vast note, *ibid.* IIIb, Suppl. 1 (1954), 125–37; see also Ehrenberg, *A.J.P.* LXVI, 123–7. The version of the story by Pausanias (1. 23. 10), which seems to be founded on Androtion, has hardly any independent value (cf. Jacoby, 127).

[4] See above, 43; cf. the criticism of the generals who negotiated the surrender of Potidaea (70. 4), though they do not seem to have been prosecuted.

criticism could have led to a prosecution in 430. It is impossible to prove that he was not prosecuted in that year,[1] but there are no positive reasons for believing that he was. On the other hand, the report of Thucydides on the appointment of Asopius in 428 presupposes that Phormio could not be sent to Acarnania, and the fragment of Androtion supplies a satisfactory reason, namely that because of his ἀτιμία he was ineligible for public office.[2] Androtion was perhaps deliberately filling in the strange gap left by Thucydides. It is true that, when according to Androtion Phormio was relieved of his ἀτιμία by a legal manœuvre, he was thereafter presumably eligible to take command; but the fragment does not state that he actually did take command,[3] and there are many possible reasons why he may eventually have been unable to do so. The legal formalities may not have been completed in time; even after the cancellation of his ἀτιμία objections to his appointment may have been raised by those responsible for his conviction; he may have fallen ill or died, perhaps a victim of the plague.[4]

The Athenian democracy was notorious for its harsh treatment of leaders whom it elected to high office, including some to whom it was deeply indebted.[5] A strategos was liable to prosecution arising from his εὔθυνα on charges which were not in practice strictly confined to financial irregularities and might extend to almost any alleged negligence during his term of office.[6] There was plenty of scope for harrying public figures by means of legal proceedings. It does not seem that before the Peloponnesian war

[1] The objections of Jacoby, *F. Gr. Hist.* IIIb, Suppl. I, 130–1, to this dating are not altogether conclusive.
[2] Jacoby, *ibid.* 137, 'the two historical witnesses supplement each other'.
[3] Nor does the version of Pausanias (I. 23. 10). To the scholiast and to Pausanias the point of the story lies in the legal manœuvre; neither is interested in the sequel.
[4] Cf. Jacoby, *F. Gr. Hist.* IIIb, Suppl. I, 134 and 136. Gomme (1), II, 235, suggests that Phormio himself may for some reason have refused to accept the command even though his ἀτιμία was removed, cf. Ehrenberg, *A.J.P.* LXVI, 125.
[5] This theme became a rhetorical commonplace, as is seen from Plut. *Arist.* 26. 5, cf. *Nic.* 6. 1.
[6] As is made clear by Arist. *Ath. Pol.* 54. 2, cf. 48. 4–5.

many eminent Athenians were brought to trial on charges relating to their discharge of public duties: a celebrated case was that of Cimon, who was prosecuted by Pericles but acquitted.[1] The outbreak of the war brought an increase in the number of trials which were essentially political, and Pericles himself was an early victim.[2] Men with political ambitions, especially demagogues, found in the law-courts a powerful instrument for attacking rivals who stood in the way of their own advancement. Paches was accused of some misdemeanour relating to his command at Mytilene;[3] Pythodorus, Sophocles and Eurymedon were convicted ostensibly of having accepted bribes, though in the eyes of the Athenians their real offence was that their campaign in Sicily had not produced the results expected of it (4. 65. 3–4); Thucydides himself was condemned after his command at Amphipolis (5. 26. 5); Laches was threatened with prosecution by Cleon, though it is most unlikely that he was actually indicted.[4] The case of Paches and, even more strikingly, that of the generals in command at Arginusae show that even successful leaders might have to face legal proceedings after their victories. Accordingly, if Phormio was prosecuted after his return from Naupactus, such an attack could not be considered exceptional; there were plenty of parallels in the same period. The evidence is confused and contains inaccuracies on points of detail, but the reason seems to be that the scholiast responsible for it was unfamiliar with the legal procedure of the fifth century and has reproduced very ineptly the substance of what Androtion wrote.[5] The circumstances leading to the imposition of a fine upon Phormio would

[1] Arist. *Ath. Pol.* 27. 1; Plut. *Cim.* 14. 3–5 and *Per.* 10. 6.

[2] See above, 38.

[3] Plut. *Nic.* 6. 1, cf. *Arist.* 26. 5.

[4] Such is the conclusion of Jacoby, *F. Gr. Hist.* iiib, Suppl. 1, 500–1, after a careful examination of the evidence.

  Demosthenes (3. 98. 5) and Nicias (7. 48. 4) showed themselves to be well aware of the personal risks run by a general in returning to Athens after an unsuccessful expedition.

[5] The version of Pausanias (1. 23. 10), though derived, directly or indirectly, from Androtion, is even more deplorable.

doubtless have been clear if the *Atthis* of Androtion had survived. The narrative of Thucydides shows that, although Phormio had won notable successes, his strategic planning was at least open to criticism. Hostile feeling could well have been stirred up against him after his return, perhaps by a demagogue, on the ground that he had taken unjustifiable risks and sustained avoidable losses in the second of his battles. Whatever the charge—which was not necessarily related to the true cause of complaint against him—he is likely to have been at a disadvantage in attempting to establish his innocence. There is no evidence that he ever aspired to political leadership:[1] his reputation, like that of Demosthenes and of Lamachus, seems to have rested solely upon his military qualities, and, despite his popularity with the men under his command, he probably lacked the support of a strong political following.

The silence of Thucydides on the fortunes of Phormio immediately after his period of service in the west would not have been at all remarkable if the passage reporting his return to Athens (2. 103. 1) had been the last in which he was mentioned. Biographical detail is normally excluded from his *History*, and some important characters, including Archidamus, are allowed to disappear from its pages without explanation. The career of Phormio as a war leader was now at an end, and whatever ended it might justifiably be regarded as a personal matter. It is, however, surprising that, when introducing the mission of Asopius (3. 7. 1), Thucydides chooses to refer to the Acarnanian request for a son or relative of Phormio and yet, having included a detail by no means essential to his narrative, omits to explain why Phormio himself could not be sent.

Here the question arises whether Thucydides is guilty of bias in his presentation of Phormio. It might be argued that he goes

---

[1] The attempt by Sealey, 69-70, to represent him as a political ally of Pericles is largely dependent upon the belief that his tribe was Pandionis. This view, which rests upon slender evidence, has been further weakened by the arguments of D. M. Lewis, *J.H.S.* LXXXI (1961), 118-19, based upon a new fragment of an inscription.

out of his way to mention the request from the Acarnanians because it was creditable, while deliberately suppressing the reason why Phormio was not available because it could be thought discreditable. There is indeed some justification for concluding that in this one passage, which is a sort of postscript, and for a special reason, which will be mentioned below, he has not been strictly impartial. First, however, since the question of bias has been raised, it is necessary to point out that, while he obviously admired Phormio, his general presentation of him is not in the least prejudiced. His account of the naval operations against the Peloponnesians is thoroughly objective, and no one reading it carefully can fail to conclude that Phormio was completely out-manœuvred in the opening phase of the second action. This unfavourable point could have been concealed or glossed over if Thucydides had so wished. He could also have avoided the implication that the military career of Phormio both before and immediately after his two naval victories was by no means distinguished. There is independent evidence from contemporary sources showing that Thucydides was not alone in admiring Phormio. Old Comedy, which tends to reflect public opinion, though often minority opinion, pictures him as a gallant leader who served his country with old-fashioned dedication and made himself popular with his men by sharing with them the discomforts of active service. Aristophanes refers to him briefly but with warm approval in three extant plays,[1] and Eupolis evidently adopted a similar tone in the *Taxiarchs*, in which he was one of the characters and apparently played a major role.[2] This evidence does not prove conclusively that Thucydides was justified in admiring Phormio; it does suggest that the latter long enjoyed an honoured reputation with a considerable number of Athenians.

---

[1] *Knights* 562, *Peace* 347-8, *Lys.* 804, cf. fr. 86 and 382.

[2] The evidence about this play is collected by J. M. Edmonds, *Fragments of Attic Comedy*, I (1957), 400-6 (fr. 250-64). The date accepted without question by many scholars, namely 427, appears to rest only on the unwarranted assumption that the play must have been produced soon after Phormio returned from Naupactus. Eupolis mentioned him in at least one other play (fr. 40).

To return to the omission by Thucydides to explain why Phormio was not available for service in the summer of 428, the key may perhaps be found in the narrative describing his victories in the previous year. In these first naval battles of the war the Athenians are shown to have enjoyed a decisive advantage because of their superiority in seamanship. The confidence of the Corinthians before the outbreak of war that the Peloponnesians would soon match the enemy in skill (1. 121. 4) was proved thereby to have been mistaken; the prediction of Pericles that they would not (1. 142. 6–9) was abundantly confirmed.[1] To convey to the reader this general lesson, which he considered to be of great importance, must be the principal object of Thucydides in recording the Athenian victories so fully and carefully. The impact of this lesson would have been weakened if he had proceeded to record that the leader of the victorious Athenians was subsequently convicted on some charge arising from the direction of the campaign. As has been already noted, he had no cause to refer to this prosecution when concluding his main narrative of the naval operations, in which he maintains his usual standards of impartiality. On the other hand, in the passage on the appointment of Asopius he does expose himself, perhaps unconsciously, to an accusation of bias by omitting a reference, which is required by the context, to the ἀτιμία of Phormio. This lapse on the part of Thucydides may be judged with more indulgence since, as was pointed out at the beginning of this chapter, Phormio interests him not so much as a prominent personality, or even for the quality of his leadership, but rather because he personified the spirit and skill of the Athenian navy. μέγα γὰρ τὸ τῆς θαλάσσης κράτος (1. 143. 5).

---

[1] How much leeway there was to be made up at the time when these speeches were delivered is well illustrated by the account of the battle of Sybota (1. 49).

CHAPTER V

CLEON

CLEON stands apart from other leading personalities in the *History* because he is somewhat differently presented. He is the only major contemporary figure whose general character and conduct Thucydides expressly condemns, as has already been seen.[1] Similarly he is the only major contemporary figure to whom Thucydides imputes discreditable motives and feelings (4. 27. 3–4; 28. 2–4; 5. 7. 2–3; 16. 1), except for one remarkable passage about Nicias.[2] Some element of personal animosity has undoubtedly influenced Thucydides in his treatment of Cleon, causing him to renounce in some degree his normal standards of impartiality. His bias against Cleon has been noted by very many scholars and is indisputable. Its origin, which may have been complex, can only be guessed. There is nothing improbable in the suggestion, which has often been made, that Cleon was responsible, or partly responsible, for the banishment of Thucydides. Athenian strategoi were exposed to violent criticism in the assembly by demagogues and, if unsuccessful in military commands, were sometimes prosecuted.[3] Cleon, as may be seen especially in the *Knights*, had a reputation for the violence of his attacks on those in authority. It is true that elsewhere Thucydides seems to have refused to allow his judgement to be influenced by personal feelings, but in the case of Cleon emotion arising from a conviction that he himself had suffered an injustice may have been too strong to be controlled. On the other hand, this explanation is not supported by evidence in which any confidence can be felt,[4] and his treatment of other demagogues,

---

[1] See above, Chapter II.   [2] See below, 93–6.   [3] See above, 55–6.

[4] The statement of Marcellinus (*Vit. Thuc.* 46) that Thucydides was banished διαβάλλοντος αὐτὸν τοῦ Κλέωνος is very nearly worthless. It is almost certainly a mere inference from the *History*, such as might have been drawn by any reader at any time since it was written, and indeed has been drawn by many.

Athenagoras and Hyperbolus,[1] though very much briefer, is no gentler than his treatment of Cleon.

It is not directly relevant to the present study to debate whether the prejudice of Thucydides has led him to represent Cleon as more brutal, unscrupulous and dishonest, more misguided politically and incompetent militarily, than he really was. The problem of the real Cleon is one for historians. The purpose of this chapter is rather to consider how the presentation of Cleon differs from that of other leading figures in the Archidamian war; what effect the prejudice of Thucydides has had upon it; whether this prejudice has caused him to devote more attention than usual to personal characteristics; to what extent he has forsaken his self-imposed principles in regard to the interpretation of evidence. In particular, an attempt will be made to show that his presentation of Cleon is curiously lacking in uniformity, since the element of personal antipathy, which gives rise to unmistakable bias, becomes flagrant only in its later stages.

The *History* contains full accounts of four episodes in which Cleon played a major role. Three are debates in the Athenian assembly, one of these being concerned with Mytilene and two with the situation at Pylos; the fourth episode is the campaign in the north-east culminating in his defeat and death at Amphipolis. These episodes will now be examined in chronological order, but a preliminary point may conveniently be made here. It will be observed that all the main appearances of Cleon are public ones. He is not seen taking part in conferences at Athens attended by a small number of persons, such as meetings of the strategoi, although he was almost certainly a member of the board in the year in which Thucydides is known to have served on it.[2] On such occasions he must have made his presence felt and provided plenty of evidence to anyone studying his personality. While serving at Pylos he evidently conferred several times with

[1] See above, 10 and 13.
[2] Gomme (1), III, 505–6 and 526–7, questions whether Cleon was strategos in 424/3, but his objections are not conclusive.

Demosthenes (4. 30. 4; 36. 1; 37. 1), and together they negotiated with the surviving commander of the Spartan garrison (38. 1); but none of these consultations receives more than a bare mention from Thucydides, though Demosthenes may well have supplied him with information about them. Hence Thucydides does not in the case of Cleon adopt a practice which will be seen to be common in the second half of the *History*, namely to portray leading individuals partly by means of reports on conferences in which they were involved.

1. *The Mytilene debate*

The debate on Mytilene (3. 36. 6–50. 1) does not, and is not designed to, throw much light upon the personality of Cleon. Although Thucydides reports the debate in the form of an anti-logy, he does not take advantage of this form to contrast the personalities of the two speakers, as he does so brilliantly in the antilogy between Nicias and Alcibiades on the Sicilian expedition. It is not so much that Cleon has as his opponent the otherwise unknown Diodotus, who is too shadowy to provide an effective contrast; in yet another antilogy Athenagoras, whose folly and violence serve to underline the wise statesmanship of Hermocrates, is little less shadowy than Diodotus. It is rather that Thucydides does not imply wholehearted approval of what Diodotus says,[1] though he could have chosen to do so if he had been determined at all costs to bring discredit upon Cleon. The antilogy presents two contrasted points of view rather than two contrasted individuals.[2] The speech of Cleon confirms the description of him as βιαιότατος τῶν πολιτῶν, but Thucydides uses it mainly to enlighten his readers on aspects of a political creed,

---

[1] A. Andrewes, *Phoenix*, XVI (1962), 78–9, points out that Thucydides does not identify himself with the viewpoint of Diodotus. He also notes (*ibid.* 71–2, cf. Gomme (1), II, 324) that a third attitude towards the decision to punish the Mytileneans with extreme severity is not represented in the report on the debate, namely that of Athenians influenced by humanitarian feelings (36. 4).

[2] Cf. F. M. Wassermann, *T.A.P.A.* LXXXVII (1956), 27–41, whose study of the debate stresses the general lessons arising from it.

the political creed of the demagogues which large numbers of Athenians came to accept in the period after the death of Pericles. If some other demagogue, such as Hyperbolus, had spoken on the punishment of the Mytileneans, his speech, or at any rate the Thucydidean version of it, would, one feels, have left the reader with much the same impression as the reported speech of Cleon.

A surprisingly large proportion of both speeches is concerned with the habits of the Athenian assembly in conducting its debates. Cleon makes a bitter attack on speakers who tried to display cleverness and novelty rather than to offer good advice; he also criticises the Athenians for encouraging such exhibitions by regarding debates in the assembly as competitions in sophistic rhetoric (37. 3–5; 38. 2–7; 40. 2–3). To modern readers this tirade against sophistic rhetoric strikes a slightly ludicrous note, because the language and style in which it is delivered are precisely those used by the practitioners of sophistic rhetoric. This incongruity is, however, only the outcome of conventions not more unrealistic than those of tragedy. It is most improbable that the attack on sophistic rhetoric is wholly the invention of Thucydides. There may well have been rhetorical displays in the debate on the previous day, and Cleon would naturally wish to discourage their resumption. Demagogues were realists who normally relied upon forceful appeals to common sense and abhorred sophistic subtleties. Cleon was, or posed as being, a blunt man who despised both intellectuals and anyone admiring intellectuals.[1] He doubtless made some pungent comments on the way in which debates were conducted in the assembly, but it is difficult to believe that this topic really played so large a part as it does in the Thucydidean version of his speech. Thucydides has not made clear, to modern readers at least, why he lays so much stress on what can hardly have been more than a side-issue. Perhaps he wishes to suggest that after the death of Pericles the demagogues

---

[1] He was himself a convincing speaker (3. 36. 6; 4. 21. 3; Aristoph. *Knights* 626–31), but his methods were certainly crude (cf. *Knights* 137; *Wasps* 36 and 1034; Arist. *Ath. Pol.* 28. 3; Plut. *Nic.* 8. 6), though their crudity was doubtless exaggerated by the comic poets.

discouraged the assembly from listening to the rational arguments ably presented by intellectuals.[1] At all events he seems to be trying to convey a general lesson.

A second subject discussed at some length in this antilogy is more obviously relevant to the occasion of the debate. The assembly met to reconsider the punishment of the Mytileneans (36. 5), but the particular issue at stake was manifestly bound up with the much wider problem of relations between the Athenians and the cities of their empire. Thucydides found this problem absorbingly interesting and evidently welcomed opportunities to introduce discussions of it. Here he is able to present to his readers two different attitudes towards it, both based on expediency and making no concessions to humanitarian feelings. Cleon advocates a policy of brutal repression designed to act as a deterrent to allied cities contemplating revolt (39-40); Diodotus rejects this policy, not because it is brutal, but because in his view it is misguided and will damage Athenian interests (44-8). The attractiveness of this debate for Thucydides, and the chief reason why he chose to include *oratio recta* reports of its two principal speeches, was primarily that he could use it to enlighten his readers on the problems of Athenian imperialism. That it also provided an opportunity to disparage Cleon, by drawing attention to his brutality and by presenting him in a situation where he suffered a defeat, cannot have been unwelcome, as is shown by the introductory description of him (36. 6), but seems to have been a secondary consideration. The occasion was not even one which, without gross distortion, could be used to bring much discredit upon Cleon personally. He was not alone in his brutality: a majority in the assembly had on the previous day supported his motion on the punishment of the Mytileneans (36. 2 and 6), and in the end the vote went against him by only a narrow margin (49. 1).[2] Nor was his policy of repression anything very novel.

---

[1] See the excellent discussion by Andrewes, *Phoenix*, XVI, 73-5.

[2] G. Mathieu, *Mélanges Radet* (1940), 245-8, maintains that, because the recommendations of Diodotus (48. 1) were not accepted *in toto*, the ultimate decision on the punishment of Mytilene (50) was to some extent a compromise.

Pericles had advised the Athenians to keep a tight hold upon the allies (2. 13. 2), and his treatment of Histiaea (1. 114. 3), though it did not involve wholesale executions,[1] is included by Xenophon (*Hell.* 2. 2. 3) in a catalogue of oppressive acts for which the Athenians at the end of the war expected to suffer reprisals.[2] The well-known verbal echoes between passages in the speech of Cleon and passages in the last speech of Pericles,[3] which are undoubtedly intentional, must be designed to show that the attitude of Cleon towards the empire was based upon the principles of Pericles, though he believed in applying them with greater harshness. Here Thucydides has chosen to draw attention to the affinity between the policies of Pericles and Cleon rather than the contrast between their personalities.[4] This choice is not without significance.

2. *The first debate on Pylos*

The lengthy report of Thucydides on the Pylos episode includes accounts of two debates in the assembly in which Cleon was the central figure. The first debate took place when Spartan envoys were received at Athens soon after the conclusion of the temporary truce at Pylos (4. 16. 3). Their speech is reported in *oratio recta* (17–20); they are then informed of the terms on which the Athenians, at the instigation of Cleon, insist as a prerequisite to the conclusion of peace (21. 3); they propose that they should discuss these terms in private with an Athenian delegation (22. 1); Cleon attacks them on the ground that their request for secret talks is proof of their insincerity (22. 2); accordingly they withdraw from Athens, realising that they cannot conduct in public delicate negotiations involving the interests of their allies and that

---

[1] Cf. de Romilly (1), 163.
[2] As pointed out by Gomme (3), 107.
[3] Gomme (3), 107–8; Andrewes, *Phoenix*, XVI, 75.
[4] de Romilly (1), 171, rightly points out that Thucydides 'makes no effort at all to mark the contrast between Pericles and Cleon', whereas in 2. 65 he 'seems particularly concerned to underline the difference between Pericles and his successors'.

the Athenians are not prepared to make peace on reasonable terms (22. 3). Thucydides explains why the Athenians took an unfavourable view of the Spartan overtures—he includes the much quoted phrase τοῦ πλέονος ὠρέγοντο (21. 2)—before he mentions the influence of Cleon upon the Athenian reaction. He is, however, only seizing the opportunity to contrast the Spartan and Athenian attitudes towards the conclusion of peace (21. 1–2); he is not implying that the Athenians had made up their minds at the outset to reject whatever proposals were put forward. On the contrary, the influence of Cleon was, in his opinion, paramount (21. 3, μάλιστα δὲ αὐτοὺς ἐνῆγε Κλέων), and the rest of his account serves to confirm this interpretation.

The narrative suggests, though it does not expressly state, that Cleon, wishing to wreck the negotiations, adopted a stratagem designed to ensure the attainment of this aim: he persuaded the Athenians to make demands which were not in the circumstances unreasonable[1] but involved the interests of Spartan allies,[2] anticipating that the envoys would ask to discuss these demands in private and thus give him the opportunity to challenge their sincerity. A similar, though more complex, stratagem was successfully used by Alcibiades in 420 to discredit another Spartan embassy (5. 44. 3–45. 4). In narrating that episode Thucydides is far more explicit, and he explains in some detail the highly personal reasons of Alcibiades for wishing to prevent closer friendship with Sparta (5. 43. 2–3).[3] Here there is no suggestion that Cleon was actuated by personal motives, though he is later charged with having opposed peace moves for his own disreputable ends (5. 16. 1). There is nothing palpably malicious, or unfair to him, in the account of this debate. Nor is any criticism

---

[1] ἐπὶ μετρίοις in 22. 3 does not refer specifically to the terms defined in 21. 3, since the envoys after hearing these were prepared to continue negotiations (22. 1). It suggests rather that the envoys expected the Athenians, egged on by Cleon, to demand more and more concessions.

[2] Wilamowitz, S. B. Berlin (1921), 309, points out that the envoys at the end of their speech (20. 4) hint that they are willing to make concessions at the expense of their allies.

[3] See below, 212–15.

implied of the methods whereby he handled the situation in the assembly. The successors of Pericles, because they lacked his authority, could not afford to be so frank with the assembly as Pericles himself had been (2. 65. 8–10), and they had at times to use subterfuges of various kinds. The successful stratagem of Alcibiades mentioned above and the unsuccessful stratagem of Nicias when trying to deter the assembly from undertaking the Sicilian expedition (6. 19. 2–24. 2) are recorded by Thucydides without any perceptible disapproval of their fraudulence. In this instance it is not the tactics of Cleon, or his character, that Thucydides condemns, but his policy.

Abortive peace moves involving the sending of embassies were made on other occasions in the course of the Archidamian war, but Thucydides barely mentions them (2. 59. 2; 4. 41. 3–4, cf. 5. 15. 2). He does not report in any detail even the successful negotiations leading to the One Year's Truce (4. 117. 1–2) and the Peace of Nicias (5. 17. 2). He must therefore have considered the negotiations conducted at Athens during the truce at Pylos to have been in some way exceptionally important or instructive and for this reason have described the scene in the assembly at some length. His account shows beyond any doubt that he did consider the occasion to have had the most profound significance and that he did not merely use it as an excuse to present a dramatic picture.

The key to many Thucydidean episodes is to be found in the content of a speech or speeches, but this episode does not seem to be one of them. It is true that the speech of the Spartan envoys (4. 17–20) presents ideas, some of them relevant beyond their immediate context, on what would today be called peaceful co-existence. There is, however, no cogent reason for believing that Thucydides agreed with these general ideas, still less that they are really his own, incorporated rather incongruously here for the edification of his readers. The somewhat academic tone of the speech is indeed appropriate to the envoys, even though they are Spartans, because of the embarrassing situation in which they find themselves. It gives the impression, which is doubtless authentic though perhaps somewhat overstressed by Thucydides, that they are trying to conceal behind a pretentious but rather transparent façade the weakness of their position; that they would be prepared, if pressed, to make concessions far beyond their vague promises of lasting friendship (19. 1–2; 20. 3).

It is, however, not the speech of the envoys but the reception of it that Thucydides found so important. He was convinced, rightly or wrongly, that the Athenians made a disastrous mistake in accepting the bad advice of Cleon and so lost a great opportunity of concluding a favourable peace—just as he was convinced that shortly before the outbreak of war they made a wise decision in accepting the good advice of Pericles to fight rather than yield to Spartan pressure.[1] For the first time the Spartans were now making a serious offer of peace,[2] and for the first time the Athenians were, according to Thucydides, taking a decisive step on the wrong path. The operations at Pylos were not in themselves inconsistent with the principles of Pericles; but the refusal to consider further the possibility of exploiting in the diplomatic field the advantages offered by the military situation was a grave error to anyone so convinced as Thucydides was that Periclean strategy could have won the war (cf. 2. 65. 13). To him the Athenians were now in a much stronger position, and had much better prospects of concluding a lasting peace on favourable terms, than in 421, when they entered into negotiations largely because of recent defeats (5. 14. 1–2). In 425, despite the unforeseen handicap of the plague, they had suffered no serious defeat and had preserved their empire intact, while Peloponnesian invasions of Attica had not produced the results expected of them. In many respects this lost opportunity was a turning point of the war.

[1] See above, 29–30.
[2] Many scholars have inferred, from Aristoph. *Acharn.* 652–4, that they made an offer in 426, but even if this inference is valid, which is disputable, very little progress can have been made towards a settlement.

Whether Thucydides was right in holding these views is a debatable question;[1] that he did hold them and wished to instil them into the minds of his readers is clear from his whole presentation of this scene in the assembly. It is equally clear that he laid the blame on Cleon;[2] that he agreed with those Athenians who shortly afterwards were displeased with Cleon for having caused the breakdown of the negotiations (4. 27. 3). Nevertheless, he does not imply that Cleon was guilty of anything worse than an error of judgement, though it was, in his view, a disastrous error. As has already been pointed out, there is no suggestion that Cleon was acting dishonestly or was misleading the Athenians in order to promote his own interests.

3. The second debate on Pylos

The second debate was held when the Athenians, disappointed by the lack of progress at Pylos and fearing that the Spartans on the island might yet escape, began to regret that they had allowed Cleon to prevent the acceptance of the Spartan peace offers (27. 1-3). The account of this second debate (27. 3-29. 1) strikes a much more personal note than that of the first. It is not so much the policy of Cleon that Thucydides here seeks to expose but his character. Each move made by Cleon is minutely examined and interpreted to his discredit, so that he is represented as having exhibited within a few minutes all the defects traditionally associated with demagogues by their detractors.[3]

Historically the outcome of the second scene in the assembly is far less important than that of the first. That Cleon rather than

[1] The masterly treatment of this whole issue by E. Meyer, *Forschungen zur alten Geschichte*, II (1899), 343–51, who believes that Thucydides was right, is, in my opinion, preferable to any more recent discussion.

[2] It is significant that he does not state whether the issue of peace or war was actually put to the vote in the assembly. According to a corrupt and confused fragment of Philochorus (*F. Gr. Hist.* 328 F 128) a vote was taken, but this may be an unwarranted inference from Aristoph. *Peace* 665–8 (F 128 is quoted by scholia on these lines).

[3] Woodhead, 314.

someone else was appointed to take command at Pylos does not appear to have decisively influenced the course of the military operations there, which were planned and conducted largely by Demosthenes.[1] It is true that Cleon chose Demosthenes to be his colleague (29. 1), whereas he could presumably have tried to discharge his mission alone; that he left Athens with commendable promptitude; that he took with him specialist troops whose skills were most likely to prove effective in the peculiar terrain of Sphacteria.[2] There is, however, no reason to believe that any tolerably competent Athenian, if entrusted with this responsibility, would have acted very differently, though doubtless no one else would have committed himself to the notorious 'mad promise' of Cleon (28. 4; 39. 3). As noted above, Thucydides gives accounts only of such debates as seemed to him to have some particular significance or to teach some important lesson. In this instance he could have chosen to report the appointment of Cleon in a few words without describing how it came about. The scene in the assembly was highly dramatic, but it provides the basis for only one general lesson, namely the irresponsibility of the Athenian assembly (28. 5), to which Thucydides draws attention without laying much emphasis upon it. The attractiveness of this scene to him, and the reason why he has chosen to include a detailed account of it, undoubtedly lie in the opportunity that it affords of underlining the personal failings of Cleon, an opportunity of which he avails himself with skill and relish. Nowhere in the first half of his *History* is the personal element so prominent,[3] and nowhere in his whole work is a major figure presented so unfavourably.

That Thucydides is here guilty of bias against Cleon has been demonstrated many times and does not require further demonstration. On the other hand, the method whereby he builds up his prejudiced picture is worth studying, and indeed very relevant

---

[1] See below, 110–11.
[2] See below, 110.
[3] Except in excursuses on the distant past and perhaps in 5. 16. 1 (discussed below, 93–6).

to the present investigation, since it is so markedly at variance with his normal practice in presenting leading individuals. Its peculiarities can best be illustrated by giving a summary of the part played by Cleon in which references to his motives and feelings are differentiated from the factual narrative by being printed in italics. This summary is as follows:

(i) he charges the messengers from Pylos with having made a false report, *because he realises that he is being criticised for having wrecked the peace negotiations* (27. 3);

(ii) when chosen to go to find out the truth, he advises the Athenians not to waste time by sending observers, *because he knows that he will either have to retract his charges or make a false report himself*; he urges them to send reinforcements, *because he sees that they themselves wish this to be done* (27. 3–4);

(iii) he attacks Nicias, accusing the generals of faintheartedness and asserting that if he were in command he would already have captured the Spartans (27. 5);

(iv) when the Athenians bid him go to Pylos and when Nicias, in the name of the generals, offers him the command, he at first accepts, *because he does not believe Nicias to be in earnest* (28. 1–2);

(v) he tries to withdraw, *because he is alarmed and has not expected Nicias to go to such lengths as to resign the command to him* (28. 2);

(vi) when Nicias presses him more insistently and is supported by the clamour of the mob, he continues his efforts to withdraw (28. 3);

(vii) *because he cannot devise any further expedient for evading the consequences of what he has said,* he accepts the appointment; he then states what troops he will take with him and makes his famous promise to capture or kill the Spartans on the island within twenty days (28. 4).

If shorn of the sections italicised above, the account of the debate would not be strikingly uncharacteristic of Thucydides. It would still prompt the reader to form an unfavourable judgement on the behaviour of Cleon, but it would do so by the normal Thucydidean method of suggestion and implication. In this instance the presentation of the facts is perhaps somewhat dishonest on one point. At the end of the debate Cleon gives details of the troops which he intends to take to Pylos (28. 4). He can hardly have produced this statement of his requirements on the spur of the moment, as is implied; though not serving on the board of strategoi, he must surely have had knowledge of reports sent from Pylos, doubtless by Demosthenes, in which the need for light-armed troops and archers was explained.[1] There is, however, no reason to suspect that Thucydides has given a fictitious or distorted account of what actually happened in the course of the debate.

The attribution of undisclosed and almost wholly discreditable motives and feelings to Cleon is very remarkable. It is almost more remarkable that Thucydides tacitly claims to see into the mind of Cleon and to know precisely why he acted as he did at each stage of the debate. In some passages in which Thucydides seeks to account for the actions of individuals he confesses uncertainty or includes a caveat that he is only expressing his own opinion;[2] here he does not. It is very difficult to believe that he can have possessed incontestable evidence. If Cleon was actuated by the motives and feelings ascribed to him here, he can hardly have divulged them to anyone except his intimate friends, and Thucydides can hardly have been one of these or indeed have associated with them. It is conceivable that by some lucky accident Thucydides may have obtained confidential information from a trustworthy source, but the possibility is very remote. There can be hardly any doubt that he has inferred the quite

[1] See below, 110. The view once widely held (cf. Busolt, 1101 n. 2) that before the debate took place Cleon was already working in close co-operation with Demosthenes should probably be rejected (Schwartz, 296–7; Gomme (1), III, 471).

[2] Cf. 5. 65. 3 (Agis); 8. 46. 5, 56. 3 and 87. 4 (Tissaphernes); 8. 94. 2 (Agesandridas).

considerable catalogue of motives and feelings included in this passage from what he knew, or claimed to know, about the character of Cleon.[1] Other historians commonly draw inferences of this kind about individuals from general indications of character, and indeed the practice is almost unavoidable when writing about the distant past. Thucydides, it seems, adopts it only here and in one other equally remarkable passage (5. 16. 1), which is abnormal in several respects.[2]

He may well be perfectly right in his interpretation of each move by Cleon throughout this episode; the available evidence certainly does not provide adequate grounds for believing that any of his interpretations must be wrong. On the other hand, because he is so obviously antipathetic towards Cleon and because he presents him in a very unusual way, some uneasiness may justifiably be felt. It is by no means self-evident that Cleon must, because no other explanation is feasible, have been actuated by motives attributed to him at each stage of the debate. Other explanations are indeed feasible. Cleon could have sincerely believed that the official report from Pylos was too pessimistic (4. 27. 3); it may have represented the viewpoint of Eurymedon and Sophocles, who had at the outset opposed the plan to occupy Pylos (4. 3. 3–4), rather than that of Demosthenes, who was already preparing for an assault on Sphacteria (29. 2–30. 3). Cleon could also have sincerely believed that to send observers to test the accuracy of the report (27. 4) would necessitate delays likely to prove fatal to the success of any attempt to capture the Spartans on the island (cf. 27. 1). In first expressing willingness to take command, then trying to withdraw and finally accepting (28. 3–4) Cleon undoubtedly exposed himself to charges of vacillation, but he was not necessarily showing himself to be a bungler and a coward. That he had no wish to be appointed cannot be assumed

---

[1] If he was himself present at the debate, as is not improbable, he could observe the behaviour of Cleon and form his own conclusions; but these would be as subjective as his opinions on the general character of Cleon.

[2] See below, 93–6.

to be beyond doubt. He had not, so far as is known, served hitherto on the board of strategoi, and he may well have welcomed the opportunity of holding an office to which demagogues were not normally elected. He may have resented their exclusion as an injustice which could now be rectified. Lack of experience in military leadership was not likely to prove a serious handicap in this instance, because the attack on Sphacteria could be left largely to Demosthenes, as indeed it was. Such could have been his feelings when he initially accepted the challenge of Nicias. He could then have sensed—his influence depended largely on his capacity for judging the mood of the assembly—that many of his political opponents were reluctant to support the unorthodox proposal of their leader Nicias; that they would probably vote against his appointment unless they could somehow be led to believe that he was being jockeyed into it against his will.[1] For this reason he may have adopted the subterfuge of pretending to be unwilling. At all events, if, as seems to be beyond doubt, Thucydides has based his own interpretations solely upon acquaintance with the character of Cleon, his judgement is largely subjective, and other interpretations are not necessarily to be excluded.

In the famous account of the Athenian assault on Sphacteria Cleon is not at all prominent. Before it was launched, he and Demosthenes tried without success to induce the Spartans on the mainland to order the surrender of the troops on the island (30. 4). The tactical plan was the work of Demosthenes (32. 3–4), but Cleon apparently played some part in its execution (36. 1). In the final phase of the operation they decided to hold back their forces with the intention that the surviving Spartans should be captured and not killed (37. 1). This decision may have been largely due to the influence of Cleon, who, as a politician, perhaps appreciated more clearly than Demosthenes the advantage of securing a substantial number of prisoners. Both conferred with the Spartan commander during the armistice leading to the surrender

---

[1] Cf. the feelings ascribed τοῖς σώφροσι τῶν ἀνθρώπων in 28. 5.

of the survivors (38. 1), but Cleon was probably the principal negotiator. The general impression created by the narrative is not unfavourable to Cleon: he evidently had the good sense to leave the military side of his mission almost entirely to the experienced Demosthenes, confining his own contribution mainly to diplomatic activities.[1] Yet, as soon as Thucydides has completed his account of the military operations, he resumes his tone of patent hostility against Cleon. Without a word of comment on the achievement of Demosthenes, he makes his well-known statement that 'the promise of Cleon, mad though it was, was fulfilled' (39. 3). If he had provided some evidence in support of this judgement, it would have carried more conviction. It rests only upon the impression created by his prejudiced account of the second debate in the assembly with its attributions of motive. Throughout the latter part of his narrative on the Pylos episode all other considerations are subordinated to his desire to expose the unworthiness of Cleon.

4. *The Amphipolis campaign*

The last of the four major episodes in which Cleon plays a leading part is the campaign culminating in his death in battle at Amphipolis in 422 (5. 2–3 and 6–11).[2] It is presented in much the same way as the debate leading to his special mission to Pylos. Again the personality of Cleon dominates the narrative, and again his defects are exposed. These defects are represented as almost wholly responsible for the Athenian defeat, and they are even

---

[1] If Thucydides had been determined to lose no opportunity of damning Cleon, he could have accepted and subtly suggested to his readers the charge, which is made several times in the *Knights* (54–7 and elsewhere), that Cleon stole the credit owed to Demosthenes. This view must have been known to Thucydides, but he seems to have rejected it. 5. 7. 3 could mean that Cleon claimed to have proved himself a skilful soldier at Pylos, but the interpretation of the passage is uncertain, cf. Gomme (1), III, 639.

[2] Between 425 and 422 Cleon is mentioned only once by Thucydides, namely as the proposer of the decree condemning the rebels at Scione to death (4. 122. 6). It is unlikely that Thucydides would have named the proposer at all if he had not been provided thereby with an opportunity to draw attention to what he evidently regarded as a typically inhuman act on the part of Cleon.

more prominent than the virtues of Brasidas with which they are contrasted.[1] Again Thucydides claims knowledge of what Cleon thought, and again the feelings attributed to him, which are for the most part discreditable, are apparently inferred from a general assessment of his character and not based upon specific information from a trustworthy source. It is hardly credible that anyone can have been in a position to report to Thucydides what was in the mind of Cleon shortly before he died. The most influential single factor in determining the result of the campaign was doubtless that Cleon was guilty of miscalculations and allowed himself to be outwitted by Brasidas. There are, however, grounds for believing that bias has caused Thucydides to exaggerate his faults and to pay an unusual and indeed excessive amount of attention to the influence of personal factors.[2]

Cleon sailed for the north-east with an expeditionary force of troops and ships 'after persuading the Athenians' (2. 1). This phrase saddles him at the outset with the main responsibility for an enterprise which ended in failure and cost Athens serious losses. He took the initiative in urging it upon the Athenians, and he was in sole command. It is represented as his personal expedition rather than theirs, although they voted for it and might indeed be thought to have prejudiced its chances of success by not appointing a second general with greater knowledge and experience of military leadership.

Cleon wasted no time at Scione, which the force left by Nicias and Nicostratus was still trying to reduce by blockade, but launched a vigorous offensive against other rebel cities. Torone, the most important of these with the exception of Amphipolis, was captured by storm at the first assault (2. 3–3. 4). The narrative of Thucydides shows that this operation was intelligently planned and skilfully executed, exploiting the weakness of the enemy by

[1] See below, 162–3.
[2] The attitude of Thucydides towards Cleon in the narrative of this episode has been examined by Gomme (3), 112–21 and Woodhead, 304–10. The general conclusions of both are, in my opinion, valid, though I disagree on some points of detail.

means of simultaneous attacks by land and sea. It is, however, described much less fully than the fall of the same city to Brasidas in the winter of 424/23 (4. 110–16); and Pasitelidas; the Spartan commander of the garrison, is at least as prominent as Cleon. Thucydides seems almost to be suggesting that Cleon did not really accomplish anything very impressive because Brasidas was absent (5. 2. 3) and failed to reach Torone before it fell. Cleon did in fact perform a feat very rare in this period and never achieved by Brasidas: a walled town of considerable size was taken by storm without any assistance from traitors.[1] Apart from an unsuccessful attack on Stagirus and a successful one on Galepsus (6. 1), the capture of Torone is the only military operation undertaken by Cleon to which Thucydides refers before the final battle at Amphipolis. There is, however, conclusive evidence from epigraphical sources that other rebel towns were recovered in the course of this campaign.[2] While Thucydides cannot be found guilty of failing to mention any major achievement, the cumulative effect of these small gains must have been appreciable. Relectance to give any credit to Cleon seems to have led him to create a somewhat misleading impression.

The defeat of the Athenians at Amphipolis influenced their attitude towards the war and their relations with Sparta. It caused a deterioration of their morale, already weakened by their defeat at Delium, and it led them to abandon their intention of restoring their authority in and around Chalcidice before concluding a lasting peace. Thucydides draws attention to its consequences (14. 1; 16. 1), but to him the battle was significant mainly as the last triumph of Brasidas and the last discomfiture of Cleon. The personal qualities of which both gave evidence during the battle and its antecedents are stressed and contrasted. The account of the battle (6–10) falls below the normal standards of Thucydides. It contains obscurities and inconsistencies, and these may be partly

[1] Gomme (3), 114.
[2] Woodhead, 304–6, who convincingly interprets this evidence originally assembled by A. B. West and B. D. Meritt, *A.J.A.* xxix (1925), 59–69.

due to a readiness on his part to accept information from prejudiced eyewitnesses, in violation of his declared principles (1. 22. 2–3), because of his eagerness to convict Cleon of incompetence and cowardice.[1]

The decision of Cleon to wait at Eion with his army until his Macedonian and Thracian allies joined him, and not to march at once to Amphipolis, was doubtless strategically prudent. He was, however, forced to alter his plans, Thucydides explains, by the restiveness of his troops, who complained to one another that he was lacking in military skill and enterprise; they compared his leadership unfavourably with that of Brasidas and declared that they had been unwilling from the outset to serve under him; it was because of these complaints, and because he feared the consequences of further inactivity, that he determined to conduct a reconnaissance in force in the neighbourhood of Amphipolis (5. 7. 2–3). There is no reason to doubt that there was grumbling against Cleon; charges of incompetence and faintheartedness, whether justified or unjustified, were brought against generals by their own troops as commonly during the Peloponnesian war as in other periods of history.[2] Thucydides must have received reports about this criticism of Cleon, probably originating from soldiers who had themselves been among the grumblers and were therefore inclined to exaggerate its extent. He does not commit himself to any expression of opinion on the question whether the charges were well-founded or not. Elsewhere he tends to disparage the collective judgement of the masses, whether civilian or military;[3] but throughout this episode he contrasts the leadership of Cleon with that of Brasidas in skill and daring, and that is precisely the point made by the discontented soldiers. Hence he appears to be suggesting that their opinion had at least some foundation.

[1] Gomme (3), 118–19.

[2] Cf. the complaints against Agis (5. 60. 2; 65. 2), against the Argive Thrasyllus (5. 60. 5–6) and against Astyochus (8. 78; 83. 3–84. 3). Thucydides does not record gossip for its own sake, but in all these instances he believed that it influenced the course of events.

[3] Cf. 2. 65. 4; 4. 28. 3; 6. 24. 3; 6. 63. 2; 8. 1. 4; 8. 86. 4–5.

On another question, which is a crucial factor in any judgement on the generalship of Cleon, Thucydides makes a quite categorical statement, though it is a question on which there would seem to have been at least some room for doubt. He states that Cleon was compelled (ἠναγκάσθη) to abandon his intention to wait at Eion because he learned of the charges directed against him by his troops (7. 1–2).[1] If this was the real reason, it was so discreditable that he is not likely to have disclosed it even to his staff. He said openly (ἔφη, 7. 3) that he was going to Amphipolis on reconnaissance (κατὰ θέαν... τοῦ χωρίου); his expectation that he would not be attacked (οὐδὲ ἤλπισεν) may also have been communicated to others. What he said must have been reported to Thucydides by someone who heard it; what he thought, namely that he could not avoid taking action against his will because of pressure by his troops, can be no more than an inference from his character, as interpreted by Thucydides.[2] Such inferences, as has been already noted, are not above suspicion. In this instance there is a particular reason for misgiving: from the rest of the narrative Cleon would seem to have been by no means unwilling to undertake a reconnaissance of the area round Amphipolis.[3] There were obvious advantages to be gained by it if he intended, as Thucydides states (7. 3), to attempt to take the city by storm when the reinforcements from his allies arrived and if, as Thucydides also states (7. 4; 10. 3), he believed that he could withdraw at will. The account

---

[1] If οὐ βουλόμενος (7. 2) is taken independently (H. Schütz cited by Steup, *Anhang*, 242–3, who disagrees), which seems very probable, the phrase underlines the unwillingness of Cleon to leave Eion before his allies arrived.

[2] Cf. Woodhead, 308. On the other hand, the sentiments ascribed to Cleon on reaching Amphipolis (7. 5) may well have been openly expressed and those ascribed to him at the beginning of the battle (10. 3–4) could legitimately have been deduced from his orders to his soldiers.

[3] Woodhead, 307, suggests that Cleon may really have sought to precipitate a battle, in which the superiority of the Athenian forces would give him an advantage, and that he may therefore have tempted Brasidas to attack. This view could well be right, but to accept it necessitates rejecting the statement attributed to Cleon that he was only on reconnaissance (7. 3)—unless he was deliberately concealing his real intention from his own men for reasons of security.

of the battle itself leads the reader to conclude that Cleon was defeated because he fell into the trap skilfully laid by Brasidas and because he handled his troops incompetently, and not because he was forced by their criticism to take a foolish risk against his better judgement in making his reconnaissance.[1]

The Athenians were defeated because they were caught at a great disadvantage at the moment when Brasidas delivered his attack. Thucydides makes clear that, in his opinion, errors by Cleon were responsible for this situation, but he fails to define at all precisely what these errors were. His narrative is, as has already been noted, not wholly satisfactory: it has given rise to controversy on topographical points,[2] and it is rather brief and confused, so that there is uncertainty about the position of the two Athenian wings and the movements made by them. Modern readers suffer from the further handicap that the system whereby commanders of hoplite armies communicated orders to their troops by signals and other means is very imperfectly known. Cleon may have committed an elementary blunder by issuing a signal ordering retreat and, at the same time as the signal, verbal instructions explaining how the movement was to be conducted (10. 3).[3] Contemporaries familiar with the techniques of hoplite warfare could perhaps easily infer from the narrative that Cleon was guilty of an error in this respect.[4] This criticism, however, if indeed it is made, does not appear to be much stressed. The point which strikes the reader most is a less technical one: Cleon

---

[1] There is some inconsistency between his rather spiritless submission to the clamour of his troops (7. 2) and his over-confident attitude towards the enemy (7. 3). It is also strange to find that Brasidas, who expected Cleon to march to Amphipolis without awaiting reinforcements because the defending army was so weak (6. 3), made a correct forecast but for a totally wrong reason.

[2] W. K. Pritchett, *Studies in Ancient Greek Topography*, I (1965), 30–45, has discussed the topographical problems.

[3] J. K. Anderson, *J.H.S.* LXXXV (1965), 1–4, interprets the passage in this way after examining evidence on procedures for transmitting orders. He concludes that Cleon 'had not troubled to make himself properly familiar with the basic techniques of commanding hoplites in the field'.

[4] Thucydides often fails to bear in mind his own claim to be writing for posterity (I. 22. 4).

thought, up to the moment before the attack, that he had time to withdraw without fighting, and he was proved to have been wrong.

It is not only in generalship that Cleon is found wanting but also in physical courage. There may be room for doubt whether he was guilty of cowardice in battle; there is no doubt whatever that the narrative of Thucydides conveys that impression. The contrast with Brasidas is sustained to the end: Brasidas died the death of a hero (10. 6, 8, 11), Cleon that of a coward (10. 9). It is not the practice of Thucydides to concern himself with the personal bravery of generals in battle, since it seldom influenced the result. In accounts of actions in which a general was killed he very rarely provides much information about the circumstances; usually, especially in the first half of the *History*, he makes no reference to the death of a general until the end of his account when he gives the casualty figures.[1] His methods are very far removed from those of rhetorical historians like Ephorus, whose battle pictures seem to have credited almost all generals killed in action, including Cleon, with conventionally heroic deaths.[2] Here, however, Thucydides forsakes his usual practice: he describes how Brasidas was wounded at an early stage in the battle (10. 8) and died soon after learning that victory had been won (10. 11), and how Cleon εὐθὺς φεύγων καὶ καταληφθεὶς ὑπὸ Μυρκινίου πελταστοῦ ἀποθνῄσκει (10. 9). This phrase must mean that

---

[1] Cf. 1. 63. 3 (Callias); 2. 79. 7 (Xenophon and two colleagues); 4. 101. 2 (Hippocrates); 5. 74. 3 (Laches and Nicostratus); 6. 101. 6 (Lamachus); 7. 52. 2 (Eurymedon). In the last two instances Thucydides gives somewhat fuller information; but Plutarch (*Nic.* 18. 2–3) provides much more detail about the death of Lamachus, and Diodorus (13. 13. 4) a little more about the death of Eurymedon.

[2] Cf. Diod. 11. 31. 2 (Mardonius); 12. 74. 2 (Brasidas and Cleon); 13. 51. 6 (Mindarus); 13. 99. 5 (Callicratidas); 15. 21. 2 (Teleutias); 15. 55. 5 (Cleombrotus); 15. 80. 5 (Pelopidas); 15. 87. 1 (Epaminondas); 16. 7. 4 (Chabrias). The source is very probably Ephorus in each case. In view of this list of passages, which is not exhaustive, it is impossible to believe (as is suggested very cautiously by Woodhead, 309–10) that Ephorus may have possessed independent information about the death of Cleon which led him to reject the version of Thucydides.

Cleon ran away and was struck down while running away;[1] even if it could be interpreted in a less derogatory sense,[2] it is undoubtedly designed to convey the impression that Cleon acted in a cowardly way. Cleon is contrasted not only with Brasidas but also with his own hoplites on the right wing, who tenaciously beat off two or three attacks before their resistance was broken by local cavalry and peltasts (10. 9). Thucydides has chosen to represent the shameful death of Cleon as a fitting climax to the whole campaign.

The last reference to Cleon occurs in a discussion of the reasons why Athens and Sparta were ready to make peace in 421. After a sketch of public feeling on both sides (5. 14-15) Thucydides goes on to consider the influence of leading individuals: he points out that the deaths of Brasidas and Cleon at Amphipolis removed the most determined opponents of peace on each side, and he states, without any caveat or qualification, why both had wished the war to continue (16. 1). The motives attributed to Cleon are thoroughly discreditable: ὁ δὲ γενομένης ἡσυχίας καταφανέστερος νομίζων ἂν εἶναι κακουργῶν καὶ ἀπιστότερος διαβάλλων. This picture of Cleon and the language used of him closely resemble those of the *Knights*, where he is very frequently charged with knavery and slander:[3] indeed in one passage (801-9) Aristophanes makes the same point that the distractions of the war enabled Cleon to exert his evil influence more effectively than would have been possible in time of peace. Once again Thucydides cannot have possessed incontestably trustworthy evidence of the motives attributed to Cleon and must have inferred them from a subjective assessment of his character. It is true that Thucydides here proceeds to describe much more fully the private feelings of Nicias

---

[1] Adcock, 63: 'it is no doubt true that Cleon ran away, for only so would he be killed by a peltast in the conditions of a normal battle' (though the battle had some abnormal features, cf. 11. 2).

[2] As by Gomme (3), 118-19, cf. (1), III, 652, whose views on this point do not convince me.

[3] Knavery (Aristophanes prefers πανουργεῖν and πανοῦργος): 45, 56, 247-50, 450, 684, 803, 823. Slander: 7, 45, 64, 288, 486, 491.

and Pleistoanax (16. 1–17. 1), whom he names as the principal advocates of peace, and that the personal tone of the whole passage is abnormal, indeed almost unique, in the *History*.[1] It is, however, interesting to note that this brief final reference to Cleon maintains the features seen in the accounts of the second debate about Pylos and of the campaign ending in his death. His personal feelings, and his personal defects as Thucydides saw them, are again given unusual prominence.

The presentation of Cleon is very exceptional and has been examined in some detail in order to show how exceptional it is. Its most remarkable feature is that Thucydides does seem to have relaxed his usual scrupulousness in the use of evidence. Normally, as has already been pointed out, he is chary of committing himself openly, especially in the first half of the *History*, on the merits or demerits of individuals, even where his information about their actions is evidently abundant and has satisfied him that it is trustworthy. Approval and disapproval emerge almost imperceptibly from narrative and speeches. Cleon, on the other hand, is treated very differently. He is introduced in very uncomplimentary terms (3. 36. 6), and in the accounts of the debate on Mytilene and the first debate on Pylos he is presented with unmistakable disfavour. It is, however, in the accounts of the second debate on Pylos and the campaign at Amphipolis that the condemnation of him becomes much sharper and more personal in tone and the bias against him becomes glaring. Here Thucydides has allowed his judgement to be swayed by emotion. He includes statements which must surely either be derived from sources open to some degree of suspicion or be assumptions of his own based upon the character of Cleon as he saw it. His bias is most clearly discernible, as has been shown above, in passages where he attributes to Cleon discreditable motives and feelings. Elsewhere, in the first half of the *History* at least, he does not attribute motives and feelings of any kind at all freely,[2] and,

---

[1] See below, 93–6. [2] See below, 96 n. 2.

where he does, they are normally those of persons, such as Demosthenes and Brasidas, about whom he possessed full information, some of it confidential. In the case of Cleon he has certainly been less punctilious. The second half of the *History* contains a somewhat larger number of passages attributing motives and feelings, but they are neither discreditable nor, it appears, based solely upon assessment of character. Hence it would be a mistake to imagine that in his presentation of Cleon Thucydides is anticipating the methods adopted in the second half of the *History*, where he lays greater emphasis on personality.[1]

The difference in tone between the reports on the first pair of episodes in which Cleon was involved and those on the second pair is very marked, if there is any validity in the findings of the investigation conducted in this chapter. To account satisfactorily for this change is extremely difficult—perhaps an insoluble problem. Its origin may lie partly in the professional pride of Thucydides as a member of the exclusive officer class which had hitherto virtually monopolised the Athenian High Command. While Cleon was trying to influence the decisions of the assembly on the punishment of the Mytileneans and on the Spartan peace offer, he was performing his proper function as a popular leader, and indeed exercising a right to which every citizen of the Athenian democracy was entitled. When, however, he aspired to military command, he was stepping outside his rightful sphere and undertaking responsibilities for which, as other strategoi doubtless complained, he was totally unfitted. In the circumstances it was only to be expected that he would fall into the errors of a novice and suffer an ignominious defeat. Sentiments of this kind may well underlie the account of the campaign at Amphipolis; but they are less likely to have influenced the account of the second debate on Pylos, in which, although the episode led to the first

---

[1] Another objection to this view is that, as already noted (see above, 61), he does not adopt in his accounts of Cleon a practice common in the second half of the *History*, namely that of using reports of conferences to throw light upon individuals.

appointment of Cleon to a military command, he was, according to Thucydides at any rate, forced against his will into accepting it.

Another explanation which suggests itself may be thought to be more probable, though it must remain conjectural. Thucydides may have begun his account of Cleon intending to exclude from it any tinge of his own personal antipathy and to picture him as the demagogue *par excellence*, the prototype of the new leaders whose influence in Athenian politics after the death of Pericles he believed to have been calamitous (2. 65. 7–10). Since he disapproved so strongly of demagogues, his portrayal of Cleon would be extremely uncomplimentary, and deservedly so in his opinion; but it could follow the same pattern and observe the same principles as are inherent in his treatment of other leaders in the first half of the *History*. Later, however, partly because his picture of Cleon was not turning out to be so damning as he believed that it ought to be, but mainly because his personal malice got the better of him, he altered his approach and abandoned his normal standards of impartiality. This may be the reason why in the first pair of episodes he seems to disapprove of Cleon because he was a demagogue, in the second pair to abominate him because he was Cleon.

CHAPTER VI

NICIAS

NICIAS is prominent in the *History* as a soldier and statesman from the first reference to him as the leader of a
small expedition in the summer of 427 (3. 51) to the
report of his execution at Syracuse in 413 (7. 86. 2–5). Apart from
Demosthenes, he is the only major figure in the *History* who
played a leading role both before and after the Peace which came
to bear his name.[1] The record of his career thus provides a test
case in the present investigation; it affords a better opportunity
than any other for observing whether the treatment of individuals by Thucydides remains constant throughout the *History* or
undergoes some modifications in the second half. It is true that
during the Archidamian war Nicias was one among many
Athenian generals appointed to conduct relatively modest and
brief expeditions in the Aegean area, whereas in the Sicilian
campaign he led very large forces operating in a distant theatre of
war and was for a long time in sole command. This difference of
circumstances has naturally influenced the presentation of him by
Thucydides in the two phases of his military career. He was,
however, entrusted with heavy responsibilities in the last six years
of the Archidamian war and was appointed to conduct military
operations more frequently than any other Athenian general, even
Demosthenes.[2]

---

[1] Hermocrates, despite his speech at Gela (4. 59–64) to which Thucydides attaches
much importance, was not a major figure in the Archidamian war. Eurymedon,
though he held some important commands, was not, to Thucydides at any
rate, a major figure at all.

[2] Long ago I published a paper on 'Nicias in Thucydides' (*C.Q.* xxxv [1941],
58–65) designed to show that Thucydides is not, as some scholars have believed,
prejudiced in favour of Nicias. Here I discuss Nicias from a different point of
view, but there is necessarily a certain amount of overlapping. I do not find
that my opinions have altered fundamentally.

According to Plutarch (*Nic.* 2. 2) Nicias served on the board of strategoi during the lifetime of Pericles and was often appointed to independent commands. This statement, though certainly exaggerated, doubtless contains some element of truth, but it may well be based largely upon an inference, and a justifiable one, by Plutarch or some earlier writer that a man of his temperament cannot have leaped suddenly into prominence. It is noteworthy that he is not mentioned by Thucydides until his reputation was established and he was on the point of becoming the most frequently re-elected of Athenian strategoi. The narrative of Thucydides does not throw much light on his qualities of leadership, either military or political, during the Archidamian war, and no speech of his in this period is reported in *oratio recta*.

His first recorded mission was directed against Minoa, an island off the Megarid (3. 51. 1). The aims of this attack, which took place in 427, are carefully defined, but the account of the fighting is so condensed that it lacks clarity (51. 2–4).[1] Nicias was apparently successful in gaining the limited objectives of this minor operation. In the following summer he commanded a force of sixty ships, carrying 2,000 hoplites, which after failing to reduce Melos was more successful in a raid on the territory of Tanagra, where his troops were joined by the rest of the Athenian army marching from Attica. The fleet then sailed on and plundered the coast of Opuntian Locris (3. 91).

Thucydides does not state the aims of these operations, which have a thoroughly Periclean flavour. The attack on Tanagra was probably intended to counteract the unfavourable impression created by the fall of Plataea and to encourage the sympathy towards Athens and hostility towards Thebes felt by many Boeotians. The account of this expedition suggests that it accomplished little except the devastation of enemy territory, a form of

---

[1] A. J. Beattie, *Rh. Mus.* CIII (1960), 21–43, has examined the obscure topography of this area and has shown that Minoa and Nisaea were very close to each other.

warfare[1] in which Thucydides seems to have had little confidence.[2]

The next appearance of Nicias is in the celebrated account of the debate in the Athenian assembly in the summer of 425 when the task of capturing the Spartans trapped on Sphacteria was proving more difficult than had been anticipated (4. 27–28). Cleon, not Nicias, is the central figure of the episode, which has already been considered above in relation to the presentation of Cleon by Thucydides.[3] It has often been noted that the behaviour of Nicias in this debate is not at all creditable:[4] he is seen to have been willing, even eager, to shirk his duty and resign his command, thereby transferring responsibility for a vitally important enterprise to a man possessing, it appears, no experience or knowledge of military leadership (28. 1–3). Thucydides neither condemns nor defends the attitude of Nicias;[5] he ignores it. He is following his normal practice of directing the attention of the reader to the most significant aspect of an episode—in this instance the mixture of reprehensible qualities exhibited by Cleon —and avoiding all distractions. He does, however, refer to the conduct of the Athenians gathered in the assembly (28. 5), whose reactions and feelings seem to have been of greater interest to him than those of Nicias.

[1] Such plundering raids might have proved effective if frequently repeated over a considerable period, cf. *C.Q.* xxxix (1945), 82.

[2] From Plutarch, *Nic.* 3. 5–7, it seems that Nicias must have played an important part in the purification of Delos in 426, to which Thucydides refers (3. 104) without mentioning Nicias. This omission is not perhaps of much significance, but it may be noted that Thucydides has chosen to use the purification as the starting-point of an antiquarian digression, whereas he might, it appears, have used it to throw light on the personality of a prominent individual (cf. 89 n. 1 below). The piety of Nicias later influenced a crucial decision affecting the fortunes of the Athenian expedition to Sicily (7. 50. 4).

[3] See above, 69–74.

[4] *C.Q.* xxxv (1941), 60 with n. 2; Gomme (1), iii, 469 and (3), 113; Woodhead, 313–14; A. Andrewes, *Phoenix*, xvi (1962), 79.

[5] It is expressly condemned by Plutarch (*Nic.* 8. 2–5). A contemptuous reference to it in a fragment of Aristophanes (fr. 100), which Plutarch quotes, is probably introduced merely to raise a laugh and does not necessarily reflect popular opinion.

Immediately after the conclusion of the operations at Pylos Nicias and two colleagues conducted an attack on the western coastline of the Saronic Gulf. A force of Athenian and allied troops, including some cavalry, was landed in Corinthian territory, and it defeated an army of Corinthians near Solygeia. When a second Corinthian force approached, the Athenians withdrew to their ships, which took them to Crommyon where they plundered the countryside. They then made landings further south, at a point in Epidaurian territory and then at Methana, where they established a garrison on the isthmus linking the peninsula to the mainland (4. 42–5). Thucydides describes this expedition in detail and very vividly; indeed the suggestion has been made, not without some reason, that he took part in it himself.[1] In one respect, however, his account is puzzling and unsatisfactory. When he gives detailed information about military episodes, and also in many instances where his narrative is quite brief, his practice is to define carefully the aims and plans of the generals, often those on both sides.[2] Here he includes no statement of Athenian aims in making this expedition, and they do not emerge in the course of his narrative. The result is that he leaves his readers in doubt whether the whole operation was largely successful or largely unsuccessful. If the Athenians intended to occupy and fortify Solygeia,[3] their principal objective was not achieved; if, on the other hand, their chief aim was the establishment of a garrison at Methana and their landings elsewhere were mainly diversionary, the expedition was a success.[4] It might be

---

[1] Gomme (1), III, 494. The anecdote about the recovery of the two Athenian bodies left behind when the Athenians withdrew after their victory (44. 5–6) is very remarkable (though, unlike Plutarch, *Nic.* 6. 5–7, Thucydides does not use it to throw light on the character of Nicias).

[2] This characteristic is minutely examined by de Romilly (2), 107–79 in an illuminating chapter on accounts of battles.

[3] This view of their intentions is suggested by Busolt, 1114–16, but rejected by Gomme (1), III, 494.

[4] Aristophanes, *Knights* 595–610, pays a tribute to the horses carried in transports on this expedition (cf. 42. 1). Even a comic poet could hardly, it may be felt, have pictured the exploits of these horses with so much enthusiasm unless the whole operation had been thought to have been at least moderately successful.

argued that Thucydides had for some reason no access to trust-worthy information, even after the event, about the aims of Nicias and his colleagues,[1] whereas he was able to give a full and graphic account of the fighting in Corinthian territory either because he was himself serving as a cavalryman or hoplite or because he had plenty of reliable reports from others not holding any position of authority.[2] There are, however, difficulties in supposing that Thucydides had no knowledge of Athenian aims. It is hard to believe that, when strategos in the following year, he was unable to discover the plans of his predecessors, if they were not already known to him. He could presumably have consulted Nicias, who was one of his colleagues. Indeed he some-how learned that the Athenians evacuated their position near Solygeia in the mistaken belief, which must have been that of the generals, that a body of troops seen advancing towards them was a reinforcement for the Corinthians drawn from neighbouring Peloponnesian states (44. 5). The omission of any reference to Athenian aims, whatever the reason for it may be, suggests that for Thucydides the importance of this episode did not lie in the light that it might have thrown upon the leadership or personality of Nicias. This impression is strengthened by the fact that Nicias is not mentioned by name after the opening sentence (42. 1). The narrative technique of these chapters, which has perhaps a flavour of Xenophon at his best, is not altogether typical of Thucydides.

In the summer of 424 Nicias, with Nicostratus and Autocles as colleagues, was entrusted with the command of another sea-borne expedition. Its principal objective was Cythera. The Athenians successfully overran the island and after establishing a garrison at its port of Scandeia conducted plundering raids at a considerable number of points on the mainland. Thyrea, where the Aeginetans expelled from Aegina had been given a home by the Spartans, was captured and burnt, and the survivors were

---

[1] It is quite possible that they improvised to a considerable extent (cf. Gomme (1), III, 494).

[2] Some details (cf. 42. 3; 44. 4) seem to have been derived from Corinthian sources.

removed to Athens (4. 53–7). A little more attention is devoted to the part played by Nicias than in the account of his expedition in the preceding summer. Thucydides mentions that, before the Athenians attacked the town of Cythera, Nicias was negotiating with some Cytherians. Although these negotiations hastened the end of resistance, it appears that the Athenians would have derived more benefit from military action alone without any admixture of diplomacy; for they evidently felt that the diplomatic moves of Nicias imposed upon them a moral obligation to refrain from expelling any Cytherians from the island except for a few suspects (54. 2–3; 57. 4). In the account of the attacks on the mainland after the surrender of Cythera the Athenian generals are not mentioned either collectively or individually. To Thucydides the expedition marks a further step in the development of the strategy from which the Athenians were now reaping so much advantage. Its importance for him lay principally in its effect on Spartan morale, already at a low ebb in consequence of the disaster on Sphacteria. He dwells upon the dejection and timidity of the Spartans arising from their unexpected adversity and their inability to devise any effective method of countering the Athenian offensive (55. 1–56. 1). This passage is inserted at the point at which the Athenians were at the height of their success just before the balance was redressed by their series of failures in Sicily, in Boeotia and in the north-east.

In the following spring Nicias was one of the three strategoi who took the oath on behalf of the Athenians when the One Year's Truce was concluded (4. 119. 2). Laches was the mover of the decree approving this armistice (118. 11), but Nicias was undoubtedly in favour of it, and although evidence is lacking, he probably played a leading role in negotiating its terms and securing its acceptance by the Athenian assembly.[1] Thucydides does

---

[1] Gomme (1), III, 605, rightly points out the error of assuming that strategoi signing a treaty necessarily approved of its contents; but his comment is influenced by his salutary though somewhat excessive horror of any suggestion that anything resembling political parties existed at Athens (cf. *ibid.* 593).

not mention the attitude of individual Athenians towards the armistice and refers only to the generally favourable mood of public opinion (117. 1).

Shortly after the conclusion of the armistice Nicias was again on active service. The revolts of Scione and Mende, which were supported by Brasidas, caused the Athenians to send an expedition to Pallene under the command of Nicias and Nicostratus (129. 2). In recording the events in this area after the armistice, Thucydides has chosen to direct the attention of his readers mainly to the fortunes of Brasidas,[1] as the arrangement of his narrative shows. Apart from two references to retaliatory preparations by the Athenians (122. 6; 123. 3), he gives no information about their expedition until he has described the Lyncestian campaign of Brasidas, who on returning from Macedonia found Mende already in Athenian hands (129. 1). Thucydides then proceeds to report the course of events in Pallene, mainly from the standpoint of the rebels and their Peloponnesian allies (129. 3–131. 3). While advancing against Mende, both the Athenian generals found themselves in difficulties; their army barely avoided defeat and had to retreat (129. 3–5). Soon, however, an uprising against the Peloponnesian garrison took place inside the city; through this stroke of good fortune—it was not the outcome of negotiations with Nicias (130. 5–6)—the gates were opened and the revolt collapsed. The Athenians then stormed a hill near Scione and began to build an encircling wall round the city (131. 1–2). At the end of the summer, when the wall was completed, the generals left some troops to maintain the blockade and returned home with the rest of their army (133. 4). The military results of this expedition were not altogether satisfactory, and Scione continued to resist until the summer of 421 (5. 32. 1). Nicias is, however, credited by Thucydides with a diplomatic success of considerable importance: it was partly through his representations that Perdiccas, who had again come to terms with the Athenians, exerted effective pressure upon some Thessalian friends to prevent a

---

[1] These are considered below, 155–8.

Peloponnesian force, which was on its way to join Brasidas, from marching across Thessaly (4. 132. 2).

The record of the part played by Nicias in the history of the war up to this point is somewhat colourless, even superficial. It suggests that, although no other Athenian was so frequently entrusted with duties which offered opportunities to display powers of leadership, his contribution did not appear to Thucydides to be particularly important, original or instructive and could not be used as the foundation of general lessons about war and politics; that his personality and his attainments were less interesting than those of some other leading figures. If, as is likely, Thucydides felt but deliberately resisted a temptation to include purely personal information when writing about Brasidas or Demosthenes, he evidently found no need to practise any such restraint when reporting the part played by Nicias in the Archidamian war. His habit of focusing attention upon events which seemed to him most significant may have led him to be a little unjust to Nicias. It was mainly because the almost desperate situation in which the Spartans found themselves in the middle of 424 (55. 1–56. 1) was largely the outcome of their debacle at Pylos that he has chosen to narrate that episode in great detail. The less spectacular operations conducted by Nicias certainly helped to consolidate the advantage which the Athenians had gained at Pylos, as Thucydides acknowledges (55. 1). Yet the reader is left with the feeling that his leadership was not such as was likely to bring about final victory in the war, even victory of the rather negative kind which Pericles had sought.

There is, however, one most remarkable passage in which Nicias seems to be rated as a much more influential and interesting figure than he is elsewhere in the first half of the *History* and his personal feelings about war and peace are described in detail (5. 16. 1). This passage belongs to a lengthy review of the reasons why in the winter of 422/21 both Athens and Sparta were favourably disposed towards making peace (14–17. 1). Thucydides begins with an analysis of public feeling on both sides (14–15), but he goes on to discuss the feelings of individuals (16. 1-17. 1). Death has now removed the principal opponents of peace on each side, Cleon and Brasidas, to whom personal motives for having wished the war to continue are ascribed. Consequently the two principal advocates of peace, Pleistoanax and Nicias, pursue their common aim with increased eagerness,[1] and their motives, which are no less personal than those of Cleon and Brasidas, are explained at much greater length. The treatment of Pleistoanax, which is not relevant here, is even more surprising than that of Nicias: a sketch of his chequered career containing personal touches is included, even though his influence upon the course of the war seems to have been, except on this one occasion, almost negligible (cf. 5. 33; 75. 1). The treatment of Nicias, if on a smaller scale, is also abnormal.

Thucydides first refers to the success of Nicias as a military leader, πλεῖστα τῶν τότε εὖ φερόμενος ἐν στρατηγίαις (16. 1).[2] This phrase might appear to be in conflict with the impression created by the reports, which have been discussed above, on the military expeditions of Nicias. It is not, however, a particularly warm tribute. There is no suggestion that his success was necessarily the result of good leadership. Entrusted with a considerable number of commands, he had suffered no actual reverse, except at Melos in 427, and no other contemporary general on the Athenian side could claim even that modest record. The motives by which he was influenced in his desire for peace are then stated: βουλόμενος, ἐν ᾧ ἀπαθὴς ἦν καὶ ἠξιοῦτο, διασώσασθαι τὴν εὐτυχίαν, καὶ ἔς τε τὸ αὐτίκα πόνων πεπαῦσθαι καὶ αὐτὸς καὶ τοὺς πολίτας παῦσαι καί τῷ μέλλοντι χρόνῳ καταλιπεῖν ὄνομα ὡς οὐδὲν σφήλας τὴν πόλιν διεγένετο, νομίζων ἐκ τοῦ ἀκινδύνου ταῦτα ξυμβαίνειν καὶ ὅστις ἐλάχιστα τύχῃ αὑτὸν παραδίδωσι, τὸ δὲ ἀκίνδυνον τὴν εἰρήνην παρέχειν. There are very few passages in the *History* in which

---

[1] The sense of this passage (16. 1) is much improved by accepting the emendation of Stahl, μάλιστ' αὐτήν for μάλιστα τήν ἡγεμονίαν.

[2] εὖ φερόμενος occurs also 15. 2, cf. 2. 60. 3 (καλῶς φερόμενος), and Xen. *Hell.* 2. 1. 6.

the motives of an individual are so penetratingly and so candidly analysed. That the principal and indeed almost sole aim of Nicias is stated to have been to safeguard his own reputation is not particularly remarkable.[1] With characteristic frankness Thucydides normally assumes that cities and their leaders were influenced mainly by self-interest;[2] and selfish motives are attributed to the three other individuals mentioned here, including even Brasidas.[3] There is no suggestion that Nicias was deliberately sacrificing Athenian interests in order to further his own: undoubtedly he was convinced that peace would benefit Athens. Nevertheless, if the motives ascribed to him are not discreditable because of their selfishness, they are discreditable for another reason. They reveal a thoroughly unenterprising, almost feeble, way of thinking of which Thucydides certainly disapproved. It has affinities with the viewpoint of Archidamus and is entirely contrary to Periclean doctrine.[4] Yet the most striking feature of the passage is not so much that it suggests to the reader an unfavourable judgement of Nicias as that the feelings ascribed to him are almost exclusively personal.

The passage may also be deemed to be exceptional in another respect. Because Thucydides was in exile in 421, he cannot have obtained information about the feelings of Nicias by means of personal enquiries in Athens; and no other passage provides even the smallest indication that he was able to consult anyone closely associated with Nicias towards the end of the Archidamian war.[5] Hence he has probably relied here solely upon inferences from personal knowledge of Nicias gleaned in the period before his own banishment: he almost certainly attended meetings of the strategoi in 424 at which Nicias was present, and he may well

---

[1] The only reference to the public interest is καὶ τοὺς πολίτας παῦσαι, cf. Gomme (1), III, 663.

[2] de Romilly (1), 100 and 256.

[3] de Romilly (1), 45–6.   [4] Gomme (1), III, 663.

[5] The sixth and seventh books, on the other hand, contain much information about the motives and feelings of Nicias during the Sicilian expedition which can only have been learned from some trusted subordinate or subordinates (see below, chapter XI).

have had private conversations with him as well. If there is any validity in this suggestion, he is here deviating from what appears to have been his normal practice. Passages in which he reports motives or feelings not publicly disclosed fall mainly into groups, each group giving those of a single leader in one, or more than one, episode;[1] and he seems to have based these reports not upon general inferences from what he knew about the character of each leader but upon specific evidence derived from a trustworthy source.[2] It seems to be only in excursuses when writing about great figures of the distant past that he is content to infer motives from knowledge of character, because he has no alternative;[3] but in his treatment of Nicias in this passage he appears to have applied much the same method to a contemporary. Indeed the unusually personal and biographical tone of his whole discussion about the reasons why Nicias and Pleistoanax desired peace (16. 1–17. 1) has perhaps more affinity with that of his major excursuses than with that of his narrative of the Archidamian war. Why he has chosen to write in this way is obscure, and speculation on the problem would be unprofitable.

[1] Examples are the case of Aristeus, which I have discussed in *C.Q.* XLI (1947), 25–30, and that of Demosthenes in the Archidamian war, to which I refer below, 96 with n. 2. The treatment of Cleon is exceptional in this respect as in others (see above, 83–4).

[2] Such passages are very few before the last chapters of the third book (cf. *ibid.* 28) and are much less common in the first half of the *History* than in the second.

[3] Cf. I. 128. 3 and 131. 2 on Pausanias.

CHAPTER VII

DEMOSTHENES

THE military operations and plans of Demosthenes in the Archidamian war, both successful and unsuccessful, are reported by Thucydides more fully than those of any other Athenian leader. There is no doubt that Thucydides was in possession of abundant and authentic information about him: not only are accounts of events in which he took part unusually full of graphic details,[1] but references to motives which cannot have been widely known and to unfulfilled intentions are frequent and illuminating.[2] Many modern scholars have felt, and with good reason despite the absence of conclusive evidence, that Thucydides obtained much of this information from Demosthenes himself,[3] who was one of his colleagues on the board of strategoi in 424/423 and must have been personally known to him.[4] Nevertheless, Thucydides nowhere specifically assesses the ability of Demosthenes or the value of his services to Athens, and the general impression given by the narrative is equivocal. That he believed Demosthenes to have been brave, energetic and enterprising, an inspiring leader of men and normally a good tactician, is perfectly clear, but he apparently also regarded him as inclined to be impetuous and found his strategy occasionally unsound and too optimistic. It may be that Thucydides, after careful consideration of all the evidence, has designedly chosen to present

[1] Some of these will be noted below.
[2] In the north-west: 3. 95. 1; 96. 2; 97. 2; 98. 5; 109. 2. At Pylos: 4. 9. 2; 29. 3–30. 1; 30. 3. In the Megarid (in association with Hippocrates): 4. 69. 1; 73. 4.
[3] Cf. Busolt, 654 n. 1 and 1067 n. 1; Schwartz, 293; Finley, 188; Grundy, I, 26 and 343, II, 172.
[4] He may even have been connected with Demosthenes by marriage, since a Θουκυδίδης ᾿Αλκισθένους ᾿Αφιδναῖος (the patronymic and deme are the same as those of Demosthenes) is attested by an inscription from the second half of the fourth century (*I.G.* II², 1678, 31).

Demosthenes to his readers with precisely this mixture of approval and disapproval. He seems, however, in some parts of his narrative strangely reluctant to give Demosthenes due credit for the originality and imaginativeness which he undoubtedly showed. These qualities, in the military sphere at least, bore some resemblance to those of Themistocles, which Thucydides praises so warmly (I. 138. 3). In modern times it has been maintained that Demosthenes was the most progressive and inventive general of his time, the creator of a new kind of warfare; and this claim, though somewhat exaggerating his merits, has at least some foundation.[1] It has also been suggested that Thucydides has done Demosthenes an injustice by withholding recognition of his high qualities.[2] The principal reason, in my opinion, for the somewhat grudging treatment of Demosthenes by Thucydides, which is in striking contrast to his treatment of Brasidas, is this: Demosthenes was obviously not a disciple of Pericles in the military sphere and sought means of breaking away from Periclean strategy, in which Thucydides believed so fervently.

Before trying to substantiate this view a preliminary point must be briefly considered. The career of Demosthenes as described by Thucydides is exclusively military, apart from purely formal activities.[3] There is no evidence from other sources that he was a politician; he seems, like some other strategoi including Phormio, Eurymedon and Lamachus, to have had only military aspirations and to have exercised little or no political influence. Modern scholars have held that he was associated with the extreme democrats and acted as their military instrument,[4] partly because of his partnership with Cleon in the later stages of the operations at Pylos, and partly because he, like the extreme democrats, favoured a more offensive strategy than that of Pericles.

---

[1] M. Treu, *Historia*, v (1956), 420–47, who seems to me to have overstated a good case. Sealey, 80, describes Demosthenes as 'the one general of the Archidamian war who could make careful strategic plans for territorial warfare on a large scale'.
[2] E. C. Woodcock, *Harv. Stud.* xxxix (1928), 93–108.
[3] See below, 119 n.1.
[4] Grundy, I, 353; Woodcock, *Harv. Stud.* xxxix, 94.

There is, however, nowhere any indication that he shared the political views of Cleon and the extreme democrats or that he was closely linked with them in any way.[1] In planning the two offensives in 424 he co-operated with Hippocrates, who was a nephew of Pericles and is unlikely to have been an associate of Cleon.[2] More important, when on two occasions military projects conceived by Demosthenes were unsuccessful, he apparently had no means of regaining popular favour by using political influence. After his defeat in Aetolia he was afraid to return to Athens (3. 98. 5) and only reinstated himself by his victories in Amphilochia (3. 114. 1), while after the failure of the plan to win Boeotia in 424 he was not, so far as is known, entrusted with the direction of any military operations, except for a single minor one (5. 80. 3), until he was sent to Sicily in 413. This evidence suggests that he neither had much political influence himself nor could rely on the support of any political leader or faction. He was important only as a general.[3]

1. *Campaigns in the north-west*

Demosthenes is first mentioned as one of two strategoi appointed to command a fleet of thirty ships sent round the Peloponnese in the summer of 426 (3. 91. 1). The Athenians from this fleet were being used to help the Acarnanians and other allies against Leucas (94. 1–2) when the Messenians of Naupactus approached Demosthenes with the suggestion that he should undertake an invasion of Aetolia (94. 3). Thucydides seems to imply that there was a fair

[1] K. J. Dover, *C.R.* IX (1959), 196–9, draws attention to the weakness of the assumption that in the opening scene of the *Knights* the two slaves consistently reproduce the characteristics of Demosthenes and Nicias. Hence the scene does not necessarily imply that Demosthenes disapproved of Cleon. Nevertheless, the joke that Cleon stole from Demosthenes the credit for the victory at Pylos (54–7, cf. 742–5, 778, 1200–1), which must surely have had some foundation if it was to be dramatically effective, hardly suggests that they were political allies.   [2] Sealey, 80, with n. 106.

[3] Even A. B. West, *C.P.* XIX (1924), 142 and 209, who tends to reconstruct the affiliations of Athenian strategoi rather speculatively, cannot attach Demosthenes to any political group.

prospect of reducing Leucas by blockade (94. 2) and that the Acarnanians were not acting unreasonably in refusing to assist Demosthenes in invading Aetolia because it meant the withdrawal of Athenian support from their own attempt to blockade Leucas (95. 1–2). The plan put forward by the Messenians for the conquest of Aetolia, as outlined by Thucydides (94. 3–5), seems feasible, though evidently based on the assumption that the Acarnanians, whose light-armed troops could have been especially valuable,[1] would take part in the expedition. In accepting the plan, however, Demosthenes enormously extended its range by an addition of his own, fully reported by Thucydides: after reducing Aetolia he would advance through Doris and Phocis and invade Boeotia from the north-west (95. 1). Readers have felt that this ambitious enterprise was unsound and too optimistic, and there is no doubt that Thucydides deliberately suggests an unfavourable verdict.[2] Some information on the views of Procles, the colleague of Demosthenes (91. 1), about the prospects of the expedition would have been instructive,[3] but Thucydides has chosen to give the impression that Demosthenes alone was responsible for planning and conducting it.[4] Although Demosthenes apparently had no mandate from the assembly for this campaign, he could hardly be criticised on that account. The orders issued to Athenian commanders tended to be deliberately vague,[5] and they were expected to follow their own judgement in using their forces in the best interests of Athens.

---

[1] For Acarnanian light-armed troops see 2. 81. 8; 7. 31. 5 and 67. 2.

[2] de Romilly (2), 169 n. 1 finds criticism of Demosthenes in the phrase τῶν Μεσσηνίων χάριτι πεισθείς (95. 1). This interpretation is questionable. The Messenians were free allies who controlled the vital base at Naupactus, and Demosthenes was surely justified in seeking to please them, provided that he believed their advice to be sound.

[3] H. Schaefer, *R.E.* XXIII (1957), 180, suggests that Procles was young and belonged to an aristocratic family; if so, he had perhaps had less experience than Demosthenes in subordinate commands and owed his election to family connexions. Both suggestions are, however, conjectural.

[4] Procles is mentioned only as the most notable victim of the expedition (98. 4).

[5] Cf. those issued to Eurymedon, Sophocles and Demosthenes himself in 425 (4. 2. 2–4).

The defeat of Demosthenes near Aegitium (97. 3–98. 4), which brought the campaign to an abrupt end, is attributed almost entirely to the disadvantage suffered by his mainly hoplite army when attacked in mountainous and wooded country (cf. 4. 30. 1) by more mobile Aetolian javelin throwers. He had arranged with his allies the Ozolian Locrians that they should meet him with their full force in the interior of Aetolia, and much emphasis is laid upon the value of the benefits which their aid was expected to produce (3. 95. 3, ὄντες γὰρ ὅμοροι τοῖς Αἰτωλοῖς καὶ ὁμόσκευοι μεγάλη ὠφελία ἐδόκουν εἶναι ξυστρατεύοντες μάχης τε ἐμπειρίᾳ τῆς ἐκείνων καὶ τῶν χωρίων). When the Athenians reached the agreed meeting place, the Locrians had not yet arrived, and Demosthenes pressed on towards Aegitium without waiting for them (97. 2). Some blame attaches to the Messenians, who despite the absence of the Locrians repeated their advice to Demosthenes that he should hurry on with all speed before the Aetolians could concentrate their scattered forces (97. 1). Thucydides, however, makes his own verdict exceptionally plain, namely that Demosthenes was gravely at fault in listening to the Messenians and was guilty of an easy optimism verging on irresponsibility (97. 2, τῇ τύχη ἐλπίσας, ὅτι οὐδὲν αὐτῷ ἠναντιοῦτο); and the value of the light-armed Locrians is again stressed. Few passages in the *History*, except for those condemning demagogues, are so critical of an individual. Attention is again drawn to the culpability of Demosthenes when the Athenian casualty figures are reported (98. 4). The dead numbered 120, heavy losses in relation to the total force of Athenians engaged, which was 300, but much lighter than those sustained in other defeats.[1] Thucydides adds that they were 'the best men from the city of Athens killed during this war'. Whatever may have prompted him to make this remarkable comment, it is hardly creditable to Demosthenes. Although the episode was not on a great scale, even judged by the standards of the Archidamian war, and did not weaken the Athenian cause very seriously, Thucydides seems determined to impress upon his

---

[1] Gomme (1), II, 407–8.

readers that Demosthenes sustained a defeat through his own errors. He adds that Demosthenes was afraid to return home because of this defeat (98. 5) but fails to make clear, here or later, whether it led to deposition from office.[1] He may have been reluctant to mention a case where the Athenians were in his view justified in dismissing a general (cf. 4. 65. 3–4).

The leadership of Demosthenes is seen in a very different light in the narrative of events in the north-west during the remainder of this year (426). The difference is not solely that he failed in Aetolia and was victorious in Amphilochia, since Thucydides does not assess qualities of leadership by the criterion of success and failure alone. His first achievement, which was to save Naupactus (3. 100. 1–102. 5), did not involve any fighting but demanded considerable skill in the diplomatic field. When Naupactus was threatened by the Spartan Eurylochus, who led a mixed force of 3,000 men and was joined by the Aetolians, the only chance of preserving this important base lay in obtaining help from the Acarnanians. They alone among the allies of Athens in this area had a large and tolerably efficient army. Demosthenes succeeded in persuading them to send 1,000 hoplites, whose arrival deterred Eurylochus from attempting to take Naupactus by storm (102. 3–5). Thucydides dwells on the difficulties of Demosthenes in securing aid from the Acarnanians which arose from their recent disagreement with him at Leucas (102. 3); and their reluctance was doubtless all the greater in that they were being asked to help the Messenians of Naupactus, whose proposals had caused Demosthenes to withdraw his support from their own attempt to blockade Leucas.

The campaign of the following winter, in which Eurylochus and the Ambraciots tried to overrun Amphilochia and Acarnania, is very fully and graphically described (105–14). Admiration for the leadership of Demosthenes, who won two brilliant victories

---

[1] D. M. Lewis, *J.H.S.* LXXXI (1961), 119–20, and H. B. Mattingly, *C.Q.* XVI (1966), 174 with n. 6, are probably right in maintaining that Demosthenes was in fact dismissed.

despite the handicap of leading a force certainly inferior in numbers (107. 3) and probably also in quality,[1] is implicit in the narrative of Thucydides at many points. The Acarnanians were being hard pressed when they sent to ask Demosthenes to help them (105. 3). The situation had deteriorated when he arrived because they had failed to prevent Eurylochus and his troops from joining an Ambraciot expeditionary force at Olpae (105. 2; 106, 3), and it would have become almost desperate if the enemy had been further strengthened by the arrival of a second Ambraciot force which had been summoned from the city of Ambracia (105. 4). Demosthenes responded speedily to the Acarnanian appeal, taking with him such forces as he could muster, and it was doubtless through his agency that the assistance of twenty Athenian ships operating round the Peloponnese was also enlisted (105. 3; 107. 1–2). Although the Acarnanians had invited him to be their leader (105. 3), they do not appear to have granted him an official status superior to that of their own generals;[2] but they wisely left the direction of operations to him. The decisive factor in the ensuing battle at Olpae was an ambush in which troops were concealed beside a road through a scrub-covered valley: Demosthenes was alone responsible for this ambush (107. 3), and to Thucydides the victory was his achievement.[3] It is made abundantly clear that, had there been no ambush, the Peloponnesians and Ambraciots, who gained an initial advantage on both wings, would have won the battle (107. 3–108. 3). On the following day the surviving Spartan commander tried to negotiate terms whereby the remnants of his troops should be allowed to withdraw unmolested. Both the refusal to permit the withdrawal of

---

[1] Cf. 108. 2 on the military reputation of the Ambraciots and 111. 3 on the indiscipline of the Acarnanians. The success of Demosthenes in directing and controlling a mixed and unmanageable force is in striking contrast to the failure of Cnemus at Stratus in 429 (see below, 137–8).

[2] μετὰ τῶν σφετέρων στρατηγῶν in 107. 2 must mean precisely the same as μετὰ τῶν ξυστρατήγων in 109. 2. The natural inference is that Demosthenes had no overriding authority in either military or diplomatic matters.

[3] de Romilly (2), 128–9, in a brief analysis of the narrative, shows that the predictions of Demosthenes were precisely fulfilled.

the whole army and the secret agreement granting this permission to the Peloponnesians alone are attributed to Demosthenes and the Acarnanian generals jointly (109. 1–2). Clearly, however, Demosthenes suggested this course of action and the Acarnanians merely accepted his recommendations. The motives underlying the secret agreement, which was designed to bring the Peloponnesians into disrepute in this area for having selfishly betrayed their allies, are expressly those of Demosthenes.[1] It was a shrewd diplomatic move, which could have yielded valuable results if the completeness of his military successes had not alarmed the allies of Athens.

His victory at Idomene over the other Ambraciot army advancing from the city of Ambracia was an even greater triumph (110; 112). He was able to achieve complete surprise by taking advantage of the inefficiency by which armies drawn from backward parts of Greece were usually handicapped. These Ambraciots pressed on in ignorance of what had happened at Olpae (110. 1), and because they evidently omitted to conduct any reconnaissance, they encamped at Idomene without being aware that enemy forces were in the neighbourhood. Demosthenes was therefore able to deliver a totally unexpected attack at first light, and he shrewdly arranged that his Messenians, who like the Ambraciots spoke Doric, should be the first to make contact with the enemy and were accordingly mistaken for friends (112. 3–4). The rout was complete and the casualties appallingly heavy (112. 5–8).

Thucydides lays great emphasis on the magnitude of this disaster, although its influence upon the course of the war was evidently slight. It was, he states, the greatest sustained by one Greek state within a few days throughout the war,[2] and he

---

[1] In 109. 2 the plural main verb σπένδονται followed by the singular participles βουλόμενος and χρῄζων suggests in a characteristically Thucydidean manner that, while the Acarnanians were jointly responsible with Demosthenes, the plan was his. To emend σπένδονται to σπένδεται (cf. Steup n. *ad loc.*) would destroy this subtle effect.

[2] κατὰ τὸν πόλεμον τόνδε (113. 6) refers to the Archidamian war only, cf. Gomme (1), II, 425.

refuses to give the casualty figures reported to him because they were incredible in relation to the population (113. 6). He is fond of pointing out that certain events are for some special reason the greatest of their kind,[1] and this consideration has doubtless influenced him here. He may also intend to draw attention to the military lesson that, where forces including mobile light-armed troops were operating in mountainous country, the losses suffered by a defeated army might be relatively far heavier than those of conventional hoplite battles. The extent of the disaster does, however, illustrate how successful Demosthenes had been in planning and directing the campaign, and this is certainly one reason why so much emphasis is laid upon it.

Thucydides also declares that, if the Acarnanians and Amphilochians had followed the advice of Demosthenes and attacked Ambracia, they would have captured it at once (113. 6). This view was, one imagines, expressed by Demosthenes to Thucydides, who accepted its validity (οἶδα ὅτι). The Acarnanians, however, were now afraid that their own autonomy might be endangered if Ambracia fell into Athenian hands. Accordingly they refused to take the offensive and later concluded a defensive alliance with the Ambraciots (114. 3). Their reaction to the proposal of Demosthenes shows that his influence over them, though doubtless increased by his victorious leadership, was still limited. Although the Athenians might have benefited more if the Ambraciots had been less decisively crushed, Thucydides does not appear to impute any error of judgement to Demosthenes in allowing his military victory to be too complete to serve political ends. Athenian prestige had been enhanced, and Spartan prestige damaged, at very little cost to Athens in manpower or finance, and the western base at Naupactus was now thoroughly secure. Relations with the Acarnanians were not seriously impaired by the disagreement on the proposed invasion of Ambracia: a dozen years later they were willing to serve as mercenaries in Sicily

[1] Cf. 1. 1. 2; 10. 3; 50. 2; 5. 74. 1. L. Pearson, *T.A.P.A.* LXXVIII (1947), 47–8, gives a general collection of *optima* and *maxima*.

'through friendship for Demosthenes and good-will towards the Athenians' (7. 57. 10, cf. 31. 5). The value of his achievements in the north-west, after his defeat in Aetolia, is fully acknowledged in the narrative of Thucydides.

2. Pylos

The account of the next episode in which Demosthenes was involved, namely the operations at Pylos, is even more celebrated than that of his campaigns in north-western Greece. Both are outstanding examples of Thucydidean technique combining accurate and dramatic description with analysis of the decisive factors in each situation. There is, however, one marked difference between them. Whereas the narrative on the campaigns in the north-west gives the reader every confidence that his judgement is being guided with complete frankness and impartiality, that on Pylos does not inspire the same degree of confidence. Because Cleon played a major role in the episode, the whole presentation of it is full of inhibitions, arousing suspicion that Thucydides is being less frank and impartial than he normally is.[1]

In three sections of the narrative Demosthenes is given a prominent part: the first describes how the Athenians came to occupy and fortify Pylos (4. 2. 2–5. 2), the second how it was successfully defended against Peloponnesian assaults (9–12), the third how the Athenian landing on Sphacteria was planned and executed (29–38). These sections are so packed with graphic detail and palpably authentic information, including some known at the time to very few persons, that they are surely based to a large extent upon reports by Demosthenes himself or at any rate by someone closely associated with him during the whole episode. Thucydides must also have had access to Peloponnesian sources,[2] but on the Athenian side he seems to have been much less fully

---

[1] See above, 65–75.

[2] Schwartz, 293–4 (though his view that Peloponnesian sources are wholly responsible for the defects of the account is not altogether convincing); Gomme (1), III, 485.

informed about events in which Demosthenes was not personally involved.[1]

The first section in which Demosthenes plays a leading part conveys the impression that, although his plan for taking advantage of his mandate to use the Athenian forces in operations round the Peloponnese (2. 4) was admirably conceived, he was very lucky to have had the opportunity to put it into effect. Eurymedon and Sophocles, who were strategoi whereas he was not (2. 2–4), objected to his proposal to land at Pylos and would certainly have overruled him if it had not happened (κατὰ τύχην) that a storm forced the fleet to seek shelter there (3. 1). When Demosthenes pointed out to them the advantages of fortifying Pylos, they rejected his plea with contempt, and he was no more successful when he sought to persuade the taxiarchs (3. 2–4. 1). His first disagreement with Eurymedon and Sophocles, when they refused to put in at Pylos, is reported in a few words, but a fuller account is given of his discussion with them when the fleet was storm-bound. It is not the normal practice of Thucydides in the first half of his work to include reports of private discussions between leaders.[2] Perhaps he intends here to contrast the far-sightedness of Demosthenes with the short-sightedness of the two strategoi, but his purpose seems rather to focus attention at the outset upon the element of chance, which is a feature of the whole narrative describing the course of events at Pylos, and to show that it was largely by accident that the episode took place at all. This feature has perhaps been exaggerated by some modern scholars,[3] but there is no doubt of its prominence. Thucydides

[1] The account of the naval engagement after the main Athenian fleet under Eurymedon and Sophocles returned to Pylos (14. 1–4) is inferior to the rest of the narrative, nor is the reader told whether, as seems likely, they tried and failed to intercept the Peloponnesian fleet on its voyage from Corcyra (Finley, 191).   [2] See below, 311–12.

[3] Cf. F. M. Cornford, *Thucydides Mythistoricus* (1907), 88–94; Luschnat, 34; de Romilly (1), 174. It is rightly pointed out by Gomme (1), III, 488, that 'τυγχάνειν does not necessarily mean that an event was accidental, but that it was contemporaneous'; but by no means all the references to fortune in the narrative and in the speech of the Spartan envoys can be removed by applying this explanation.

seems determined to suggest that the situation leading eventually to a victory for which Cleon received most of the credit was to a large extent brought about by a series of accidents.

What happened after Eurymedon and Sophocles had vetoed the fortification of Pylos, and the taxiarchs had supported their decision, is not made altogether clear. Thucydides states that Demosthenes ἡσύχαζεν ὑπὸ ἀπλοίας, μέχρι αὐτοῖς τοῖς στρατιώταις σχολάζουσιν ὁρμὴ ἐνέπεσε περιστᾶσιν ἐκτειχίσαι τὸ χωρίον (4. 1). This rather cryptic statement has been much disputed. It seems that, openly at least, Demosthenes took no further steps to implement his plan because the weather was such that the fleet could not in any case sail for some days; and during this period boredom caused the troops, as he anticipated, to undertake the work of fortifying the peninsula.[1] It is likely enough that he surreptitiously predisposed them to do what he wished without actually exposing himself to a charge of insubordination. Thucydides could doubtless have been more explicit about the part played by Demosthenes if he had so desired; but what evidently interested him most was the contribution of fortune, and not the contribution of Demosthenes, to the development of a situation which had unexpectedly far-reaching consequences. This passage illustrates his habit of focusing attention upon factors lending support to conclusions which he wishes to impress upon his readers.

The account of the Peloponnesian attack on Pylos and the successful defence by Demosthenes and his garrison is a typical example of a Thucydidean battle narrative (9–12): first a report of the preparations of Demosthenes and the reasons for them, then his speech of encouragement, and finally a description of the fighting, including some graphic touches and a comment on the unusual circumstances of the conflict (12. 3).[2] There is no suggestion that the success of Demosthenes was in any way due

---

[1] I am much indebted to T. J. Quinn, whose note on this passage I was privileged to read before its publication in *Hermes*, xcv (1967), 378–9. I agree with him that the best solution of the textual difficulties is to delete τοὺς στρατιώτας, as suggested by H. Köstlin supported by Steup.

[2] The part played by Brasidas in this action will be mentioned below, 149.

to good fortune; it is attributed rather to his intelligent planning of defensive measures and the stout resistance of the Athenians (cf. 12. 2).[1] The Spartan attack from the sea was made where he had anticipated (9. 2; 11. 2), and his decision to station at this point a force of picked troops outside the wall and on the edge of the sea (9. 2–4; 10. 3–5)[2] was abundantly justified by the course of the battle (11. 4–12. 2). In this phase of the episode, when he was in sole command and was committed by circumstances to fighting a defensive action, the merits of his leadership are acknowledged unreservedly, as in the case of his achievements in Amphilochia. He showed himself to be capable of intelligent improvisation, a quality to which Thucydides attaches great importance in men of action. His speech, however, is a largely conventional παρακέλευσις (10). He argues that the superiority of the enemy in numbers is more than counterbalanced by the strength of the Athenian position, which will prevent them from taking advantage of their superiority. The speech gives the reader some assistance in understanding the main factors of the situation, though it is less instructive in this respect than the preceding report on the preparations of Demosthenes. Unlike some later speeches, it throws hardly any light on the personality of the speaker.[3]

When the Spartans who had been landed on Sphacteria were marooned there through the victory of the Athenian fleet, Demosthenes must at least have been consulted about the local truce concluded to enable the Spartans to send envoys to Athens (15. 2–16. 3). He is not, however, mentioned until after the report of the discussions at Athens. When Cleon had been appointed to

[1] The arrival of the Messenians, who contributed forty hoplites, is not regarded as accidental, since οἳ ἔτυχον παραγενόμενοι (9. 1) means 'who had just arrived', as Gomme (1), III, 444–5, points out.

[2] It was to this force that his speech was addressed (Luschnat, 34 n. 1).

[3] The exhortation in the opening sentence to be ἀπερισκέπτως εὔελπις instead of trying to be thought clever by assessing the extent of the danger may perhaps be characteristic of Demosthenes (H. Swoboda, R.E. V [1903], 169; Luschnat, 35–6), who perhaps liked to be thought a plain soldier rather than an intellectual. The rest of the speech, however, virtually contradicts this sentiment by analysing Athenian prospects with typically Thucydidean penetration, cf. Gomme (1), III, 446.

take command, he 'chose one of the generals at Pylos, namely Demosthenes, to be associated with him' (29. 1, προσελόμενος). This phrase must mean that Cleon and Demosthenes were in joint charge of the operation against the Spartans on Sphacteria, while Eurymedon and Sophocles were excluded from any responsibility for it. Cleon had heard that Demosthenes was planning to land troops on Sphacteria and chose him for that reason (29. 2). Thucydides gives a lengthy account of the reasons why Demosthenes had hitherto considered an attack on the island to have little prospect of success but now changed his mind after an accidental fire had destroyed most of the scrub which provided the Spartans with cover (29. 2–30. 3). Demosthenes must have communicated this appreciation of the military situation to the board of strategoi at Athens and doubtless at the same time asked for a force of light-armed troops and archers.[1] Whether or not he would have attacked Sphacteria if he had received no aid from Athens is not altogether clear. He was, however, making preparations and assembling troops from local allies before he heard that Cleon was on the way (30. 3–4). Most probably, therefore, he intended to make the assault even if he were to receive no light-armed troops and archers from Athens, though doubtless with less confidence of success. Thucydides has not chosen to provide any information on this point.

Although Cleon took part in the landing on the island (36. 1; 37. 1), the tactical plan was the creation of Demosthenes, who devoted great care to every detail (32. 3–4).[2] In the first phase of the action (33–4), which is described mainly from the Spartan point of view, the calculations of Demosthenes were almost wholly fulfilled.[3] In the second phase (35–6), when the Spartans

---

[1] See above, 70.

[2] Cornford, *Thucydides Mythistoricus*, 117 n. 2: 'Thucydides seems to emphasize the skill of Demosthenes, as if he were half aware that the Pylos narrative hardly did him justice.'

[3] de Romilly (2), 129–31. This is an excellent example of a narrative in which the plans laid by a commander of one army are seen in operation from an account based mainly on information about their effect upon the opposing army.

withdrew to the ancient fortification near the northern end of the island, his plan suffered a temporary check. It was only after the leader of the Messenians had sugested and carried out a bold and intelligent move whereby light-armed troops reached the rear of the enemy position that the Spartans had to choose between death and surrender. Yet this manœuvre only hastened the collapse of their resistance; they could not have held out much longer because they had no food (36. 3).[1] Thus the plan of Demosthenes proved completely successful, its development being delayed only by one setback. Thucydides, however, makes only two comments on the outcome of the whole episode: his celebrated statement that 'the promise of Cleon, mad though it was, was fulfilled' (39. 3),[2] and a brief report, supported by an anecdote, on the shock to public opinion throughout Greece caused by the decision of the Spartans to surrender (40. 1–2). Nowhere does Thucydides assess, or even refer to, the contribution of Demosthenes to one of the most decisive and most valuable victories in Athenian history. That contribution is to him only a subsidiary issue.

3. Offensives against Megara and Boeotia

The last two episodes in which Demosthenes was prominent during the Archidamian war were the operation in the Megarid in the summer of 424 (66–74) and the ambitious attempt to win control of Boeotia in the autumn of the same year (76–7; 89–101). Thucydides is well acquainted with the Athenian plans for both these enterprises: he was now one of the strategoi and may have attended meetings of the board when the plans were discussed. His account of the fighting in the Megarid, which is detailed and graphic, may be based partly on reports from Demosthenes himself, though he also had information from Peloponnesian sources.

---

[1] Gomme (1),I II, 477, points out that their main food store was doubtless at their main camp in the middle of the island (31. 2), which had already been overrun (cf. 39. 2).

[2] See above, 75.

It somehow lacks the quality of his best narrative passages, but its defects do not appear to be caused by any shortage of reliable evidence.[1] The situation at Megara, as it developed, became complex and somewhat confusing, involving many groups of civilians and soldiers, whose hopes, actions and reactions are described; and it ended indecisively, since neither side was prepared to take the initiative in forcing a major battle. Another factor is that no significant lesson, military or political, emerges from it to which the attention of the reader may be drawn. When the scheme against Boeotia was put into operation in the autumn, Thucydides had very probably left Athens to take up his command in the northern Aegean, and it is most unlikely that he ever met Demosthenes again. Information about the only major action of this campaign, the battle of Delium, for which Thucydides seems to have been dependent largely on Boeotian sources, could not have been obtained from Demosthenes, who was at the time of the battle in command of a naval and military force in the Corinthian Gulf. It is, however, noteworthy that the two failures of Demosthenes during this campaign, his abortive landings at Siphae (4. 89) and in Sicyonian territory (101. 3–4), are very briefly described. Light is thrown on the methods of Thucydides in assembling the substance of his *History* by the abrupt cessation, from 424 onwards, of the hitherto abundant material derived very probably either from his own observations at Athens or from consultations with leading Athenians.

Although Demosthenes, with Hippocrates as his colleague, led the Athenian forces engaged in the fighting in the Megarid, the operation was not undertaken at his suggestion. The initiative came from democratic leaders at Megara, who, fearing the probable restoration of some oligarchs then in exile, entered into secret negotiations with Demosthenes and Hippocrates (66. 3). The Athenian generals must already have been organising their offensive against Boeotia (76–7), but evidently they felt that the

---

[1] It is unfortunate that an important passage (73. 2–4) is very obscure and probably contains textual corruptions.

opportunity of winning Megara was not one to be neglected, especially as success there would greatly improve their prospects in Boeotia. Nevertheless, their Fabian tactics in the final stage of the struggle in the Megarid suggest that they were unwilling to devote more than a limited time to these operations, or to run the risk of incurring heavy losses there,[1] through fear of damaging their chances of success in their more important Boeotian venture.[2] It is indeed likely that the fighting at Megara caused the Athenians to postpone their move against Boeotia, thus increasing the danger that the plan would be betrayed and contributing to the ultimate failure of the whole enterprise.

The tactical plan agreed between the democratic leaders at Megara and the Athenian generals is characteristic of Demosthenes and bears unmistakable traces of his influence. It was ingenious and bold; it was well-suited to make full use of every favourable element in the situation for which it was designed; it was somewhat too complicated to be easily workable in the primitive conditions of Greek warfare, which seldom permitted communications to be satisfactorily maintained. At first all went well. Demosthenes led a force of light-armed Plataeans and Athenian frontier guards which hid by night near the more easterly of the two Long Walls joining Megara to Nisaea (67. 2).[3] When through an agreement with the Megarian traitors a gate in the wall was opened before dawn, the troops of Demosthenes rushing in seized the gate and admitted a body of hoplites under Hippocrates, which had also been in hiding. The Pelopon-

---

[1] Cf. 73. 4, ἢ σφαλέντας τῷ βελτίστῳ τοῦ ὁπλιτικοῦ βλαφθῆναι.

[2] Gomme (1), III, 535 hints at this. The decision of the Boeotians to send to Megara only a small part of the large army mobilised at Plataea and to retain most of it in Boeotia (72. 1), which is very remarkable, may have been due to fears of attack from Attica aided by treachery. The explanation of Steup n. *ad loc.* and Gomme (1), III, 532 that the Boeotians took this step on hearing that Brasidas was on his way to Megara is hardly adequate: the prospect of defeating the Athenians would obviously have been greater if the entire Boeotian army had marched into the Megarid.

[3] The topographical problems of this area are discussed by A. J. Beattie, *Rh. Mus.* CIII (1960), 21–43 (29–34 deal with the operations of 424).

nesian defenders were taken by surprise and fled to Nisaea, leaving the Long Walls in Athenian hands (67. 3–68. 3). In the morning, when another Athenian force had arrived, the situation inside Megara did not develop as had been planned. The conspirators there found themselves unable to open the gates as had been arranged with the Athenian generals, who accordingly turned their attention to Nisaea, where the Spartan commander of the Peloponnesian garrison somewhat surprisingly capitulated (68. 4–69. 3).[1] The expectation of the Athenian generals that the surrender of Megara would quickly follow that of Nisaea (69. 1) was unfulfilled, mainly through the arrival of Brasidas, who was near the Isthmus assembling troops for his mission to the northeast (70. 1).[2] The Athenian generals could scarcely have known that he was in the neighbourhood, and it was a stroke of ill-luck that he was; but they might, one imagines, have anticipated a speedy and vigorous intervention by the Boeotians, whose cavalry was allowed to take the Athenians by surprise, though in fact the ensuing cavalry engagement was indecisive (72). Thucydides may perhaps imply criticism of Demosthenes and Hippocrates here, but the implication, if there is one, is not altogether clear.[3]

Meanwhile both factions in Megara were awaiting the result of the expected battle between the Athenians and the forces sent to relieve the city (71. 1). No battle, in fact, took place. When Brasidas arrived with an advance guard and was refused admission to Megara, he brought up his main army and stationed it in a strong position awaiting an attack by the Athenians, which did not materialise (71; 73).[4] Thucydides evidently believed that

[1] Despite shortage of food, poor prospects of being relieved and the danger of further treachery (69. 3) the situation hardly appears to have been so desperate as to necessitate immediate surrender. The mildness of the terms offered to the members of the garrison who were not Spartan is perhaps a further indication that the Athenian generals were in a hurry.   [2] See below, 150.

[3] Busolt, 1138–9, points out that the Athenians were insufficiently informed about the approach of the relieving army.

[4] Beattie, *Rh. Mus.* CIII, 33, suggests that each army, if it were to attack the other, would have to expose its flank.

Brasidas was wise to remain on the defensive (73. 2–3), even though the Peloponnesians and Boeotians now outnumbered the Athenians. His defensive strategy saved Megara for the Peloponnesian cause, since, after the Athenians had withdrawn to Nisaea, the Megarians admitted him within their walls. His principal aim was attained, and he was certainly justified in abandoning his earlier plan (70. 2) to recover Nisaea, which, together with the Long Walls, was firmly held by the Athenians. What Thucydides thought of the decision by the Athenian generals to decline battle is less clear. The claim attributed to them to 'have been successful in most of their aims' (73. 4) is surprising:[1] although it was a valuable achievement to have gained Nisaea and the Long Walls, their main objective was undoubtedly Megara itself. Thucydides does not appear to imply any judgement, favourable or unfavourable, on their decision, or indeed on the question whether or not the whole operation brought credit to Demosthenes, whom he does not mention by name in his account of its later stages.

Soon after the Athenian withdrawal from the Megarid Demosthenes sailed to Naupactus with a fleet of forty ships (76. 1). This move was a preliminary step in the elaborate scheme planned by himself and Hippocrates for an attack on Boeotia, which must have been in an advanced state of preparation when the operations at Megara began and may, as has been suggested above, have had to be postponed because of the fighting there. Thucydides describes the scheme very fully. Demosthenes and Hippocrates were in touch with some Boeotians who wished to establish democratic government in their country and had made secret plans for Siphae, which was the port of Thespiae, and Chaeronea to be betrayed to the Athenians. Some Phocians were also involved in the plot for betraying the latter town, which lay near the Phocian border (76. 2–3). On the same day Athenian forces

---

[1] Cf. Gomme (1), III, 535. This claim could well have been made by the generals in self-justification either to their troops, who might have felt that an opportunity to gain a decisive advantage was being wasted, or in a report to their colleagues on the board of strategoi.

were to cross the border of Attica and Boeotia near its eastern end and to seize and fortify Delium, which lay a few miles inside Boeotia. Simultaneous action at three points would prevent the Boeotians from concentrating all their forces at any one of them. The Athenians would then control three bases in Boeotia from which they could ravage the rest of the country and spread political unrest (76. 4-5). It was evidently intended that these bases should perform much the same function as Pylos and Cythera,[1] but they seemed likely to be much more effective because the oligarchies then in control in Boeotia were not very securely rooted.

This scheme was both ambitious and ingenious—too ambitious and too ingenious, apparently, to win the approval of Thucydides. If it had developed as planned, the Athenians might soon have controlled much of Boeotia without having committed themselves to a pitched battle of the conventional hoplite type against the Boeotian federal army, which included troops of very high quality. The recent successes achieved by similar methods against the Spartans, combined with the recollection of the rapid collapse of oligarchical governments in Boeotia some thirty years earlier,[2] doubtless encouraged the colleagues of Demosthenes and Hippocrates to accept their scheme. It seemed to provide plenty of opportunity for disentanglement without risk of serious losses if parts of it were not successful. Whether Thucydides, who was a member of the board, was in favour of it at the time can only be guessed, but his account of it exposes its weaknesses very plainly. It had to be disclosed, at least in part, to many Boeotians and some Phocians for a considerable time before it was put into operation, so that the chances of betrayal were dangerously high; and success was unlikely unless its three sections could be exactly synchronised. It was much more carefully and realistically planned

---

[1] Busolt, 1141; Gomme (1), III, 538-9.

[2] That both sides had the events of this period in mind is suggested by the speeches of Pagondas (92. 6) and Hippocrates (95. 3) before the battle of Delium.

than the attempt by Demosthenes to attack Boeotia from Aetolia in 426. Nevertheless, its failure does not come as a surprise to the reader.

Demosthenes was entrusted with the task of collecting at Naupactus a force of Acarnanians and other allies and of landing them, together with some Athenian troops, from his ships on an appointed day at Siphae, which was to be betrayed to him (77. 1). He succeeded in assembling a substantial army, including a contingent from the Agraeans (cf. 101. 3) who had hitherto been hostile to Athens (77. 2). When, however, he arrived with his fleet off Siphae, he found himself unable to carry out his part of the scheme and apparently did not even attempt a landing. The plot had been betrayed by a Phocian, and the Boeotian government sent strong forces to Siphae and Chaeronea with the result that at neither town did the intended uprising take place (89. 1–2). A mistake was also made in the timing of the operation: Demosthenes appeared off Siphae before Hippocrates crossed the frontier to occupy Delium, so that the Boeotians were not, as had been planned, compelled by simultaneous threats at separate points to divide their main army. Thucydides does not make clear to his readers whether Demosthenes arrived too early or Hippocrates too late.[1] Possibly he lacked reliable information on this point, but a more likely explanation is that he did not consider the apportionment of blame for the error in timing to be particularly important. Nor does he state whether it was the error in timing or the betrayal of the scheme that was principally responsible for the failure of Demosthenes at Siphae: both are expressed by genitive absolutes in the same long sentence (89. 1). Demosthenes apparently remained in the vicinity of Siphae for some days after most of the Boeotian troops had left the district: his unsuccessful raid on Sicyonian territory, which he must have

---

[1] πρότερον πλεύσας, used of Demosthenes in 89. 1, can hardly mean 'too early' (though some scholars have interpreted it in this way, cf. G. P. Landmann in his translation). ὕστερος ἀφικνεῖται, used of Hippocrates in 90. 1, could much more easily mean 'too late' (cf. 2. 5. 3; 7. 27. 2) but more probably means only 'later'.

undertaken in the hope of accomplishing something to offset his failure against Boeotia, took place after the battle of Delium had been fought (101. 3-4), and he seems to have crossed the Corinthian Gulf without returning to Naupactus. He may have remained off Siphae expecting that despite the betrayal of the scheme the town would still be surrendered to him by the conspirators after the main Boeotian army had withdrawn to meet the invasion from Attica. The narrative of Thucydides is here compressed and somewhat obscure. His interest in the failures of Siphae and Chaeronea lay almost wholly in their effect on the third section of the scheme, namely the occupation of Delium by Hippocrates.

The military reputation of Demosthenes, which was at this time greater than that of any Athenian general throughout the Archidamian war, was shattered by the failure of the scheme to gain control of Boeotia. Unlike the generals who had returned from Sicily some months earlier without achieving what the Athenians expected of them (65. 3), he was apparently not put on trial,[1] but he was not again entrusted with an important command until 413. It is very likely that the Athenians acted with characteristically ill-considered hastiness in discarding Demosthenes, whose energy and experience in unconventional methods of warfare might have proved valuable against Brasidas in the north-east. Their slowness to regain confidence in him is much more remarkable.[2] While there was every justification for hold-

---

[1] Some scholars have inferred from Antiphon fr. 8-14 (Blass–Thalheim) and [Plutarch] *Lives of the ten orators* 833 e that Demosthenes was prosecuted after the battle of Delium (cf. Sealey, 80). There is, however, no means of dating the speech of Antiphon against Demosthenes, and Harpocration, who has preserved all these singularly uninformative fragments of it, states that they were contained ἐν τῇ πρὸς τὴν Δημοσθένους γραφὴν ἀπολογίᾳ, which suggests a very different setting (cf. Schmid–Stählin, *Gesch. der gr. Lit.* I, 3 [1940], 101 with n. 11). It is also possible that the author of the *Lives of the ten orators* may be wrong in identifying the Demosthenes involved in these proceedings with the well-known general.

[2] Cf. the much quoted ἐν ᾿Αθηναίοις ταχυβούλοις . . . πρὸς ᾿Αθηναίους μεταβούλους in the *Acharnians* (630-2). Despite the period of nominal peace after 421, there were plenty of occasions between 424 and 413 when the services of an energetic and experienced commander ought, one feels, to have been very welcome.

ing him largely accountable for the unsoundness of the general scheme against Boeotia, it was unreasonable to blame him, as they seemingly did, for their severe losses in hoplite manpower at Delium. For these losses Hippocrates, who could not be made a scapegoat because he was killed in the battle, seems to have been wholly responsible. Demosthenes had every reason to expect that, after completing the fortifications at Delium, the army of Hippocrates would retire without fighting unless favourable news from other parts of Boeotia offered opportunities for further action. A safe withdrawal from Delium could and should have been achieved without any great difficulty; the battle took place because Hippocrates was insufficiently informed about the movements of the Boeotian army. It was fought in the late afternoon of the fifth day after the forces under his command had left Athens and the third day after they had begun to fortify the temple at Delium (90. 3; 93. 1). Although he had no means of ascertaining quickly what had happened at Siphae and Chaeronea, he ought, it seems, to have guessed that the enemy would concentrate most of their strength against him. He was apparently unaware that contingents from Boeotian cities were massing at Tanagra (91), which was close to Delium, or indeed that the enemy were in the neighbourhood at all, until very shortly before they attacked him (93. 1–2). These conclusions may be drawn with some degree of confidence from the evidence supplied by Thucydides, but neither in his narrative nor in the short speeches of Pagondas and Hippocrates does he provide the reader with much guidance. On the part played by Demosthenes in the execution of the scheme he seems to imply no judgement; the failures at Siphae and near Sicyon are reported in his briefest manner. The eclipse of Demosthenes receives no comment whatever. It is indeed known to have taken place only because, after being the most prominent of Athenian military leaders for the past two years, Demosthenes is barely mentioned for the next ten.[1]

---

[1] The only references to Demosthenes in the first half of the *History* after the report of his failure at Sicyon (4. 101. 3–4) are documentary: his name appears

Demosthenes refused to accept the inevitability of a military stalemate in the Archidamian war. The superiority of the Peloponnesians on land and of the Athenians at sea drastically restricted the use of the traditional methods prevalent in Greek warfare, namely battles between large armies of hoplites or large fleets of triremes. Accordingly he tried to break the military stalemate by creating opportunities to exploit unconventional methods: the development of ἐπιτειχισμός; the use of light-armed troops, in which he made himself an expert; efforts to turn to the advantage of Athens political unrest in cities allied to the Peloponnesians and feuds between backward peoples in the more remote areas of Greece. None of these methods was entirely new, and none was in principle inconsistent with Periclean strategy. Yet in trying to apply them in such a way as to secure a decisive advantage for Athens, Demosthenes tended to rely upon elaborate and ambitious plans exposing the Athenians to risks of sustaining serious losses, risks of which Pericles would certainly have disapproved. Though showing some interest in the personality of Demosthenes, Thucydides is far more concerned with drawing attention to the lesson of his chequered career in the Archidamian war. This lesson is that not even an energetic and intelligent leader with original ideas could successfully break the military stalemate; that Periclean strategy, which accepted this stalemate as inevitable and even desirable, was right and that any other strategy was wrong. It is mainly for this reason that Demosthenes scarcely receives from Thucydides the recognition to which his qualities of leadership appear to entitle him, except when engaged upon unimpeachably Periclean undertakings in which any risk of involving the Athenians in crippling losses was avoided. To charge Thucydides with unfairness is hardly justifiable, since he did not deem

in the list of seventeen delegates who took the oath on behalf of Athens in 421 when the peace with Sparta (5. 19. 2) and the subsequent alliance (5. 24. 1) were concluded. It is known from an inscription (*I.G.* II², 2318, 124) that he was *choregos* in the same year. While the Athenians evidently refused to entrust him with military commands (perhaps unwisely), he does not seem to have been in any sense in disgrace.

it to be a primary duty to assess the ability of Demosthenes. Nevertheless, some sympathy may be felt for Demosthenes because his reputation has been judged by posterity largely by the yardstick of Periclean strategy. It has also been affected to some extent, as has been noted above, by his association with Cleon at Pylos. Although he was the most interesting of military leaders in the Archidamian war, Thucydides does not allow himself to show more than a limited and almost reluctant interest in him.

CHAPTER VIII

ARCHIDAMUS

THUCYDIDES was convinced that the difference in temperament between Athenians and Spartans exerted a profound influence upon the course of the war. Because he considered this factor to be fundamental and wished his readers to appreciate its importance, references to it, whether direct or by implication, are many both in narrative and in speeches.[1] It is more prominent in the first half of his work than in the second. It has undoubtedly affected his presentation of the principal Spartan leaders in the Archidamian war, who are seen to have exhibited typically Spartan qualities: they are slow, cautious, conventional, lacking in inspiration and imagination. There seems to be no reason to accuse Thucydides of having deliberately distorted his pictures of these leaders in order to substantiate his general theory. It would, however, be unwise to be dogmatic on this point, since evidence from independent authorities, which might have been used to rebut the charge, is almost entirely lacking. He has not chosen to treat these Spartans primarily as individuals, and, in seeking to fit them into his pattern of Spartan leadership, he sometimes tends to judge them a little unsympathetically.[2] Another factor has had similar consequences: in addition to contrasting them with Athenians, he also contrasts them with Brasidas, whom, as will be shown in a later chapter, he represents as the antithesis of the typical Spartan leader.

The first and most important of these Spartan leaders is

---

[1] It is the central idea in the speech of the Corinthians at the first congress of the Peloponnesian League shortly before the outbreak of war (1. 68–71, especially 69. 4–5; 70. 2–4; 71. 1). It is also implicit in much of the Funeral Speech (2. 37–41).

[2] Cf. P. Cloché, *Ét. class.* XII (1943), 105: 'un jugement méprisant et dur (peut-être même parfois injuste).'

Archidamus. He had already long experience of kingship, having succeeded to the throne probably in 469/68,[1] perhaps the year in which he came of age.[2] He first appears in the *History* as a speaker in the Spartan assembly when the Spartans were debating whether to go to war with Athens, and he is introduced as ἀνὴρ καὶ ξυνετὸς δοκῶν εἶναι καὶ σώφρων (1. 79. 2). This phrase describes his reputation, mainly no doubt at Sparta but also perhaps elsewhere. To interpret it as a personal judgement by Thucydides is, as has already been noted,[3] an error, though to infer from δοκῶν that he necessarily disagreed with this estimate would be equally mistaken.[4] He has not chosen to express what he himself thought. If asked for an opinion he would perhaps have answered that Archidamus possessed both integrity and intelligence as those terms were understood at Sparta,[5] but not intelligence[6] and perhaps not even integrity as understood elsewhere. His attitude towards Archidamus is not unsympathetic, but a clear-cut assessment nowhere emerges from narrative or speeches. He does not appear to have felt himself to be under any obligation to provide one.

The speech of Archidamus in the Spartan assembly (1. 80–5) falls into two parts. In the first part (80–3) he draws attention to the difficulties likely to be encountered by the Spartans if they decide to embark at once upon a war against a power possessing financial and naval resources so formidable as those of Athens. He urges them to continue negotiations in the hope of reaching a satisfactory settlement and meanwhile to build up their strength where they are now weak, so that they may be better equipped to

[1] K. J. Beloch, *Gr. Gesch.* I, 2 (1913), 184.
[2] H. T. Wade-Gery, *Essays in Greek History* (1958), 264 n. 6.
[3] See above, 6–7.
[4] Cf. 4. 81. 1, ἔν τε τῇ Σπάρτῃ δοκοῦντα δραστήριον εἶναι ἐς τὰ πάντα, where Thucydides undoubtedly agreed with the Spartan assessment of Brasidas to which he refers.
[5] Archidamus defends Spartan slowness by arguing that it was σωφροσύνη ἔμφρων (1. 84. 2).
[6] It will be seen that after the war began almost all his predictions proved to be wrong.

go to war in two or three years if their demands are not met. In the second part of the speech (84-5) he argues that the traditional slowness and caution of the Spartans brought positive advantages, and he seeks to refute the recent criticisms made in the speech of the Corinthians, which might appear to have been substantiated by his recommendations.

Archidamus delivered his speech to the Spartans only: the Corinthians and other allies, together with the embassy from Athens, had withdrawn (79. 1). Accordingly Thucydides may have experienced some difficulty in obtaining information about its content, and it is likely that he supplied τὰ δέοντα himself (cf. 22. 1) more freely than in some other speeches. There is, however, no reason to believe that he invented almost the whole of it. Archidamus must have answered the criticisms of Sparta by the Corinthians (68-71), and the arguments attributed to him in defence of Spartan caution are consistent with his own record of military leadership after the war began. These arguments are, it is true, presented in an unrealistically intellectual form. Their tone is curiously out of harmony with the doctrine, expounded in a complex and difficult passage, that the traditional discipline of the Spartans is to be preferred to cleverness in thought and speech (84. 3). There are, however, similar incongruities in other Thucydidean speeches.[1]

The practical advice, both positive and negative, offered by Archidamus in this speech (82; 85. 1-2) strikes a perfectly authentic note. The same cannot be said of a basic argument which he uses in support of his recommendations. In the first part of his speech he preaches a doctrine (80. 3-81. 6, cf. 83. 2-3) which is essentially Thucydidean and Periclean in its principles. The theory that only states possessing wealth and naval power are capable of waging effective war on a large scale is the keynote of the Archaeology and is implicit in the sketch of the Pentecon-

---

[1] The closest parallel occurs in the speech of Cleon in the debate on the Mytileneans, where he disparages sophistic rhetoric (see above, 63-4); there are even some verbal echoes.

taetia. To find much the same conception in the speech of a Spartan king is indeed a surprise, however shrewd he may have been and however experienced in inter-state relations. Equally strange is his profound grasp of Periclean strategy at a time when it had not yet been put into operation.[1] Admittedly this strategy was the natural outcome of a policy already pursued for at least a decade with the intention of building up Athenian power. It is also true that Archidamus was on friendly terms with Pericles (2. 13. 1). Nevertheless, in reporting this speech, Thucydides has evidently been at pains, perhaps to an even greater degree than usual, to instruct his readers about the essence of the situation and has been less concerned to make the content appropriate to the speaker. To a large extent the speech is a rejoinder to the call for action which the Corinthians had addressed to the Spartans and allies (1. 68-71). At the same time, however, the doctrine on which Archidamus bases his plea for delay foreshadows, in a characteristically Thucydidean manner, the optimistic assessment of Peloponnesian prospects contained in the speech of the Corinthians at the second congress at Sparta (121. 2-122. 1), which is directly answered in the first speech of Pericles (141. 2-143. 2). On this subject, to which Thucydides attaches great importance, the course of events during the opening phases of the war showed Archidamus and Pericles to have been very largely right and the Corinthians very largely wrong. Consequently Archidamus seems to be credited with statesmanship of almost Periclean quality, an estimate incompatible with his subsequent record as a war-leader. His speech fulfils an important function as a link in the elaborate chain of speeches in the first book. It is not designed, primarily at least, to throw light on the personality or the ability of the speaker.

Archidamus next appears as the leader of the Peloponnesian army mobilised at the Isthmus in the spring of 431 in readiness to

---

[1] Finley, 130, in an excellent discussion of the speech (129-33), is to a large extent justified in maintaining that the first speech of Pericles 'virtually repeats what Archidamus has said here'.

invade Attica if the Athenians refused to yield (2. 10. 2–3). Here he addressed a meeting of senior officers, and Thucydides gives a summary of his speech (11). It is thoroughly conventional and uninspired and probably reflects the real character of Archidamus more accurately than the speech assigned to him in the first book. It is mainly a warning against over-confidence. He warns his audience against underestimating the power of the enemy and against assuming that their own superiority in numbers will deter the Athenians from daring to fight a pitched battle to protect Attica from devastation. He even commits himself to a forecast, which proved to be mistaken, that the Athenians will come out and fight when they see their property being destroyed. He ends with an exhortation to maintain strict disclipine, which may reflect the contempt felt by the Spartans for their Peloponnesian allies. It is not altogether clear why Thucydides includes a summary of this speech, which does not appear to provide any very significant elucidation of his narrative. Perhaps he wishes to stress the rather heavy-handed attitude of Archidamus towards his mission, which was to be rendered to a large extent ineffective by the intelligent foresight of Pericles.

Archidamus was not in any hurry to lead his army into Attica. He first attempted to reopen negotiations, believing that the Athenians might make concessions when the Peloponnesians were known to be on the march. When this approach was firmly rejected, he advanced to the frontier of Attica (12. 1–4). He did not, however, choose the most direct route but made a détour by way of Oenoe, a fortress on the frontier of Attica and Boeotia.[1] Here he spent a considerable amount of time in preparing and delivering attacks on the walls, but despite the use of siege engines these attacks failed (18. 1–2; 19. 1). There were sound strategic reasons why it was desirable for the Peloponnesians to capture Oenoe, though Thucydides does not mention them. It was

---

[1] N. G. L. Hammond, *B.S.A.* xlix (1954), 112, discusses the route taken by Archidamus, locating Oenoe at the modern Villia (*ibid.* 121). J. Wiesner, *R.E.* Suppl. viii (1956), 370, locates it further east at Myupolis.

important that, while their army was operating in Attica, they should keep intact their communications with Boeotia, which must have been one source for supplies.[1] These communications were vulnerable, since they could be threatened both from Plataea and from Oenoe; if the latter were captured, demands on manpower to safeguard the maintenance of supplies would obviously be much reduced. It was doubtless with the same considerations in mind that the Athenians chose to defend Oenoe on this occasion and to maintain a garrison there,[2] though it was not an integral part of their strategy to hold frontier posts. Thucydides doubtless understood the value of Oenoe and the military reasons why Archidamus wished to take it. His omission to mention them is typical of him. He is following his normal practice of seeking to make a situation easily intelligible to his readers by directing their attention exclusively to its most important factors. In this instance these are the remarkably slow progress of Archidamus in his mission and the possibility that he may have delayed deliberately because he still had hopes of a satisfactory settlement without bloodshed.

While the army was at Oenoe, Archidamus was severely criticised by his troops, whose complaints are recorded fully and in very striking terms by Thucydides (18. 3–5). He had, they declared, shown a lack of energy and enthusiasm[3] while the preparations for war were in progress and had even favoured the Athenians. He had been dilatory in delaying at the Isthmus, on the march towards Attica, and especially now at Oenoe, since by wasting time in attacking the fort he had given the Athenians a respite during which they could withdraw their movable property

[1] Cf. Hammond, *ibid.* 112, who points out that an invading army, such as that of Archidamus, could not feed itself on supplies brought with it or seized in enemy territory and was partly dependent on food transported from a distance, normally in waggons.

[2] 8. 98. 2–4 shows that it was still garrisoned twenty years later, and an incident mentioned in this passage illustrates its value to Athens.

[3] μαλακός, cf. 2. 85. 2 (the commanders of the Peloponnesian fleet against Phormio); 5. 7. 2 (Cleon at Amphipolis); 5. 72. 1 (two polemarchs at Mantinea); 8. 29. 2 (Therimenes); 8. 50. 3 (Astyochus).

to safety. This passage is remarkable for the accumulation of abstract nouns denoting slowness or hesitancy: ἐπιμονή, σχολαιότης, ἐπίσχεσις, μέλλησις.[1] Thucydides goes on to refer to a report (18. 5, ὡς λέγεται) that Archidamus deliberately chose to dally because he expected the Athenians to be now ready to make concessions to save their territory from devastation. This motive is the same as is attributed to him, without any qualification, when he made overtures to them before he started out from the Isthmus (12. 1–4).[2] The phrase ὡς λέγεται does not indicate merely that Thucydides is quoting hearsay which is not necessarily trustworthy: he seems to be referring to statements said to have been made by Archidamus, or by his friends, in repudiation of the charges against him, possibly at Oenoe but more probably later at Sparta, where his handling of the whole campaign must have been the subject of discussion and criticism. λέγεται is similarly used in other passages dealing with debatable decisions by Spartan commanders, one of them (20. 1) relating to further criticisms of Archidamus at a later stage of the same invasion, as will be seen below.[3] It may be noted that, if on this occasion he expected Athenian determination to crumble, his expectations were unfulfilled.

At last the Peloponnesians left Oenoe and advanced into Attica, where they first ravaged the Thriasian plain. They then moved on to Acharnae, which remained their headquarters for some time while they were conducting further plundering (19. 2). They did not, however, approach Athens itself and left the plain in the immediate vicinity of the city untouched (20. 1 and 4). Again Archidamus was censured: by lingering so long at Acharnae he had, it was thought, squandered opportunities of inflicting more

[1] Only the last is used elsewhere by Thucydides. ἐν τῇ καθέδρᾳ (5) might be added, though Gomme (1), II, 69 thinks that it means only 'during this siege'.
[2] Cf. the similar point made in his speech to the Spartan assembly, 1. 82. 3.
[3] Other passages are 2. 93. 4 (see below, 141) and 3. 79. 3 (see below, 146). Doubtless one reason for the parallelism between these passages is that it was difficult to obtain reliable information about the intentions of Spartan leaders or even about their discussions with other Spartans.

widespread damage. His alleged motives are again recorded: they are more complex but are introduced in much the same way (20. I, λέγεται). His first and most important point was that the Athenians would now be prepared to risk a battle in order to prevent further devastation. Because the Acharnians, who formed a substantial section of the population, would be the first to suffer, they, he felt, would be especially eager to fight and would stir the rest of the Athenians to action. A second consideration was that, if no battle took place and the Acharnians had their property destroyed, they would be less willing in subsequent invasions to take up arms to protect the property of others, and their attitude might lead to internal discord (20. 2–5).[1] This second point proved to be entirely without foundation, but the prediction that the Athenians might under provocation commit themselves to a battle, already put forward in more general terms in the speech at the Isthmus (11. 6–8), was almost fulfilled. As has been shown in an earlier chapter,[2] it was only with great difficulty that Pericles succeeded in restraining the Athenians from abandoning his strategic plan.

Thucydides seems to be suggesting that, although Archidamus was proved to have been mistaken in his calculations, his military planning was neither unreasonable nor wholly the outcome of over-caution.

The invasion was now virtually over. Because of the strategy adopted by both sides it could no longer produce decisive results. It is for this reason that Thucydides is content to give a brief and purely factual account of its closing stages. The Boeotians won a minor victory over an Athenian cavalry squadron, which was supported by allies from Thessaly (22. 2). Eventually the Peloponnesians moved north-eastwards from Acharnae and after some further plundering withdrew into Boeotia through the territory of Oropus (23. 1 and 3).

[1] The passage has some of the features of a Thucydidean speech, cf. γνώμῃ δὲ τοιᾷδε at the beginning and τοιαύτῃ μὲν διανοίᾳ at the end.
[2] See above, 32–3.

The views of Thucydides on the handling of this invasion by Archidamus are not so clearly conveyed as his judgements normally are. It may well be that this portion of his work was among the first to be written, when he had not yet fully mastered the technique, which he later perfected, of combining narrative with commentary, information with evaluation.[1] Archidamus is presented to a large extent as a typical Spartan. He is seen to have practised only too faithfully what he preached in his speech at Sparta and to have given abundant evidence that he possessed the Spartan qualities which he himself considered to be virtues. The remarkable emphasis laid upon his slowness and lack of enterprise shows that Thucydides was disposed to accept the validity of the charges brought against him by his troops. Thucydides is not, however, content to conclude that he acted as he did almost by instinct because he was a conventional Spartan. The emphasis laid upon his alleged motives, which are reported in some detail, suggests that he may have shown a certain amount of shrewdness in accommodating his movements to the expected reactions of the Athenians. What is not made clear is whether these reported motives are mere excuses put forward in order to defend a course of action to which his Spartan caution would have committed him in any case, or whether they reflect a calculating appreciation of the whole situation by a man of some intellectual quality. It is regrettable that Thucydides has not included any reports of staff conferences held by Archidamus after the army had left the Isthmus, though their absence may be wholly due to lack of reliable information.[2] There is, however, one indication that Archi-

---

[1] J. de Romilly, *R.É.A.* LXIV (1962), 287–99, has argued, conclusively in my opinion, that the sequence of thought in the sections dealing with the intentions of Archidamus is perfectly logical and that there is no real basis for the criticisms of scholars, including Gomme (1), II, 70 and 77, who have suggested that they belong to drafts composed at different times. Nevertheless, they do create an impression of slight awkwardness, and, more important, the sureness of touch in guiding the judgement of the reader, which is so prominent elsewhere, is somewhat lacking. These features suggest early composition.

[2] Reports of such conferences become more frequent, especially in the second half of his work.

damus was not abundantly endowed with the ability γνῶναι τὰ δέοντα, which was to Thucydides the primary requisite of great leaders. As has been pointed out, all his reported predictions proved to be incorrect; he is thus seen to have been unable to understand fully the psychology of other Greeks, a failing common among Spartan leaders with the notable exception of Brasidas. Here he is perhaps intentionally contrasted with Pericles: each sought to think out how the interests of his city might best be served, but while Pericles was, to Thucydides at least, always right, Archidamus was always wrong.

The treatment of Archidamus is instructive for another reason. During this first invasion of Attica he was in a position comparable with that of Nicias in Sicily, and he handled it in a similar way, though in outcome the campaigns bore no resemblance to one another. Each of the two leaders found himself entrusted with responsibility for an enterprise of which he disapproved, and each discharged his unwelcome duty conscientiously in accordance with his own interpretation of what the situation demanded. On the other hand, Thucydides chooses to present the part played by Nicias in Sicily in a totally different way from the part played by Archidamus in Attica. He sketches the personality of Nicias very vividly and, though not unsympathetic towards him, shows how his leadership was largely responsible for the Athenian disaster, as will be seen in a later chapter. Archidamus is hardly a character at all, and there is no palpable assessment of his quality. The dissimilarity of treatment cannot be entirely due to a difference in the volume of reliable evidence available to Thucydides in each case. It is the whole approach that is different.

Archidamus was again in command when the Peloponnesians invaded Attica in the spring of 430 (47. 2). He must either have been under orders not to repeat the delays of the previous summer or have become convinced that there was no longer any prospect of gaining advantages by holding back. The invasion of this year lasted longer and inflicted greater damage than any other during the Archidamian war (57. 2, cf. 3. 26. 3). Thucydides defines the areas devastated by the Peloponnesians (2. 55. 1) but gives no other details about this invasion, which is overshadowed by the plague and Athenian reactions to it. He is again following his practice of recording very briefly everything lying outside what he has chosen to be the central theme in any section of his narrative. He seems, however, almost reluctant to admit that a Peloponnesian enterprise had been efficiently conducted and had been very successful. His reference to a report (57. 1, ἐλέχθη), which he does not seem disposed to credit, that the Peloponnesians hastened their withdrawal through fear of infection does not necessarily denote that he was ill-informed about their intentions during this invasion.

In the following spring (429), when the Peloponnesians made an expedition against Plataea instead of invading Attica, Archidamus was once more in command (71. 1). Their decision not to invade Attica this year needs, and receives, no explanation: they were evidently unwilling to run the risk of infection. On the other hand, the failure of Thucydides to explain why they tried to reduce Plataea is a serious omission. Doubtless they were under pressure from the Thebans (cf. 71. 3), and probably they wished to ensure that, when they resumed their invasion of Attica, their communications with Boeotia should be absolutely secure. It will be remembered that Thucydides also fails to give any strategic reason for their attack on Oenoe in 431, which probably had a similar motive. In the case of their attempt on Plataea he may have neglected to mention their strategic aim because of preoccupation with a wider issue upon which he wishes to focus attention. He was intensely interested in problems of inter-state relations and in the disputes to which they frequently gave rise involving legal and moral principles. He reports some of these disputes in dialogue form, mainly in *oratio recta*. The outstanding example is the Melian Dialogue, but there are others, including that of the dispute which now arose on the question whether the threat to Plataea was a breach of faith on the part of the Spartans

(71–4).[1] It is presented in the form of a dialogue mostly in *oratio recta* between Plataean representatives and Archidamus.[2] The Plataeans claim that their independence has been guaranteed for all time by the declaration sworn fifty years earlier by all the Greek cities whose forces defeated the Persians in Plataean territory. Archidamus questions the validity of this claim in the present circumstances but offers to leave the Plataeans unharmed if they will renounce their alliance with Athens and remain neutral. When the Plataeans point to difficulties likely to arise from the acceptance of this offer, Archidamus makes a second, namely that, if they will evacuate Plataea for the duration of the war, Sparta will safeguard their property and return it to them intact.

While Archidamus is seen to have made every effort to create the impression that the Spartan proposals were just and even generous, Thucydides makes no secret of his own conviction that they were insincere.[3] Like the Athenians in the Melian Dialogue, Archidamus uses spurious reasoning to justify decisions already taken on grounds of self-interest, and his air of moderation and piety is sheer hypocrisy. It is at least open to doubt whether, if the Plataeans had accepted his second offer (72. 3), the Spartans would themselves have held their lands in trust for the duration of the war, as they promised. Yet, although Archidamus emerges with little credit from the report of these negotiations, which certainly do not support his reputation for integrity (1. 79. 1), his personal responsibility is not stressed. There appears to be no intention to damn his character, even by implication. He is only

---

[1] Cf. the arguments between the Athenians and the Corinthians after the battle of Sybota (1. 53. 2–4) and between the Athenians and the Boeotians after the battle of Delium (4. 97. 2–99). The latter is presented in *oratio obliqua*, as are the briefly reported disputes in which Brasidas was involved in Thessaly (4. 78. 3–4) and at Scione (4. 122. 2–5).

[2] The reply brought back by a Plataean embassy sent to consult the Athenians is also reported in *oratio recta* (73. 3), as well as the address by Archidamus to the gods and heroes of Plataea (74. 2).

[3] Busolt, 967 n. 1 and Gomme (1), II, 206 rightly infer from 3. 68. 1 that Thucydides believed the Spartans to have acted dishonestly.

a spokesman, doubtless briefed at Sparta before the expedition began, since the protests made by the Plataeans against the illegality of the threat to their independence must have been foreseen. Two years later, when Archidamus was dying or already dead, a similar but even more culpable policy was adopted by an unnamed Spartan commander at Plataea acting on instructions from Sparta (3. 52. 2) and by the five judges sent to conduct the trial of the surviving Plataeans after their surrender (3. 52. 3–4 and 68. 1–2). The speeches of the Plataeans and the Thebans at this trial (3. 53–67) continue the discussion of legal and moral issues begun in the dialogue reporting the negotiations before the first attack was launched. Sparta, or perhaps even mankind generally when corrupted by the stress of war, is the target for criticism here and not Archidamus personally.

The ensuing attempts to take Plataea by storm are fully and vividly described by Thucydides (2. 75–7),[1] who dwells upon the inventiveness and determination of both sides. He evidently found these operations interesting because they illustrated the important military lesson that even large armies in this period experienced great difficulties when they tried to storm quite small walled towns. The episode was also attractive to him from the dramatic point of view. He must have based his narrative largely upon information from Plataeans who later escaped to Athens,[2] but it is surprising that Archidamus is not mentioned at all, so that he receives neither credit for the planning and execution of the Peloponnesian attacks nor discredit for their ultimate failure. The arrangements for maintaining a blockade when the greater part of the army withdrew are attributed to 'the Peloponnesians' (78. 1).

The last invasion of Attica led by Archidamus in the spring of 428 is recorded by Thucydides very briefly and formally (3. 1.

---

[1] Cf. de Romilly (2), 166–7 and (Budé) II, *Notice* xxiv–xxxvi.

[2] Busolt, 968 n. 2; Gomme (1), II, 211. Only 75. 3 seems to have been derived from Peloponnesian sources, though in 77. 6 λέγεται may perhaps once more denote a reply to criticisms after the event.

1–3). He refers only to the customary attacks by Athenian cavalry, designed to protect the area near the city, and then passes on to the revolt of Lesbos, which was the outstanding event of this year. Archidamus is not mentioned again except as the father of Agis. The invasion of 427 was led by Cleomenes acting as regent for the young Pausanias (3. 26. 2), and in 426, when a Peloponnesian army assembled at the Isthmus but did not proceed to invade Attica because of earthquakes, Agis, who was in command, had already succeeded his father (3. 89. 1). Hence Archidamus was already dead in the spring of 426; he was probably still alive but too ill to command an expeditionary force in the spring of the previous year.[1] That Thucydides has not chosen to record the death of a man who, despite obvious limitations, was the leading figure on the Peloponnesian side for several years may appear remarkable and even regrettable. It is, however, symptomatic of his attitude towards individuals in the first half of his *History*.

[1] K. J. Beloch, *Gr. Gesch.* I, 2 (1913), 184–5; Gomme (I), I, 405 and II, 289.

CHAPTER IX

CNEMUS AND ALCIDAS

CNEMUS and Alcidas, who held the office of *nauarchos* in 430/29 and 428/27 respectively, may conveniently be discussed in the same chapter because, as presented by Thucydides, they are almost indistinguishable. The problems with which they were confronted and their methods of handling these problems were much the same. Cnemus was less reluctant than Alcidas to embark upon offensive action, but equally inclined to show infirmity of purpose when difficulties or setbacks were encountered. Thucydides seems deliberately to draw attention to their affinities, which he may well have exaggerated. To him they were interesting not as individuals but as typical Spartans, whose qualities of leadership afforded an instructive contrast to those of Brasidas. They are shown to have been normally as cautious and unenterprising as Archidamus without, it appears, possessing his homely good sense. They are also seen to have been incapable of effective leadership when commanding mixed forces composed mainly of allied contingents, because, like most Spartans except Brasidas, they were unable, or unwilling, to appreciate that not everyone viewed each situation from a purely Spartan angle. The narrative of the episodes in which Cnemus and Alcidas were involved illustrates the preoccupation of Thucydides, in this part of his work, with general lessons. In this instance the general lesson to which he wishes to draw the attention of his readers is, as in his presentation of Archidamus, the dearth of enterprising and imaginative leadership on the Spartan side during the opening years of the war. It was partly through the shortcomings of their *nauarchoi* that the Spartans gained an unenviable reputation in the eyes of other Greeks for poor planning and for dilatoriness which persisted until their victory at Mantinea in 418 (5. 75. 3).

1. *Cnemus*

Cnemus is first mentioned as the commander of a Peloponnesian expedition sent in 430 to attempt the reduction of Zacynthus. In this project, which is described very briefly, he was unsuccessful (2. 66). During the following summer the Ambraciots and Chaonians persuaded Sparta to sponsor and lead an expedition by land and sea designed primarily to overrun Acarnania and detach it from the Athenian alliance (80. 1). Thucydides evidently had the advantage of well-informed sources on the Peloponnesian side, since he reports in detail the plans of the Peloponnesians, including some never put into operation (80. 1; 81. 2) and gives a full list of allied contingents and their leaders (80. 5–7). Cnemus was entrusted with the direction of the entire enterprise, which must have appeared to have good prospects of success because the Athenians, weakened by the plague, might well be unable to spare any forces to support their Acarnanian allies, apart from the squadron of twenty ships under Phormio stationed at Naupactus (69. 1). Yet the Peloponnesian plan miscarried lamentably. Cnemus sailed with his force of 1,000 hoplites and successfully evaded interception by the squadron of Phormio (80. 4). Acting with much greater boldness than on any subsequent occasion throughout his tenure of office, he then decided not to wait for the Peloponnesian section of his fleet, which was expected to arrive at Leucas and occupy the attention of Acarnanians living on the coast, but to lead all his land troops, including local allies, into the interior against the Acarnanian city of Stratus (80. 8). When this mixed force was approaching Stratus in three divisions, the Chaonians and other barbarians, rushing forward without his knowledge or consent with the intention of winning for themselves alone the credit of capturing the city, fell into an ambush and were routed by the Stratians (81. 2–7). This action caused the Peloponnesians to discontinue their attempt to take Stratus. After reuniting their forces hitherto dispersed in three divisions, they remained on the defensive throughout the day, harassed by enemy slingers. At nightfall Cnemus withdrew in haste to a point ten miles from Stratus; he then made a further withdrawal to Oeniadae, where he dismissed the allied contingents (81. 8–82). He and his Peloponnesians proceeded to Leucas, whence they sailed to Cyllene in Elis (84. 5). His operations in Acarnania had accomplished nothing.

One reason why Thucydides describes this campaign in some detail is that it gives him the opportunity of drawing attention to a military lesson of some importance. It illustrates how barbarian troops, even if their fighting qualities were exceptionally high (81. 4), tended to be unreliable because of their indiscipline and impetuosity.[1] The narrative also exposes the weakness of conventional Spartan leadership, though Cnemus is nowhere expressly criticised. It is evident that he acted unwisely in permitting his army to advance upon Stratus in three independently operating divisions when one of these was composed entirely of barbarians under their own leaders. Spartan officers were sometimes appointed to command contingents from Greek states allied with Sparta (cf. 75. 3), and Cnemus could presumably have adopted this system, though the self-confident Chaonians might well have objected for reasons of prestige. Thucydides also creates the impression that Cnemus displayed a lack of determination and perseverance both in withdrawing so hurriedly from Stratus and in abandoning the whole campaign after he reached Oeniadae. It is true that at Stratus, in addition to the defeat of his barbarian troops, his hoplites found themselves at a disadvantage when under fire from the Acarnanian slingers; but his army was a large one (81. 1), which must have outnumbered the Stratians, and two of its three divisions were almost intact when he gave the order to retreat. Why he disbanded his army at Oeniadae, without attempting to resume the offensive, is not adequately explained. He is stated to have retreated thither before the main force of the Acarnanians could arrive (82), so that he seems to have felt too weak to challenge this force without the support of additional

---

[1] Cf. the views attributed to Brasidas in 4. 126.

troops. It may be that from Oeniadae he expected to make contact with a substantial reinforcement which was to have been landed by the fleet intercepted by the Athenians under Phormio; and that, when this fleet failed to arrive and he learned of its defeat, he decided, especially as the land campaign in Acarnania had little prospect of success, to devote his attention to operations at sea.[1] By failing to account for this decision Thucydides leaves his readers with the impression, which perhaps does Cnemus less than justice, that it was the outcome of irresolution.

The ignominious defeat of the Peloponnesian fleet when intercepted by Phormio outside the mouth of the Corinthian Gulf has been considered in an earlier chapter.[2] Because Cnemus had been entrusted with the direction of the whole campaign, he was held responsible for this failure at sea (85. 1–2), though he was far away in Acarnania when the battle was fought (83. 1). The Spartans were surprised and angered by the ineffectiveness of the fleet, which was mainly Corinthian, against an enemy much inferior in numbers. According to Thucydides, they concluded that there must have been some lack of energy and enterprise,[3] failing to appreciate the extent of the advantage enjoyed by the Athenians through much longer experience of fighting at sea (85. 2). The ill-success of Cnemus in Acarnania, which must also have caused dissatisfaction and given rise to criticism of his leadership there, doubtless contributed to the Spartan decision to send three advisers, including Brasidas, to assist him (85. 1).[4] Thucydides, however, attributes this decision solely to displeasure arising from the naval defeat; he does not mention any Spartan reaction to the

[1] Cf. Adcock, *C.A.H.* v (1927), 208.

[2] See above, 44–7.

[3] The word used is μαλακία (on which see above, 127 n. 3).

[4] This measure was not infrequently adopted when Spartan commanders were unsuccessful. Gomme (1), II, 220 cites other examples. Although a *nauarchos* might constitutionally be dismissed from office (8. 39. 2), there is no evidence that the Spartans ever went so far as to take this step, nor do they seem to have relieved a *nauarchos* of the main responsibility for directing a campaign when once it had begun. Pasippidas, who in 410 was banished while in command of a fleet (Xen. *Hell.* 1. 1. 32), is not stated to have been *nauarchos*.

result of the land campaign, to which at the outset the movements of the fleet had been designed only to lend support (83. 3; 87. 2). This omission is instructive. While the operations in Acarnania had no immediate sequel, the first naval battle was followed by a second, and both provided abundant evidence of Athenian superiority in seamanship. Thucydides here lays emphasis upon this factor, to which he attached great importance because of its influence upon the course of the war, whereas the attitude of the Spartan government towards Cnemus and the extent of his personal responsibility for Spartan failures were relatively insignificant topics.

Even less prominence is given to the personal contribution of Cnemus to the second naval battle and its antecedents. Thucydides assigns to 'Cnemus and Brasidas and the other generals of the Peloponnesians' (86. 6) the speech of encouragement to the Peloponnesian forces, and to 'the Peloponnesians' (90. 1) the battle-plan which compelled Phormio against his will to fight in the narrow waters of the Gulf and very nearly led to the destruction of his squadron. Whoever may have been the creator of this bold plan,[1] Cnemus deserves some credit for having consented to put it into operation. Neither Cnemus nor Brasidas is mentioned in the account of the battle, which demonstrates very clearly that the failure of the Peloponnesians to exploit their initial success was due to the inferiority of their sailors in naval technique. The Peloponnesian decision to disperse their fleet and steal away by night seems rather fainthearted despite the approach of a squadron from Athens to reinforce Phormio. Although this decision is not expressly attributed to Cnemus (92. 6), he must, as supreme commander, at least have sanctioned it. His leadership seems to have again been somewhat lacking in perseverance.

The account of his last operation as *nauarchos* (93–4) provides somewhat more tangible evidence of this defect, though even here he is not criticised directly. Shortly after their withdrawal

---

[1] See above, 48 n. 3 on the suggestion that Brasidas was responsible.

from the Corinthian Gulf 'Cnemus and Brasidas and the other commanders of the Peloponnesians' accepted a Megarian proposal that they should undertake a raid on the Piraeus, which was unguarded (93. 1–3). The crews from the Peloponnesian fleet recently disbanded were to cross by land from Corinth to Nisaea, taking their equipment, and there to embark upon forty Megarian ships. Thucydides evidently admired this plan: to him it was original and imaginative, daring without being foolhardy. It contains all the ingredients later associated with the projects of Brasidas, and the reader may feel, and is perhaps intended to feel, that, if Brasidas had been in sole command, it would have achieved much greater success. At first all went well. By maintaining strict measures of security during their preparations and by acting very rapidly the Peloponnesians took the enemy completely by surprise. No sooner, however, had they started by night from Nisaea than they abandoned their intention to attack the Piraeus and confined themselves to the far less ambitious task of raiding Salamis. Here they did a considerable amount of damage, besides causing consternation at Athens and the Piraeus, which is very graphically described. Thucydides criticises the Peloponnesians with unusual bluntness for their change of plan. He states that they became alarmed at the danger and adds in a contemptuous parenthesis καί τις καὶ ἄνεμος αὐτοὺς λέγεται κωλῦσαι (93. 4).[1] He also declares categorically that, if they had acted with any determination, they could easily have reached the Piraeus (94. 1, ὅπερ ἄν, εἰ ἐβουλήθησαν μὴ κατοκνῆσαι, ῥᾳδίως ἐγένετο, καὶ οὐκ ἂν ἄνεμος ἐκώλυσεν). He is little less critical of their hasty withdrawal from Salamis when Athenian forces were about to engage them, for he evidently does not accept as adequate an excuse that their Megarian ships had long been out of service and were unseaworthy (94. 3). It may be that they would not have caused severe or lasting damage at the Piraeus if they had per-

---

[1] The use of λέγεται in quoting answers to criticisms has already been noted above, 128. Cf. Gomme (2), 133 on the probability that Cnemus was responsible for the change of plan.

sisted in their original plan,[1] but Thucydides certainly held the view that a promising scheme was ruined by timidity and excessive caution. He does not report here, as he does on a subsequent occasion (3. 79. 3), that Brasidas advocated bold action and was overruled by an unenterprising superior. Such, however, is the impression conveyed by his account of this episode.

2. *Alcidas*

The career of Alcidas illustrates even more strikingly the defects of Spartan leadership. In the late summer of 428 he was appointed to command a fleet of forty ships which was to be sent to Lesbos (3. 16. 3), where Mytilene was already being blockaded by sea by the Athenians (6. 2) and, before the summer ended, was invested by land as well (18. 4–5). The Peloponnesian fleet did not sail until the following spring (26. 1). There is no reason to blame Alcidas for the delay in assembling and dispatching this expedition, and there is at least some room for doubt whether he was personally responsible for its strangely slow progress across the Aegean, which could have been largely the outcome of orders issued to him at Sparta.[2] Prospects of saving Mytilene would obviously be enormously enhanced if he could take the Athenians by surprise while their attention was concentrated upon the task of maintaining the blockade. Two different methods of trying to escape detection were open to the Peloponnesians during their voyage. They could press on with all possible speed, hoping to outstrip anyone who might report their approach, or they could take a circuitous and unfrequented route, making landfalls only where they could feel secure and capturing any merchantmen that

[1] Gomme (1), II, 240. During the Corinthian war Teleutias, whose naval forces were relatively much stronger by comparison with those of the Athenians, conducted a successful raid on the Piraeus from Aegina (Xen. *Hell.* 5. 1. 19–23), but the results were not catastrophic for Athens.

[2] A reference to the disappointment of the Spartans operating in Attica when they received no news from Lesbos (26. 4) does suggest that the progress of the fleet was slower than had been expected. It does not, however, necessarily inculpate Alcidas.

they sighted. By dwelling upon the slowness of their progress[1] Thucydides makes his own verdict unusually clear: that they ought to have adopted the first of these methods and that by adopting the second they threw away the last chance of saving Mytilene. The narrative does not contain any mention of Alcidas at this stage, and, in the absence of any reference to the orders issued to him by the Spartan government, the question of his responsibility for the fall of Mytilene is left obscure. The primary aim of Thucydides here is to underline the slowness and excessive caution of the Spartans generally rather than to assess the qualities of an individual.

When the Peloponnesians reached Embatum on the Asiatic coast, they received confirmation of an earlier report that Mytilene had surrendered (29. 2). They can hardly have been given instructions applicable to the new situation created by this development. Hereafter they had to act on their own initiative, and the part played by Alcidas at once becomes more clearly defined. A conference was held to consider what action should be taken; it was attended by the principal officers of the fleet, while some Ionian exiles and some Lesbians were also present (29. 2–31. 2). Thucydides was well-informed about this conference and evidently regarded it as important, since he includes in his report of it a brief speech in *oratio recta*. The speaker is Teutiaplus, an Elean, who urged the Peloponnesians to make a sudden attack by night upon the Athenians before their own arrival in Asia became known and while the Athenian forces were likely to be dispersed and off their guard because of their recent success. Alcidas refused to accept this plan. He also rejected another put forward by the Ionians and Lesbians (31. 1). They advised him to seize some town on the Asiatic coast and use it as a base for stirring up revolt in Ionia, which would increase the financial difficulties of the Athenians;[2] there was also some prospect of

---

[1] 29. 1, where the phrases οὓς ἔδει ἐν τάχει παραγενέσθαι and σχολαῖοι κομισθέντες are noteworthy, cf. 27. 1, ἐνεχρόνιζον.

[2] Cf. 19. 1, which shows that these difficulties were real enough. Hopes of widespread revolt in Ionia were perhaps over-optimistic when the fate of Lesbos

securing Persian aid. Thucydides does not mention any arguments advanced by Alcidas to justify his rejection of these proposals. He states only that the thoughts of Alcidas were directed mainly towards a speedy return home since he had been too late to save Mytilene (31. 2). The implication is that he not only lacked fortitude[1] but also chose to adhere very strictly to his instructions and was reluctant to improvise.[2]

While the fleet was still off the Asiatic coast, Alcidas put to death most of the prisoners taken during his voyage. This action led to vigorous protests from some Samian exiles, who pointed out that it belied the claim of the Spartans to be liberators and would alienate public feeling; the victims were not enemies but belonged to cities allied to Athens by compulsion. Alcidas at least had the good sense to see the cogency of this criticism and released most of the surviving prisoners (32. 1–2). This minor incident is perhaps included in order to show that he had two failings often associated with Spartan leadership, namely a tendency to senseless brutality and an inability to foresee what repercussion his actions would produce from other Greeks.

The Athenians had by now heard that an enemy fleet was in Asiatic waters, and they hastily tried to intercept it. Alcidas, however, in fear of pursuit bolted homewards across the open sea ὡς γῇ ἑκούσιος οὐ σχήσων ἄλλη ἢ Πελοποννήσῳ (33. 1), a phrase loaded with contempt. He succeeded in outstripping his pursuers (33. 3). Thucydides seems to have felt some doubt whether he could have saved Mytilene but no doubt at all that he could have inflicted severe damage upon cities in Ionia, which were without fortifications, if he had been a little less intent on escaping from the Athenians. A reference to the feelings of panic in Ionia at the prospect of Peloponnesian attack makes this conclusion abund-

had so recently given evidence that the Athenians were still able to retaliate effectively.

[1] The phrase μὴ ἀποκνήσωμεν τὸν κίνδυνον (30. 4) in the speech of Teutiaplus is significant.

[2] See below, 295, on Astyochus.

antly clear (33. 2).[1] Thucydides postpones to a later stage of his narrative the information that the Peloponnesian ships were caught in a storm and reached home waters piecemeal (69. 1). Characteristically he confines his attention to the main issue, which is their headlong flight from Asia.

The fleet of Alcidas was eventually reassembled at Cyllene, where preparations were made to send it, reinforced by thirteen ships from Leucas and Ambracia, to operate at Corcyra, now in the grip of violent revolution. Spartan disapproval of Alcidas arising from his handling of his mission to Asia is reflected in the appointment of Brasidas to serve as his adviser (69. 1-2). The stimulus of having Brasidas at his side had remarkably little effect upon Alcidas. When they arrived with their fleet in the vicinity of Corcyra, the political upheavals there had reached a critical stage (76). The Athenian squadron supporting the democratic faction amounted to only twelve ships (75. 1), and although the Corcyrean fleet numbered sixty, its efficiency, never very high, was now dangerously impaired by dissension and distrust. Hence the Peloponnesians appeared to have an excellent chance of turning the situation to their own advantage. They failed, however, to win a crushing victory in a sea-battle fought against the Athenians and Corcyreans (77-8), though the Corcyrean fleet fell into utter confusion even before the action began. The outstanding quality of Athenian seamanship is seen to have once more proved a decisive factor. Although thirty-three of the Peloponnesian ships engaged the small Athenian squadron, they were outmanoeuvred and compelled to form a defensive circle with bows facing outwards, as in the first naval battle against Phormio. The other twenty Peloponnesian ships had to break off their pursuit of the Corcyreans, whose withdrawal was then

---

[1] Paches is stated to have felt some relief that he failed to catch the Peloponnesian fleet and was therefore not put to the trouble of blockading it anywhere (33. 3). It is very unusual for Thucydides in the earlier books of his *History* to record the personal feelings of individuals (*C.Q.* XLI [1947], 28). Gomme (I), II, 295 suggests that the wording is deliberately tinged with irony directed against the Peloponnesians.

skilfully covered by the Athenians. That the Peloponnesians failed to take full advantage of a favourable situation and captured only thirteen Corcyrean ships (79. 2) was attributable to the deficiencies of their crews rather than to ineffective leadership. On the other hand, it must have been on the orders of Alcidas, though he is not named, that they sailed back to the mainland in the evening after the battle instead of launching an attack on the city of Corcyra, a decision regarded by Thucydides as timid (79. 2, οὐκ ἐτόλμησαν). On the following day, though the Corcyreans were in a state of confused panic, the Peloponnesians again refrained from offensive action against the city and were content to plunder a district in the south of the island (79. 3; 80. 2). Here Thucydides does expressly hold Alcidas responsible, for he mentions a report (ὡς λέγεται) that Brasidas urged his superior to attack the city but was overruled.[1]

At nightfall the Peloponnesians received a signal that a large Athenian fleet was approaching from the south. This news caused them to sail away at once during the night with all possible speed, and in order to reduce the risk of interception they hugged the coast and at Leucas hauled their ships across the isthmus (80. 2–81. 1). Thucydides dwells on the precipitancy of their withdrawal, perhaps suggesting a comparison with their flight from Asia. If, however, the approximate size of the Athenian fleet, which amounted to sixty ships, was known to them, as seems probable, their eagerness to escape was hardly discreditable. Even if the Corcyrean fleet were to continue to be almost impotent, they would now be outnumbered, as well as outclassed, by the Athenians. Nevertheless, opportunities had been lost during this expedition, which further illustrates the inadequacy of Spartan leadership.

Alcidas must have completed his term of office as *nauarchos*

---

[1] Again λέγεται does not appear to refer merely to hearsay (see above, 128), especially as Thucydides was very well-informed about Brasidas. It suggests rather that at some subsequent enquiry at Sparta (not necessarily of a formal kind) the attempt by Brasidas to stir Alcidas to action was cited.

soon after his return from Corcyra. In the following summer he was chosen with two others to found the Spartan colony at Heraclea in Trachis (92. 5). This mission seems to have been largely a sinecure, and the three founders apparently did not remain long at Heraclea.[1] Unlike Leon, one of his colleagues, Alcidas is not known to have been entrusted thereafter with any responsible appointment.

[1] A. J. Graham, *Colony and Mother City in Ancient Greece* (1964), 38–9.

BRASIDAS

BRASIDAS is the antithesis of the conventional Spartan leader. Wherever he appears in the narrative of Thucydides, there is action, energy and enterprise. Almost alone of Spartan leaders in the Peloponnesian war he is seen to have appreciated the value of consulting the interests of other Greeks and to have possessed a remarkable flair for winning popularity and even devotion.[1] The account of his achievements given by Thucydides is evidently based upon abundant information; at several points it betrays knowledge of motives which can have been disclosed only to a few persons;[2] it may well have been derived largely from personal contacts with Brasidas himself, or at least with one of his subordinates, when Thucydides was in exile. It is clear that Thucydides was interested in Brasidas, whose personality he found attractive, and that he allowed his interest in personality to be more prominent than usual in his narrative of the Archidamian war. Yet among the qualities of Brasidas only those distinguishing him from other Spartans and those influencing the course of the war—which are largely the same—receive much attention. His diplomatic activities are stressed,[3] and some account is given of his negotiations with Perdiccas, but apart from occasional hints there is hardly any picture of his relations with his Spartan superiors or subordinates or with the opponents of his policy at home. He is largely a public figure whose impact is on bodies of troops or populations of cities.

In seeking to establish the undoubtedly valid point that he was refreshingly unlike other Spartan leaders, Thucydides perhaps

---

[1] Cf. 4. 81. 1–3 (see above, 9). This is implicit in the whole narrative of his campaign in the north-east.

[2] The best examples are: 4. 70. 1–2; 105. 1; 120. 2; 124. 4; 5. 6. 3.

[3] L. Bodin, *Mélanges Navarre* (1935), 47–55.

tends to overestimate his services to the Spartan cause, valuable as these certainly were.

During the first seven years of the war Brasidas was not entrusted with any major command; presumably he lacked the necessary seniority. He did, however, seize such opportunities as came his way to display personal bravery and a most un-Spartan readiness to act boldly on his own initiative. In 431, when an Athenian raiding force was threatening Methone in Laconia, he saved the town by prompt and resolute action (2. 25. 2).[1] In 425, while serving as a trierarch during the Spartan assault on Pylos, he stirred his men by exhortation and example to press home their attack, and his gallantry nearly cost him his life (4. 11. 4–12. 1).[2] Between these two episodes he served as 'adviser' first to Cnemus and later to Alcidas and did his best to infuse into his superiors something of his own enterprising spirit.[3] It must have been a frustrating experience.

His first real chance to distinguish himself in an independent command came in the summer of 424 when he was sent with a force of Peloponnesians and helots to the Thraceward region.[4] Allies of the Athenians in this area, who wished to revolt, and Perdiccas, who contemplated changing sides once more, had asked for Spartan aid, and Brasidas was eager to take command (4. 79. 2; 80. 1; 81. 1; 82; 83. 4). This celebrated mission, which continued until his death two years later, influenced the course of the war very considerably and inflicted permanent damage upon the Athenian empire: at various stages it hastened and delayed the conclusion of peace. Thucydides does, however, describe it more fully than is warranted by its importance. He can hardly

[1] For his services he received the equivalent of a gallantry award. Thucydides would scarcely have reported this if he had not wished to prepare the reader for the subsequent exploits of Brasidas.

[2] See above, 108–9, on this operation. The reference to the capture of his shield by the Athenians is another almost personal detail.

[3] See above, 139–42 and 145–6.

[4] It is necessary to use this unlovely term because neither Thrace nor Chalcidice accurately represents τὰ ἐπὶ Θρᾴκης, which stretched from the Thermaic Gulf to the Hebrus.

be thought to be thereby attempting indirectly to excuse his own failure to save Amphipolis from Brasidas. His principal aim seems rather to be to build up the contrast between Brasidas and other Spartan leaders in two pre-requisites of good leadership: first, the ability to seize and exploit opportunities by imaginative and daring action and, secondly, the ability to win and retain the loyal support of others by effective use of the spoken word.

While Brasidas was still mobilising his expeditionary force near the Isthmus in preparation for his northward march, his promptitude and determination saved Megara from the Athenians (4. 70–3). In this episode, which has already been discussed from the Athenian point of view,[1] his swift grasp of an obscure and complex situation and his skilful exploitation of it without committing his troops to battle provide evidence of intellectual qualities not vouchsafed to all gallant soldiers (73. 2–3). He was not wholly successful, and Thucydides neither conceals nor excuses his failures: his hopes first of saving and then of regaining Nisaea were unfulfilled (70. 1–2), and his initial attempt to persuade the Megarians to admit him was abortive (71. 2). The same capacity for quick decision and quick action, combined with adroit and indeed unscrupulous diplomacy, is seen in the account of his successful march across Thessaly despite the disapproval of most Thessalians (78). Included in this account is a brief report of a conference at the Enipeus, where Brasidas and his Thessalian supporters, who were guiding him through the country, negotiated with other Thessalians who were members of an opposing faction and protested that he had no right to cross Thessaly without permission from the federal government. By a mixture of conciliation and duplicity Brasidas and his guides appeased their opponents and then hurried northwards before a large force could be mustered to stop their advance (78. 2–5). This account is interesting for two reasons: hitherto Thucydides has reported few small, almost private, conferences of this kind; and Brasidas is seen, not for the last time, to have practised barefaced deception

---

[1] See above, 111–15.

(cf. 85. 7; 108. 5; 122. 6). In another respect, however, the methods of Brasidas might well have been more clearly explained. As on many subsequent occasions, he was able to rely upon influential local agents (78. 1–2), whose support must have been carefully solicited long before the arrival of his army. How he enlisted these agents is not disclosed, although information on the subject would have thrown valuable light upon his personality.

Soon after he reached his destination friction developed between him and Perdiccas, who demanded his assistance against a Lyncestian prince named Arrhabaeus (83). It is comparable with the friction between the Spartans and Tissaphernes at a later stage of the war but is less fully reported. Thucydides does, however, give some account of the acrimonious exchanges with Perdiccas and also mentions consultations by Brasidas with Arrhabaeus and with the Chalcidians (83. 3–6). Brasidas was in a difficult position, for the Spartan government had apparently omitted to negotiate in advance a satisfactory agreement defining the relations between his expeditionary force and Perdiccas, who was paying half of its costs. Always an uncomfortable and unreasonably demanding ally, Perdiccas treated the Peloponnesians like mercenaries and was furious when Brasidas chose to come to terms with Arrhabaeus instead of fighting. The result was that Perdiccas reduced his subsidy (83. 6). The firmness of Brasidas seems to have been justified, even though it alienated Perdiccas: his primary duty was to embark without delay upon attempts to stir up revolt among the subject-allies of Athens in the neighbourhood.

The first revolt was that of Acanthus (84–8). At the outset the inhabitants were divided in their attitude towards Brasidas (84. 2), and it was only by his skilful handling of a delicate situation that he induced a majority of them to vote in favour of revolt (88. 1). Thucydides reports his speech in their assembly (86–7). It is mainly a plea that they should seize this opportunity of gaining their freedom by joining the Spartans, who are represented as disinterested champions of autonomy striving to liberate other Greeks from enslavement by the Athenians. He is stated to have spoken in much the same vein later at Torone (114. 3) and Scione (120. 3), so that a single speech is evidently used to sketch the broad outlines of his propaganda throughout his mission. The speech illustrates his diplomatic skill, which differentiates him from other Spartans, but its principal aim is to explain to the reader the official policy of Sparta towards Athenian imperialism. His attitude is not wholly conciliatory, for he issues a threat, which he tries to justify, that he will ravage Acanthian territory if his proposals are not accepted (87. 2-3). This threat, which was particularly effective because the grape harvest was about to be gathered, was as influential as his persuasiveness in causing a majority to vote for revolt from Athens (88. 1). Stagirus revolted soon afterwards (88. 2).

The next exploit of Brasidas was his capture of Amphipolis (102-7), which dealt the Athenians a very damaging blow.[1] The account of Thucydides has many of the same features as are found in accounts of other episodes in which Brasidas played a major role. It draws attention to his skilful exploitation of disaffection against Athens at Argilus and Amphipolis despite the loyalty of most Amphipolitans; to his enterprising unconventionality in making his attempt on a stormy night in winter; to his swiftness of movement, which enabled him to achieve surprise; to his shrewdness of judgement in offering moderate terms to the Amphipolitans while they were still affected by the confusion caused by his sudden arrival and before the fleet under Thucydides could bring aid. In all these respects he showed qualities in which other Spartan leaders were found wanting. Because the fall of Amphipolis was so important, Thucydides goes on to comment upon its effect on public opinion not only at Athens but also in neighbouring cities in the north which were subject-allies of the Athenians (108. 1-6). These allies, he declares, were so impressed by the success of Brasidas and by his considerate and

---

[1] I have discussed this episode from a different standpoint in *Hermes* XC (1962), 276-87, where I have tried to show that the treatment of it by Thucydides constitutes a subtle defence of his own part in it.

unoppressive attitude towards them that they welcomed the prospect of revolt with ill-considered optimism; they were later made to regret their error in underestimating the power of Athens.[1] It is noteworthy that Thucydides is here, as very frequently elsewhere, preoccupied with the general issue of the relations between the Athenians and their allies. He does not at the same time consider whether Brasidas himself may have been unwise in exploiting his success too eagerly. The revolts of very small towns probably proved a liability. Their military resources were slender, and the necessity to protect each of them against the danger of Athenian reprisals must have imposed a severe strain upon the small forces at his disposal.[2] It was doubtless with such considerations in mind that he asked for reinforcements to be sent from the Peloponnese. His request was refused (108. 6–7), partly, Thucydides states, because leading Spartans were jealous of him. This explanation provides a pointer to the sources from which Thucydides derived his evidence: though doubtless authentic, it almost certainly originates from Brasidas himself or someone serving under his command. A second reason why the Spartans refused to send reinforcements is that they were bent rather on the recovery of the prisoners captured on Sphacteria and on the conclusion of peace. To them his success was valuable chiefly as a means of attaining these ends (117. 2, cf. 81. 2). It is uncertain whether Thucydides is here implying criticism of them for their desire to make peace: the passage is very obscure. There is, however, no doubt that the enterprise of Brasidas is contrasted with traditional Spartan passiveness.

For a time his mission continued to prosper. Most of the small towns on Acte agreed to revolt when he appeared with his army

[1] Cf. *Proc. Camb. Phil. Soc.* VII (1961), 63–7, where I have argued that this passage refers to the period between 423 and 421, during which the Athenians recovered many of the cities which had revolted.

[2] A minor criticism of Brasidas by Thucydides, if indeed it is a criticism, is that, in order to encourage allies of Athens to revolt, he falsely claimed that at Megara the Athenians had shrunk from engaging the small force now serving under him in the north-east, whereas in reality he then led a much larger army which outnumbered the Athenians (108. 5, cf. 85. 7).

(109), though their support cannot have brought him much advantage. A much more valuable success was his capture of Torone, a prize second only to Amphipolis and won by similar methods (110–16). No major episode in the career of Brasidas is more brilliantly described by Thucydides, whose narrative technique is here seen at its best.[1] Each step in the development of a complex situation is explained with penetrating clarity, and the number of graphic touches is exceptionally large.[2] At the same time the narrative is remarkably economical and rapid. Because an Athenian garrison was stationed at Torone and put up a resolute resistance, some stiff fighting was required, in which the gallant leadership of Brasidas was again prominent (112), before the town itself and the fort of Lecythus fell into his hands. Once more, however, a well-laid plan for using a small body of local partisans, combined with skilful propaganda in conciliating the mass of the population, contributed to his success. When Torone had fallen but Lecythus was still in Athenian hands, he issued a proclamation designed to win over citizens still loyal to the Athenians (114. 1), and he made a speech in the assembly (114. 3–5). Thucydides does not give a full report but states that it was similar to the speech at Acanthus, adding in *oratio obliqua* a few further points. The keynote was insistence on Spartan good will, but Brasidas ended with a warning. He bore no grudge, he said, against Toroneans who, having no alternative, had in the past supported the Athenians and opposed him; henceforward, however, he would expect the whole population to remain faithful to Sparta and would punish any disloyalty.

The conclusion of the One Year's Truce in the spring of 423

[1] In describing the two successes of Brasidas at Amphipolis—its capture in 424 and the battle there in 422—Thucydides has not been able to suppress entirely the influence of personal feelings, since he himself was involved in the former and Cleon in the latter.

[2] Examples are: 110. 2, where only seven out of twenty light-armed soldiers sent forward to make the first entry into the town prove brave enough to obey their orders; 115. 2–3, where a house being fortified by the Athenians suddenly collapses; 116. 2, where Brasidas pays to Athena the reward promised to the first man to scale the wall (which is almost an anecdote).

was a severe blow to Brasidas, who was instigating further revolts (cf. 116. 3). He refused to abandon his plans. When Scione revolted just as the truce was being concluded, he crossed secretly from Sithonia to Pallene by night—another graphically described incident (120. 1–2). At Scione he made a speech similar to those at Acanthus and Torone, but he added a special compliment to the citizens. They had, he declared, chosen of their own free will to revolt when they could not hope for support by land from outside Pallene as long as the Athenians held Potidaea on the isthmus joining the peninsula to the mainland (120. 3). There was more general enthusiasm for revolt at Scione than in other cities, and Brasidas, who was honoured as a liberator, had no need to issue threats in order to secure unity there (121. 1). Although he was engaged on intrigues designed to bring about the revolt of Potidaea (121. 2), it seems doubtful whether he was wise in encouraging the Scioneans when he could not protect them adequately. Perhaps his hand was forced by the impending conclusion of the truce. On this point Thucydides does not provide any information.

In the subsequent dispute on the question whether Scione had revolted before or after the date on which the truce was concluded, Brasidas insisted that the revolt had taken place before that date (122. 3–6). Thucydides declares bluntly that this contention was false (122. 6): he does not explicitly accuse Brasidas of deliberate dishonesty, but such is the implication of his account. If Brasidas had not adopted this attitude, he would have been forced to leave Scione unprotected and his reputation as a staunch defender of rebel cities would have been severely damaged. Further negotiations failed to resolve the dispute and left the Athenians furious because the truce could not now be fully implemented. Accordingly they passed a resolution, which was proposed by Cleon, that Scione should be reduced and the inhabitants put to death. They then made preparations for a military expedition to Pallene (122. 6). This expedition was also directed against Mende, where a small body of intriguers forced revolt upon a reluctant majority, confidently anticipating that Brasidas would support them despite the conclusion of the armistice (123. 1-3). He did not disappoint them, asserting that he was justified in giving them aid because of violations of the armistice by the Athenians. Thucydides does not specify these alleged violations and seems to imply that Brasidas was merely seeking an excuse for illegally supporting the rebels. Some Peloponnesian and Chalcidian troops under a subordinate named Polydamidas were sent to Scione and Mende, and the women and children were evacuated (123. 4).

When the expeditionary force arrived from Athens to reduce the two rebel cities, Brasidas was absent, with most of his Peloponnesians and some of his local allies, assisting Perdiccas, who was again campaigning in Lyncestis against Arrhabaeus (124. 1). It is remarkable that, though Thucydides describes this campaign fully and graphically (124-8), he does not explain why Brasidas was compelled to take part in it at a moment critical for his allies on Pallene, where an Athenian landing was soon expected. Brasidas felt anxiety during his absence about the fate of Mende and evidently wished to escape from his obligations to Perdiccas at the earliest opportunity (124. 4); but it seems to be assumed that he had no means of refusing to commit his forces to supporting the expedition against Arrhabaeus. Perdiccas doubtless put pressure upon him by arguing that for many months he had contributed towards the maintenance of the Peloponnesians, and perhaps by threatening to reduce this subsidy further or to withdraw it altogether (cf. 83. 6). He could also claim that it was easier for Brasidas to help him while the armistice was being observed except in Pallene. The silence of Thucydides on this not unimportant issue could well be due to unwillingness to prejudice the general picture of Brasidas as an un-Spartan Spartan by presenting him in a situation in which he perhaps showed some lack of diplomatic skill or of determination—or of both. Brasidas must, it seems, have tried, and failed, to persuade Perdiccas at the outset to release him and his Peloponnesians from their obligations in view of the threat to Mende and Scione (cf. 124. 4). He might then, it appears, have decided, unless there were obstacles of which no evidence survives, to break completely with Perdiccas and to forgo the financial subsidy, hoping to make good the deficiency from his allies in Chalcidice and elsewhere, whose loyalty to him was assured. In somewhat similar circumstances another Spartan Callicratidas chose a different method of dealing with his paymaster Cyrus (Xen. *Hell.* 1. 6. 6–12).

Thucydides evidently found the campaign in Lyncestis interesting chiefly because of its military lessons. He dwells upon the skill of Brasidas in extricating his troops from a dangerous situation when deserted by their Macedonian allies; the position was aggravated because he was at loggerheads with Perdiccas (125. 1). The main theme of a speech made by Brasidas when his force was about to face a horde of Illyrians (126) is the superiority of trained hoplites over undisciplined masses of barbarian light-armed troops. The Illyrians proved to be as ineffective as he had predicted, and he succeeded in withdrawing his army safely from Lyncestis to Macedonia. He and Perdiccas were now irreparably estranged; the breach between them could not have been more complete if it had occurred before the campaign began.

Thereafter until his final and fatal victory at Amphipolis a year later Brasidas experienced nothing but frustration and failure. When he returned from Macedonia to Torone, Mende had already fallen to an Athenian expeditionary force led by Nicias and Nicostratus (129. 1), largely because most of the population had no wish to revolt from Athens (cf. 123. 2). Polydamidas, whom Brasidas had sent to take command, showed characteristically Spartan arrogance in using violence against a Mendean democrat who challenged his order to go out and fight the Athenians. This action precipitated a popular rising against the Peloponnesians and their supporters, and the city was soon in Athenian hands (130. 1–6). The report of the incident again suggests a contrast between Brasidas, who conducted public relations with so much tact, and other Spartan leaders, who used cruder methods.[1] Whether he could have saved Mende if he had been in the neighbourhood is another matter.

The Athenians moved on from Mende to Scione and were building a wall of circumvallation there when Brasidas returned from Macedonia (130. 7–131. 1–2). There was no prospect of betrayal at Scione, and the only practicable way of reducing the town was by a blockade. As Brasidas had foreseen when the revolt began (120. 3), he was unable to help the defenders: access to Pallene was impossible by land because the Athenians held Potidaea, and equally impossible by sea because they had a strong fleet (129. 2). The armistice prevented him from creating diversions elsewhere. Accordingly he made no move from his headquarters at Torone,[2] though he took steps to strengthen its defences (129. 1).[3] He was doubtless much occupied in preparing plans for the defence of other cities which would be likely to be attacked if the truce ended without the conclusion of a general peace. Only one military action undertaken by him during the remainder of the truce is mentioned by Thucydides. At the end of the winter he tried to surprise Potidaea by a night attack, which was very soon detected and had to be abandoned almost before it had begun (135. 1). There is no reference to any contacts between him and agents inside Potidaea; evidently the Athenians, who used the town as their base (129. 3), had rounded up all the Potidaeans who had earlier intrigued with him (121. 2) and might now have tried to admit his troops within the walls. This attack, which was a flagrant breach of the truce, seems to have been the outcome of desperation on the part of Brasidas, who had no other means of helping Scione, where the blockade was now complete (133. 4).

---

[1] This resort to violence against a free ally was even more culpable than the similar action of Astyochus (see below, 303–4) against mutineers in forces directly under his command (cf. Xen. *Hell.* 6. 2. 19 on a later Spartan, Mnasippus, who struck his subordinates).

[2] αὐτοῦ ἡσυχάζων (129. 1) does not mean that he did nothing, but the verb is not one that is naturally associated with Brasidas.

[3] It must have been at this time that he built the wall mentioned in 5. 2. 4.

Meanwhile there had been further developments unfavourable to Brasidas. Before the summer of 423 ended, Perdiccas decided, as a result of his breach with Brasidas, to forgo the advantages of association with the Peloponnesians and negotiated an agreement with Nicias and Nicostratus, the Athenian generals at Scione (128. 5; 132. 1). He must already have ceased to pay any subsidy to the Peloponnesians, but his decision to change sides had much more serious consequences for them. Partly through pressure from Nicias he used his influence with the Thessalians to baulk a Spartan plan to send a second expeditionary force to the Thrace-ward region (132. 2). Some leading Spartans did, however, succeed in reaching Brasidas. They included Ischagoras, who had been appointed to command the second expeditionary force and headed a commission of three charged with the duty of 'observing the situation' (132. 3). At the same time some younger Spartans were sent to serve as governors of allied cities: of these Clearidas was installed at Amphipolis and Pasitelidas at Torone.

The measures taken by the Spartan government are reported very briefly and the motives underlying them are not adequately explained. Thucydides may well have lacked reliable information from Sparta about these motives, where they cannot, for reasons of security, have been freely debated in public. Yet the person, or persons, from whom he derived his very full account of Brasidas in the north-east could, it seems, have thrown some light on the views of the Spartans at home about the problems of this area: Ischagoras and his colleagues must have communicated these to Brasidas in discussions held with him soon after their arrival. The predicament of the Scioneans must have been considered, and conferences were probably held with representatives of cities now under Spartan control. The only point in which Thucydides seems to feel any special interest is, oddly enough, a largely constitutional one, namely that to enlist younger men for service as governors was contrary to normal Spartan practice. On two much more important issues, which are closely linked, he provides his readers with hardly any guidance. First, he gives no reason why the Spartan government, after having refused only a few months earlier to send reinforcements to Brasidas—partly, he states, through jealousy (108. 7)—should now have prepared a second expedition. Secondly, he does not explain satisfactorily what the three Spartan commissioners were ordered to do, or indeed what they did.

To take the second question first, the instruction to the commissioners to 'observe the situation' (ἐπιδεῖν τὰ πράγματα) probably reproduces an official resolution, which, after the fashion of official resolutions, is designedly vague. Yet it certainly suggests dissatisfaction at Sparta with the recent activities of Brasidas.[1] Unlike the ξύμβουλοι attached to other Spartan leaders with the intention of spurring them to greater enterprise,[2] these commissioners were surely instructed to restrain Brasidas from ill-considered action likely to damage the prospects of recovering the prisoners captured on Sphacteria (117. 2) and of concluding an agreement with Athens more lasting than the present armistice (119. 3).[3] If such was the purpose of the Spartans in appointing the commissioners, it may seem strange that they intended originally to send an army with Ischagoras. They may have felt that, if the armistice ended without the conclusion of a general peace, it would be advantageous to have more troops available in the area, both to oppose the Athenians now at Scione and to encourage further revolts.[4] Another consideration, however, may have weighed more heavily with them. The 1,700 helots and Peloponnesians originally sent with Brasidas (78. 1; 80. 5) had become almost a personal army, and he had won immense popularity in the cities liberated from Athens. Hence, unless Ischagoras and his colleagues had with them a body of troops owing allegiance to themselves rather than to Brasidas, they might experience

---

[1] Busolt, 1170.　　　　　　　　　　[2] See above, 139.

[3] Ischagoras was apparently among the Spartans most eager for peace and therefore an opponent of Brasidas, cf. Gomme (1), III, 624 (the only evidence of any value is 5. 21. 1–3). Clearidas, if ever hostile to Brasidas, evidently fell under his spell and became a supporter of his policy (5. 8. 4; 9. 7; 10. 1 and 7–12; 21. 1–3).　　　　　　　　[4] Cf. Busolt, 1170.

difficulty in curbing his eagerness to find excuses for ignoring the armistice. In the circumstances, when the second expeditionary force had to be left behind, these fears seem to have proved well-founded; for his attack on Potidaea, which has been mentioned above, can hardly have met with the approval of the commissioners. If there is any validity in this reconstruction of Spartan policy, Thucydides could, it might seem, have laid further emphasis on the contrast between the enterprise of Brasidas and the cautious inertia of other Spartans by explaining the intentions of the home government fully to his readers. In this instance, however, his own integrity of judgement may well have prevented him from seeking to reinforce this general lesson to which the career of Brasidas seemed to him to point: for he may have felt himself forced to conclude that the policy of Brasidas at this stage was injudicious and much less likely than that of the home government to benefit Spartan interests. It was perhaps for this reason that he preferred to relapse into his barest and bleakest manner.[1]

Apart from the fruitless attack on Potidaea, Brasidas attempted no offensive action, so far as is known, before the armistice expired in the summer of 422. Perhaps the restraining influence of

[1] Two other points in the account of this mission (132. 3), which have given rise to much discussion in modern times (cf. Gomme (1), III, 623–4), do not seem to me to have much substance. It is thought that the appointment of Spartan officers to serve as ἄρχοντες in cities which had rebelled against Athens was a violation of the promises of autonomy given by Brasidas. The use of this term may be an example of Spartan tactlessness; but these cities might well have to defend themselves against Athenian reprisals when the armistice expired, and they probably welcomed the protection of a Spartan governor and some troops. Clearidas was in fact largely instrumental in preserving the autonomy of Amphipolis when it was to have been surrendered to Athens under the Peace of Nicias (5. 21. 1–3). The second point concerns the statement that the young Spartans sent with Ischagoras were to act as governors of the cities, which were not to be entrusted to 'any chance persons' (τοῖς ἐντυχοῦσι). This rather curious phrase (whether it reproduces the opinion of Brasidas or of others) surely reflects the contempt of Spartiates for anyone who was not a Spartiate. Brasidas had evidently not been provided at the outset with enough Spartiates to meet his needs. Thus more were now sent. That they were young is a quite separate point; Thucydides is fond of packing several ideas into a single sentence.

Ischagoras was partly responsible. When hostilities were resumed in the north-east, the initiative lay with the Athenians, who were persuaded by Cleon to send a strong force under his own command to recover their lost possessions (5. 2. 1) The part played by Cleon in the ensuing operations and the presentation of it by Thucydides have already been discussed.[1] At first Brasidas was unable to halt the successful progress of the Athenians. He was not at Torone when Cleon delivered an attack there (2. 3), and his absence is unexplained. He may have expected Cleon to remain at Scione (2. 2) and try to reduce it before proceeding against other towns. The circumstances resemble those in which Thucydides was absent from Amphipolis when it fell to Brasidas in 424,[2] and the omission of any explanation may be due to similar factors.[3] Brasidas hastened to the aid of Torone, presumably accompanied by a relieving force, but he was still five miles distant when he heard that the city had fallen (3. 3). Pasitelidas, the Spartan governor, defended the city with energy and spirit, but he was compelled to divide his very inadequate forces because the enemy, being able to land troops from ships, attacked from two directions simultaneously (2. 3–3. 2).[4] Torone was lost because Cleon exploited Athenian control of the sea so as to outgeneral his opponents, Pasitelidas tactically and Brasidas strategically, though Thucydides is evidently reluctant to suggest this conclusion even by implication.

In the account of the events culminating in his victory and death in battle at Amphipolis (6–11) Brasidas is pictured in the same light as before his year of eclipse which followed the signing of the armistice. Here, however, the contrast underlined by Thucydides is not so much between him and other Spartan leaders as between him and Cleon. His actions and decisions are brave and wise, those of Cleon cowardly and foolish. The failings of Cleon are allowed perhaps to be the most striking feature of

[1] See above, 75–82.   [2] Gomme (3), 114.   [3] Cf. Hermes, XC (1962), 285–7.
[4] The two suggestions made rather tentatively by Gomme (1), III, 632, that Pasitelidas was incompetent and that Brasidas was on bad terms with him, cannot, in my view, be legitimately inferred from the account of Thucydides.

the narrative. Brasidas, however, displays all the qualities that readers of Thucydides have been led to associate with him: a firm grasp of the strategic situation, as is seen very clearly in his speech to his troops (9. 2–8);[1] a capacity for penetrating the mind of his opponent (7. 1); skilful handling of his forces so as to counteract their acknowledged inferiority in quality (8. 2) and to commit them to battle at the right moment (10. 5–7); confidence in his own judgement (9. 2; 10. 5) and a flair for inspiring his men; dashing leadership in the action itself.[2] He could be criticised for having endangered his own life unnecessarily by choosing to lead the first charge at the head of a very small striking force (8. 4; 9. 6; 10. 6). He may well have felt, like Alexander in comparable situations, that only personal leadership and example, involving the acceptance of grave risks, could bring victory. Such at least is the impression conveyed by Thucydides.[3] Mortally wounded at the moment when his tactical plan began to be effective (10. 8), he lived long enough to learn that complete victory had been achieved (10. 11).

He was given a public funeral at Amphipolis, and every mark of distinction was heaped upon him by the Amphipolitans who regarded him as their saviour and adopted him as official founder instead of the Athenian Hagnon (11. 1).[4] That such honours

[1] de Romilly (2), 136–8, who analyses the account of the battle, points out that the foresight of Brasidas is illustrated by the fulfilment of the predictions made in his speech. The speech explains his tactical plan more fully than is usual in Thucydidean speeches of encouragement before battles. Another noteworthy feature is that he gives the allied troops a very frank picture of the unpleasant consequences to which they would be subjected if the Athenians were victorious (9. 9).

[2] His final exhortation to his troops immediately before the battle—it must have been almost the last utterance of his life—is reported in a very brief passage of *oratio recta* (10. 5). This unusual feature of the narrative is dramatically most effective.

[3] Clearidas, the governor of Amphipolis, who led a much larger body of troops in an attack from another gate, is a secondary figure barely equal to the responsible task assigned to him (9. 7–9), which he seems to have performed no more than adequately (10. 9).

[4] Similar honours were bestowed upon Timoleon by the Syracusans, cf. my *Timoleon and his relations with tyrants* (1952), 1.

11-2

should be conferred spontaneously by an allied city on a Spartan serving abroad is indeed remarkable. Thucydides reports them fully: he evidently felt that they confirmed his presentation of Brasidas as a unique figure among Spartan leaders, who by the exercise of military and diplomatic qualities had, almost single-handed, done much to nullify the advantage gained by the Athenians from the Spartan debacle at Pylos.

There is, however, something missing in the Thucydidean presentation of Brasidas. During his mission to the north-east, though orders were issued to him by the Spartan government, he held a virtually independent command. In this respect his position was similar to that of Nicias in Sicily, and, although the circumstances were totally different, not much less isolated than that of Alcibiades at the court of Tissaphernes. It is beyond doubt that concerning the activities of Brasidas in Thrace, of Nicias in Sicily and of Alcibiades in Asia Thucydides possessed plentiful information derived from persons enjoying their confidence. The personal agony of Nicias during his unwanted command is made as clear as the personal scheming of Alcibiades in pursuit of his own interests. On the other hand, very little light is thrown upon the inner feelings of Brasidas, and his attitude towards his own mission remains obscure. He made himself immensely popular wherever he went, and he caused the allies of Athens to feel a new confidence in Spartan good-will, which lasted long after his death (4. 81. 2–3 and 108. 2–5).[1] But did he see himself as the leader of a crusade to liberate fellow-Greeks from slavery under Athenian rule? Did he sincerely believe in his own propaganda, which is known principally from the report of his speech at Acanthus (4. 85–7)? Or did he seek only to promote the narrow interests of Sparta and to win for himself a glorious reputation? A passage discussing the situation after his death might seem to throw light on this question: he is stated to have been opposed to the conclusion of peace 'because he had won success and was honoured

---

[1] The former passage is almost certainly a late addition to the narrative, as stated above, 14.

as a result of the war' (5. 16. 1). This phrase, however, does not imply that he regarded the war exclusively as a means of winning personal fame and had no other thoughts about it; and the whole passage is a very remarkable one in which Thucydides dwells to a most unusual degree upon the personal motives of leading individuals on both sides, as has already been pointed out.[1] It could be that Brasidas was only a dedicated, uncomplicated soldier, but the emphasis laid by Thucydides upon his capacity for intelligent planning and negotiation suggests that he had a subtle and original mind. There does not seem to be any valid reason for believing that Thucydides acquired his abundant knowledge of the part played by Brasidas in the north-east from persons less intelligent or less perceptive than those from whom he obtained information about Nicias in Sicily or Alcibiades in Asia. The feelings of Brasidas about the broader aspects of his mission would doubtless have been much clearer if Thucydides had included reports on his consultations with the three commissioners led by Ischagoras similar to the reports on the consultations between Nicias and his colleagues. The difference of treatment is significant. It does not arise merely because the information available to him may have differed somewhat in character. It arises because his treatment of individuals is not the same in the first half of his *History* as it is in the second.[2]

[1] See above, 93–6.
[2] I agree with P. A. Brunt, *Phoenix*, XIX (1965), 276 (published when this chapter was already in draft), that Brasidas 'was probably, like Lysander after him, a powerful and ambitious political figure, and not just a romantic war-hero'. It is noteworthy that this conclusion has to be regarded as no more than a probability. If Thucydides had presented Brasidas as he presents Nicias or Alcibiades, no such qualification would have been required.

SECOND HALF

(5. 25–8. 109)

CHAPTER XI

NICIAS *(cont.)*

1. Opposition to the policy of Alcibiades in the Peloponnese

THE first appearance of Nicias in the second half of the *History* occurs in a detailed and instructive account of a conflict between him and Alcibiades on a crucial issue of Athenian foreign policy (5. 43–6). In the spring of 420, when the Peloponnese was in a turmoil, the Athenians were in doubt whether to maintain their alliance with Sparta, in spite of unresolved grievances, or to join the coalition under Argive leadership, which was hostile to Sparta. Nicias advocated the former policy, Alcibiades the latter. Thucydides makes Alcibiades the protagonist of this episode, as will be shown in the next chapter,[1] but the character of Nicias is more sharply portrayed here than in the record of his earlier career during the Archidamian war. The conflict is presented as a clash of personalities—the first of several such clashes in the second half of the *History*, which will be noted as they occur. Similar conflicts between leading individuals must have taken place during the Archidamian war,[2] and indeed Thucydides was in a much better position before his exile to obtain information about those at Athens than he was later; he doubtless witnessed some of them himself. Apart, however, from his account of the clash between Cleon and Nicias on the situation at Pylos (4. 27. 5–28. 5), the first half of the *History* contains little trace of personal rivalries between leading individuals who held opposing views on important questions of policy.[3]

[1] See below, 212–15.
[2] In 2. 65. 7–10 Thucydides refers in general terms to rivalries between the successors of Pericles. The whole tone of the *Knights* suggests that they were often very bitter and violent.
[3] The dispute between Cleon and Diodotus does not belong to this category for reasons already given (see above, 62). The disagreements of Demosthenes with

This first clash between Nicias and Alcibiades is presented with great skill. Nicias is brought into the narrative at the point at which he began, with somewhat bewildered doggedness, to play an active part. Alcibiades had by successful trickery brought discredit upon a Spartan embassy sent to seek a reconciliation with Athens, but because an earthquake caused an adjournment of the assembly, he was unable to secure the immediate conclusion of an alliance with Argos. The debate was resumed on the following day when Nicias, though outwitted by the cleverness of his younger opponent, persevered in his efforts to preserve the existing friendship with Sparta. He persuaded the Athenians not to carry their negotiations with Argos any further until they had made another attempt to get the Spartans to clarify their intentions in regard to points still under dispute (5. 46. 1–2).[1] He was himself sent to Sparta with an embassy, which tried to put pressure on the Spartans by using the threat that Athens would join the Argive coalition. The Spartans, however, refused to make any concessions to Athenian demands, and all that Nicias was able to extract from them was a renewal of their oaths to the treaty with Athens. He is stated to have requested them to do this because he was afraid to return to Athens empty-handed. The failure of his mission naturally led to the conclusion of the alliance with the Argives and their associates which Alcibiades advocated (46. 3–5). Nevertheless, the Athenians did not renounce their alliance with Sparta (48. 1) and for the next few years refused to commit themselves wholeheartedly either to the policy of Alcibiades or to that of Nicias. The account of this episode contrasts the personalities of two leading figures whose rivalry was to influence momentously the destiny of Athens.

Throughout the next four years Nicias undoubtedly persisted in his efforts to limit the Athenian involvement in the Pelopon-

Eurymedon and Sophocles at Pylos (4. 3) and of Brasidas with Perdiccas in Macedonia (4. 83. 3–6) might be cited; both are reported very briefly.

[1] In support of his proposals he is stated to have used a very characteristic argument, ὡς ἐπὶ πλεῖστον ἄριστον εἶναι διασώσασθαι τὴν εὐπραγίαν, 46. 1 (cf. 16. 1).

nese promoted by Alcibiades and to preserve friendly relations with Sparta. Yet Thucydides omits to mention the continuation of the conflict between the two leaders during this period. The reasons why he chooses to describe the activities of Alcibiades very briefly and to include hardly any information about Nicias will be considered in the next chapter.[1] He refers only to the appointment of Nicias in 417 to lead an expedition to Chalcidice. Because of disputes with Perdiccas, who was to have supported the Athenians, this project was abandoned (83. 4), probably even before the expeditionary force left Athens.[2]

2. *The first phase of the expedition to Sicily*

From the point at which Thucydides begins his account of the Athenian expedition to Sicily he gives much attention to the personality of Nicias, doubtless because of its influence upon the outcome. He was evidently fortunate enough to be able to consult persons enjoying the confidence of Nicias, but he could have omitted much of the more personal information with which they supplied him if he had believed it to be of purely biographical interest. In his reports on the debate in the assembly before the expedition started (6. 8. 3–26. 1) and on the opening stages of the campaign in Sicily the contrast between the personalities of Nicias and Alcibiades is kept in the foreground. Their speeches in the assembly present two diametrically opposite individuals as well as two diametrically opposite policies. These speeches strike a more personal note than any in the first half of the *History*, and no antilogy in the whole work reflects so strikingly the characters of the speakers. It is typical of Nicias that he is less insistent than Alcibiades upon personal factors. He does, however, claim that, while his appointment as one of the three generals brings him honour, it is not his practice to make recommendations on public

[1] See below, 219, where reference will also be made to the ostracism of 417, which Thucydides does not mention in its context (cf. 8. 73. 3).
[2] Steup, n. *ad loc.*

policy contrary to his own convictions for the sake of securing personal advancement (9. 2).[1] Here he implies that to Alcibiades self-advancement is paramount. Later he attacks Alcibiades more directly, though without actually mentioning his name. He declares that someone, appointed to take command when he is too young, is urging the Athenians to make the expedition from purely selfish motives; that this person, who is seeking to enrich himself in order to win admiration by extravagant displays of wealth, ought not to be allowed to endanger the state while promoting his private interests (12. 2).[2] A statement by Thucydides himself shows that in his opinion these charges were well-founded (15. 2).

Both speeches of Nicias in the debate throw plenty of light upon his own temperament. Their keynote is the avoidance of any risk (cf. 23. 3). He insists that it is folly to undertake an ambitious expedition to a distant land when the situation at home is precarious (10. 2–5; 11. 5–7); that the Sicilian cities have formidable resources and will not easily be subjugated (20. 2–4); that a huge expeditionary force is required in order to eliminate, so far as possible, any risk of disaster (21–3). Many of the arguments in these two speeches proved, when put to the test, sounder than those of Alcibiades, but they give the unmistakable impression that Nicias is carrying caution to excessive lengths. His debating tactics also are seen to have been mistaken. If the principal motive of his second speech was to cause the Athenians to abandon their project by insisting on a very large expeditionary force—and Thucydides has no doubt that it was (19. 2)[3]—he misjudged completely the temper of the assembly, and his manœuvre failed to

---

[1] This claim might be held to be inconsistent with the attribution of personal motives by Thucydides to Nicias in advocating the conclusion of peace in 421 (5. 16. 1); but it is highly probable that on that occasion Nicias believed the conclusion of peace to be in the best interests of Athens as well as in those of himself.

[2] Cf. 10. 2, where the unnamed Athenians accused of having caused the peace with Sparta to be ineffective are Alcidiades and his supporters.

[3] In 24. 1 an alternative motive is added: 'if he were compelled to make the expedition, he would by this means sail with the greatest degree of security.'

achieve its main purpose. The Athenians accepted his advice only too readily and became even more eager to undertake the expedition (24. 2–4). He was then urged to express his views candidly upon the size of the force required (25. 1), which he did in fairly specific terms but with reluctance, protesting that he needed an opportunity to consult his colleagues (25. 2). His unwillingness to commit himself without more ado, which is only a side issue, is surely mentioned by Thucydides because it illustrates his caution and his tendency to shun personal responsibility.

The account of this debate defines very clearly the attitude of Nicias towards the expedition and contrasts his conception of it with that of Alcibiades. He is not mentioned again until the incompatibility between the views of himself, Alcibiades and Lamachus is revealed very plainly by a report on a conference held when the expedition had almost reached Sicily. The Athenians were disappointed by the coldness of their reception at Rhegium, where this conference took place, and by the news, which did not surprise Nicias, that they had been deceived about the financial resources of Segesta (46. 1–2). Thucydides reports this conference at Rhegium rather briefly, summarising in *oratio obliqua* the recommendations of each general (47–9). Those of Nicias are characteristically cautious and unenterprising (47); they amount to little more than a strictly literal interpretation of the instructions issued to the generals when the expedition was first voted (8. 2). The Athenians ought, he declared, to sail first to Selinus. If Segesta supplied funds to finance the whole expeditionary force, they should determine what action to take; if not,[1] they should demand the subsidy already promised and should settle the dispute between Segesta and Selinus by force or by negotiation. They should next sail along the coast of Sicily giving an impressive display of Athenian power and of Athenian loyalty to friends and allies.[2] They should then return home unless an un-

---

[1] Earlier passages (12. 1; 22; 46. 2) show that Nicias had no illusions about the prospects of financial aid from Segesta.

[2] In his first speech in the assembly he had declared (11. 4) that, if the expedition were undertaken at all, it ought to be confined to such a display.

expected opportunity offered itself to spend a short time helping
the Leontines or winning the support of other cities. The summary of these proposals is certainly designed to draw attention to
their timidity. Nicias wished the generals to attempt just enough
to warrant a claim that they had carried out their official orders;
they would thereby provide themselves with a defence against
any charge of having neglected their duty which might be
brought against them in the assembly after their return.[1] Alcibiades, who rejected with contempt the plan of Nicias, himself
proposed that they should first try to gain as much support as
possible in Sicily by diplomacy (48).[2] Lamachus first called for an
immediate attack on Syracuse, but, when he found himself unable
to secure the acceptance of his own plan, he decided to vote for
that of Alcibiades, which was accordingly adopted (49–50. 1).

The report of Thucydides on this episode provides an excellent
example of his technique. To him the principal lesson of the
conference was that the three generals differed fundamentally in
character and outlook and in interpretation of their mission; that
their disunity constituted a serious handicap to the direction of
the expedition. Having singled out this disunity as the most
important factor in the situation, he proceeds to devote almost
the whole of his report to it. His insistence upon its importance is
undoubtedly justified, but his habit of laying great emphasis upon
one salient factor for the guidance of his readers has in this instance
had some unfortunate results, largely because his report is so
highly condensed.[3] It has led to oversimplification and probably
produced a somewhat misleading impression. His desire to contrast the generals and their plans schematically and briefly has
caused him to include in his summary only points of disagreement

[1] That he often had in mind the possible reactions of the Athenians at home is
seen from 7. 14. 4; 48. 3–4; 50. 3. He doubtless remembered the treatment of
the generals in command of the previous expedition to Sicily (4. 65. 3).

[2] See below, 223.

[3] It may well include arguments put forward at several conferences. The generals
seem to have held an earlier meeting immediately after their overtures had
been rejected by the Rhegines and before they received news from Segesta
(44. 4).

between them. It is difficult to believe that there were no points on which they were agreed and that none of them was willing to accept any compromise until Lamachus, in order to break the deadlock, consented to support the plan of Alcibiades *in toto* (50. 1). These doubts are reinforced by the record of subsequent action taken by the Athenians. Even in the brief period between the conference at Rhegium and the recall of Alcibiades they did not adhere strictly to his plan for a diplomatic offensive as defined by Thucydides. When they had scarcely begun their quest for allies, they twice sailed with their fleet into Syracusan waters and on the second occasion were apparently ready to fight a naval battle if any opposition had materialised (50. 4–5; 52. 1). Nor did their subsequent movements conform closely to any of the reported recommendations of the conference at Rhegium. They first embarked upon a considerably modified version of the plan suggested by Nicias (62); they then delivered an attack on Syracuse corresponding roughly to the plan of Lamachus, though again with modifications (64–71). Nicias apparently raised no objection to the launching of this attack on Syracuse and indeed seems to have been largely responsible for its strategic planning. For these reasons the views expressed by the three generals at the conference were surely less rigid and less irreconcilable than is suggested by the report of Thucydides.[1]

[1] The report has caused modern scholars to feel some misgivings and even led G. De Sanctis, *Problemi di storia antica* (1932), 127–32 (originally published in *Riv. Fil.* VII, 1929), to reject it as a fabrication designed to exculpate Nicias and Alcibiades from responsibility for sanctioning the offensive against Syracuse which ultimately brought about the Athenian disaster. This brilliantly presented view has won little acceptance (Hatzfeld, 197 n. 2; Brunt, 70 with n. 3) and need not be discussed in detail here. Its gravest weakness is the assumption that only the three generals were present at the conference and could give information about what was said. It is beyond reasonable doubt that other officers must have attended, such as Menander, later one of the generals (7. 16. 1) and certainly a survivor of the expedition (Xen. *Hell.* 1. 2. 16), who may well be one of the persons from whom Thucydides obtained, directly or indirectly, his remarkably abundant information about the plans and motives of Nicias, cf. *Proc. Class. Ass.* L (1953), 27. Nevertheless, there is, in my opinion, justification for some of the criticisms directed by De Sanctis against the report on the proposals of Nicias and Alcibiades.

The account of this conference has led to a certain amount of misunderstanding in another respect. Modern readers have assumed that the subject under discussion was the general strategy of the whole campaign, and such indeed is the impression created at first sight by the report of Thucydides, to whom the broadest issues tend to be the most absorbing. Yet both the context in which the conference is set and much of the report itself show that the primary concern of the generals was rather with a narrower and more pressing problem, namely what action they should take at once to deal with the critical situation with which they were confronted. In considering plans to meet the crisis they were evidently influenced, as is natural, by their own ideas about the strategy of the campaign, but it was to their immediate needs that they devoted much of their attention. None of the Italiot cities, not even Rhegium, had granted the support expected by the Athenians (44. 2–3), and there was as yet no assurance that they would be more warmly welcomed by any Siceliot city. The depressing news from Segesta brought even more bitter disappointment (46. 5). It would be necessary to obtain supplies, mainly of food, in very large quantities during the next few months: these might be bought at some places, as at Rhegium (44. 3), but the generals can hardly have had available sufficiently large funds to enable them to continue buying supplies indefinitely in addition to defraying other expenses.[1] If they were to remain long in Sicily, they must secure money or food, or both, by contributions from allies (cf. 88. 4)[2] or by plunder from enemies (cf. 62. 2–3).

The plans of all three generals betray consciousness of this

[1] Some epigraphical evidence about the financing of the expedition survives, but it is unfortunately very incomplete, and modern scholars have reached widely divergent conclusions, cf. W. S. Ferguson, *Treasurers of Athena* (1932), 160–1; *A.T.L.* III (1950), 356–7. Although Thucydides refers occasionally to the financial aspects of the expedition (31. 5; 74. 2; 93. 4; 94. 4), he does not discuss them in detail.

[2] The reluctance of former allies to support the Athenians was doubtless due partly to financial considerations: they feared that they might be ruined by the demands made upon them.

pressing problem, and each proposed a different solution. The first recommendation of Nicias was to defer consideration of any ambitious projects until the generals had ascertained whether Segesta could maintain the whole expeditionary force. If, as he expected, the Segestans proved unable to do this but could be induced to provide a subsidy to cover the expenditure on the sixty ships for which they had asked, the Athenians could hope to complete the very unenterprising programme outlined by him at the conference; they would then return home towards the end of the summer (47). The proposal of Alcibiades was to secure as many allies as possible, whose support would help to maintain the Athenian force: he expressly mentions that these allies were to provide food (48). When the generals knew which cities would be their allies, they could frame their plans accordingly. To Lamachus the problem could best be solved by landing troops at Syracuse and fighting a battle there. The Athenians could hope to gain plenty of plunder in the country outside the city if they acted at once and took the Syracusans by surprise (49. 3, τὴν στρατιὰν οὐκ ἀπορήσειν χρημάτων), and a victory would win for them the allegiance of Siceliots now wavering (*ibid.*), from whom he, like Alcibiades, doubtless expected to obtain contributions in money or in kind (cf. 71. 2). During the period after the conference at Rhegium the Athenians did not in fact find themselves crippled by shortages of money or of supplies. Their immediate needs were temporarily met by the support extracted from Naxos, Catana and some of the Sicels and from the windfall resulting from the sale of the prisoners captured at Hyccara (62. 4). It was not, however, very long before a request was sent to Athens for further financial support (71. 2; 74. 2).

Both features of the report by Thucydides on this conference to which attention has been drawn owe their origin largely to his practice of trying to make his account of each episode as brief, coherent and instructive as possible. In this instance the result has in each case been to mislead the reader somewhat. While the two features noted above are comparable in this respect, they differ very considerably in another respect. The apparent implication, which seems to be mistaken, that the conference was concerned more with broad strategic problems than with the immediate needs of a critical situation doubtless arises from the fondness of Thucydides for dwelling on general issues. This tendency is prevalent throughout his *History* and indeed is more marked in the first half than in the second. On the other hand, when he stresses, and probably overstresses, the disagreements of the generals arising from their differences in personality and outlook, he is giving an emphasis to the character of individuals and its influence upon the course of events which is more prominent in the second half of the *History*.

3. *Nicias and Lamachus in command*

After the majority decision to adopt the plan of Alcibiades, the task of implementing it was left mainly in his hands, but his diplomatic offensive had not made much progress when he was summoned home for trial.[1] Thucydides now shows less inclination to give prominence to the character of Nicias, partly perhaps because Lamachus had not a sufficiently colourful personality to afford a significant contrast with that of his colleague. The account of the war in Sicily hereafter for a period of nearly a year is largely a factual summary of events: it contains plenty of implied judgements in accordance with the normal practice of Thucydides, but it does not throw much light on leading figures on the Athenian side or give information about private deliberations between them. At this stage there is little to suggest that he has modified his methods of presentation in any way since writing the first half of the *History*. His narrative is no more detailed than in his accounts of some episodes in the Archidamian war, and the speeches of Hermocrates and Euphemus at Camarina (76–87) are concerned largely with the ethics of imperialism, a subject to

---

[1] See below, 224.

which he devotes far more attention in the first half of his work than in the second.

The plan of Alcibiades, which was very dependent on his own flair for diplomacy, was discontinued when he was recalled. His colleagues then sailed with their whole force for western Sicily, intending to put into operation a plan similar to that proposed by Nicias. After landing at Hyccara and storming this small Sican town, they decided to use the fleet to transport the inhabitants to Catana, where their sale as slaves realised 120 talents. This decision, which confirms that the financial needs of the Athenians were urgent, had the consequence that the fleet could not now proceed to Selinus, as had been intended. Nicias visited Segesta, where he obtained thirty talents but evidently failed to negotiate a settlement with Selinus (62. 1–4). Thucydides implies that this expedition to the west was ill-advised and largely a waste of effort.[1] He goes on to report that, combined with the failure of the Athenians to capture Hybla Geleatis (62. 5), it caused an upsurge of confidence at Syracuse (63. 2). What Nicias felt at this stage is not recorded. He must have realised that it was necessary for the expeditionary force to remain in Sicily throughout the winter: to have returned home now would have exposed the generals to the fury of the assembly. The views expressed by Lamachus in the discussions at Rhegium suggest that he was now the instigator of the decision to launch an attack on the Syracusans in the early autumn, but Thucydides gives no hint that Nicias was unwilling to take the offensive.[2]

This operation was well planned and well executed. The Athenian generals sent to Syracuse a Catanean who, posing as a supporter of the faction hostile to Athens, encouraged the Syracusans to attempt a surprise attack on the Athenian base and promised them local aid. While the entire Syracusan army was on its way to

---

[1] Cf. Plut. *Nic.* 14. 4 and 15. 3–4. See Schwartz, 338–40, for a valuable discussion of this episode.

[2] The statement of Plutarch (*Nic.* 16. 1) that Nicias delivered this attack with reluctance (μόλις) is not a legitimate inference from the narrative of Thucydides.

12-2

Catana by land to implement this plan, Athenian forces were transported by sea to the Great Harbour at Syracuse and occupied a strong position on its western shore. After the Syracusans had returned in haste, the Athenians did not engage them at once but waited until the following day when they were able to take them by surprise. Although the Syracusans resisted stoutly, the Athenians were victorious because of their superiority in military skill and experience. The strength of the Syracusan cavalry prevented the Athenians from inflicting heavy losses upon the fleeing infantry. Immediately after the battle the Athenians sailed back to Catana. Although they had established a base so near Syracuse and defeated the Syracusans, they did not feel able to maintain it throughout the winter (64–71).

The report of Thucydides on this first major clash between the Athenians and Syracusans exemplifies the characteristic merits of his technique in describing military operations. It is less prejudiced than his account of the Athenian defeat at Amphipolis in 422, more lucid than that of the fighting in the Megarid in 424. It is graphic and fairly detailed, but without superfluous ornament or rhetoric. It provides plenty of guidance whereby the reader may evaluate the strategic planning and the fighting qualities of both sides and may judge why the situation developed as it did. Nicias is named only twice: first when he exhorted his troops (67. 3), and again when, his speech ended, he led them into battle (69. 1). The summary of this speech (68) is not particularly distinctive or original, and Thucydides may perhaps have stressed its conventionality as being characteristic of Nicias. Both the conclusion that the Syracusan forces must be lured away from Syracuse before the Athenians could land there safely and the scheme to achieve this end by making use of the Catanean agent are attributed to 'the generals of the Athenians' (64. 1). Elsewhere the narrative is even less explicit: Thucydides merely states that 'the Athenians' did not seize their first opportunity of engaging the Syracusan army (66. 3) and withdrew their whole force to Catana after their victory (71. 1), though in each case responsibility for the decision must have been rested with the generals. He implies that, while the strategy of the Athenians was excellent, their withdrawal from Syracuse was an error of judgement and that the motives underlying this decision, which are recorded in some detail (71. 2), were indefensible. It has been widely assumed that, while Lamachus doubtless led part of the Athenian forces engaged in this operation, Nicias was largely responsible for planning it and also for deciding not to continue it after the Syracusan defeat.[1] There is every justification for this view. Both the use of secret negotiations to pave the way for military action and the excessive caution of the Athenian withdrawal are thoroughly characteristic of Nicias.

An important but strangely neglected passage in the seventh book throws some light upon the opinion of Thucydides about this decision to withdraw from Syracuse (7. 42. 3). He reports what Demosthenes thought, and doubtless said,[2] immediately after arriving with the second expeditionary force in 413, about the military situation at Syracuse at that time and the urgent need for energetic action. Inserted in this report is a long parenthesis criticising Nicias, as though he had been in sole command, for having committed strategic blunders at earlier stages of the campaign. These blunders include spending the winter at Catana, which must refer to the decision to withdraw thither in the autumn of 415, and failing to prevent Gylippus reaching Syracuse with forces from the Peloponnese. The strictures on the generalship of Nicias expressed in the parenthesis must represent the views of Thucydides himself as well as those of Demosthenes, because the verbs in it are indicative; if he had been merely reporting the views of Demosthenes, he would have used the accusative and infinitive construction, as he does in the clause

---

[1] Plutarch (Nic. 16. 3 and 8–9), who is probably dependent here, directly or indirectly, upon Thucydides, praises Nicias for his leadership on this occasion but criticises his faint-heartedness in withdrawing from Syracuse. Although it is natural that a biographer should focus attention on Nicias, these inferences seem to be sound.

[2] See below, 269–70.

immediately preceding the parenthesis.[1] It must, however, be admitted that he has chosen a strangely cryptic way of conveying his opinion. His habit of compression has doubtless had some influence: he has been able to make the parenthesis perform the double duty of combining the views of Demosthenes and himself. Another habit has probably been more influential, namely his tendency to avoid committing himself to a categorical declaration of his own judgement on some issues. Had he chosen to express himself rather less equivocally here, there would have been less support in modern times for the highly disputable belief that he treats Nicias too indulgently.

In describing the events of the next few months Thucydides shows even less inclination to throw light upon the personality of Nicias or to assess the quality of his leadership. He seems to have felt more interest in Hermocrates, who was engaged upon the unenviable task of organising the defence of Syracuse. He does not mention Nicias by name in his accounts of the efforts made by the Athenians to win more allies (6. 74–88), of two minor expeditions undertaken at the beginning of spring from their base at Catana (94. 1–3), and of their highly successful offensive at Syracuse, when they seized Epipolae, defeated the enemy several times and destroyed the first Syracusan counter-wall (96–100). In the narrative of these events there are only two references to

[1] G. Donini, *Hermes*, xcii (1964), 116–19, has established beyond reasonable doubt that this is the correct interpretation of the passage by examining other passages in the *History* comparable with it in various ways. Dover, n. *ad loc.* takes the same view; he also suggests that the criticisms contained in the passage may be directed either at the decision of Nicias and Lamachus to withdraw from Syracuse in the autumn of 415 or at the decision of the three generals at Rhegium to adopt the plan of Alcibiades and not that of Lamachus. There is certainly some confusion of thought, but the main criticism is of the withdrawal from Syracuse, as is shown by the references to the Athenians wintering at Catana and to the Syracusans sending to the Peloponnesians for aid (cf. 6. 73. 2). This confusion and the 'rhetorical distortion' with which Dover charges Thucydides may owe its origin to the fact that the sentence is first and foremost reporting the views of Demosthenes, which were likely to be outspoken and trenchant, in the military manner, rather than logically sound or even strictly fair to his colleague (see below, 270).

action specifically attributed to the Athenian generals (93. 4; 100. 1).

The capture of Epipolae was a notable feat of arms. Because Thucydides has chosen to describe rather how the Syracusans lost this key position than how the Athenians won it (96–7), the latter seem hardly to receive as much credit as they deserve. Their success was evidently attributable to a large extent to skilful planning and timing by their generals. It can hardly be a coincidence that they forestalled by a few hours a Syracusan plan to establish a garrison of picked troops to guard the only practicable way of access to Epipolae after first holding a review on level ground beside the Anapus. The Athenians must have learned what was intended. They also made intelligent use of their naval supremacy and were therefore able to take the enemy by surprise. The measures planned by the Syracusans suggest that they expected the Athenians to sail into the Great Harbour, as in the previous autumn, and to threaten Epipolae from the south, whereas the Athenians actually landed at Leon on the northern side. Although the Athenian troops reached the heights of Epipolae with commendable speed and defeated the Syracusans hastening to dislodge them,[1] the decisive factor on this occasion was evidently not so much their superiority in training and skill as the enlightened strategy of their leaders. The question whether this strategy was the work of Nicias or Lamachus, or both in conjunction, cannot be answered with any confidence.[2] Nicias was perhaps responsible for obtaining information about Syracusan intentions: he was at a later date in communication with traitors inside the city (7. 48. 2; 49. 1; 73. 3) and may already have established contact with them.

On the whole, it is perhaps legitimate to conclude that the planning of Athenian operations was mainly in the hands of Nicias, while Lamachus was more concerned with their execu-

---

[1] The Syracusans had already fallen into disorder because of their haste when they engaged the Athenians (97. 4).

[2] Plutarch (*Nic.* 17. 1) again attributes the whole operation to Nicias.

tion.[1] Thucydides, however, does not provide any guidance on this question.

The Athenians next built two forts and embarked upon an attempt to establish a complete blockade of Syracuse on the landward side by means of a wall across Epipolae. At first progress was rapid. The Syracusans no longer ventured to commit their forces to battle on a large scale, preferring to build a counter-wall designed to prevent the Athenians from completing the blockade (6. 97. 5–99). A small striking force of picked Athenian troops attacked and captured the Syracusan counter-wall. Each of the Athenian generals commanded one of the two sections into which the main army was divided to cover the attack by their striking force. All these troops then demolished the counter-wall (100). Shortly afterwards the partnership between Nicias and Lamachus was ended by the death of the latter. In the course of confused fighting on marshy ground beside the Great Harbour, after the Athenians had captured a second Syracusan counter-wall, he became isolated from the rest of his troops with a few companions and was killed (101. 3–6).

Thucydides tends to keep the Athenian leaders in the background, as has already been noted, in his narrative of events in Sicily after the recall of Alcibiades, when Nicias and Lamachus were in joint command. Athenian leadership during the period is found wanting in some respects: Thucydides implies that the decisions to sail to western Sicily in the summer of 415 and to withdraw from Syracuse in the autumn were errors of judgement and that a sense of urgency was lacking at other times. Nevertheless, the period ending with the death of Lamachus was for the Athenians the most successful, or at any rate least unsuccessful, of

---

[1] C.Q. xxxv (1941), 62. Freeman, 207–8, believes that, when the Athenians seized Epipolae, they were putting into operation the plan suggested by Lamachus at Rhegium. That plan, however, had envisaged the capture of Syracusans and their property in well-cultivated districts (49. 3), so that Lamachus surely intended the Athenians to establish their advance base on the western shore of the Great Harbour, as they did temporarily in the autumn of 415. He also apparently expected a conventional pitched battle (49. 1), which would most appropriately be fought in the same area.

the entire campaign. In the latest stages of this period, when they were gaining what appeared to be a decisive advantage over the enemy, Nicias is totally ignored. This fact is significant and helps to explain why Thucydides devotes so little attention to the personal contribution of Nicias towards the direction of Athenian strategy throughout the whole of this period. It is not his practice, even in the second half of the *History*, to present complex psychological studies of leading individuals. His treatment of character has more subtlety than that of Herodotus and could doubtless have been more subtle still if he had so wished; but his purpose was rather to focus attention on the outstanding characteristics of leading individuals in order that the reasons why they influenced the course of events as they did might be easily understood by his readers. His method of treating individuals thus tends to produce a certain amount of oversimplification. Undoubtedly he wished to convey to his readers an unfavourable verdict on the leadership of Nicias in Sicily.[1] He makes abundantly clear that, in his opinion, Nicias was found wanting on many occasions during the campaign, mainly through excessive caution or lack of energy, and that these grave defects of leadership, though combined with a devotion to duty which justifiably aroused sympathy,[2] were to a considerable degree responsible for the ultimate disaster. It seems probable that the moderately successful attack on Syracuse by the Athenians in the autumn of 415 and the highly successful operations on Epipolae in the following spring were mainly due to enlightened and unusually enterprising strategy on the part of Nicias, though Lamachus doubtless contributed vigour and bravery in the field and perhaps some tactical skill. If so, Thucydides must have been in something of a dilemma. He was compelled either to do less than justice to the qualities shown by Nicias at this time or to introduce a complication into his judgement on the military leadership of Nicias, which is elsewhere almost wholly unfavourable, and so run the risk of presenting his readers

---

[1] *C.Q.* xxxv (1941), 61–3.
[2] Cf. 7. 86. 5, which will be discussed below, 209–11.

with a confusing picture. Faced with these alternatives, he may well have felt the former to be the lesser evil and may accordingly have decided to give no prominence to the personal contribution of Nicias to the events of this period.

4. *From the death of Lamachus to the arrival of Demosthenes*

Nicias returns to prominence after the death of Lamachus not merely because he was now in sole command (cf. 103. 3) but because Thucydides wishes to suggest that his shortcomings were largely responsible for the rapid transformation of the situation at Syracuse, which set the Athenians on the path to ultimate disaster when they had been on the verge of complete victory. The death of Lamachus is felt to be a turning point in the campaign, although the tide of Athenian success did not reach its highest point until some weeks later. Without the support of his colleague, Nicias is seen to have drifted into inertia and to have frittered away the advantages gained by their partnership. The impetus of the Athenian offensive was suddenly lost.

It is ironical that on the day when Lamachus was killed Nicias was involved in an incident in which he showed himself to be capable of quick and ingenious improvisation in battle (102. 1–3). Because of his illness, now mentioned for the first time, he had remained in the Athenian fort on Epipolae known as the Circle. The Syracusans observed that this fort was almost undefended and tried to take it by surprise. Nicias ordered his servants to set fire to some timber lying beneath the wall of the fort, and this expedient caused the enemy to withdraw. His presence of mind saved a key position from falling into their hands.[1]

The day's fighting in which Lamachus was killed and Nicias narrowly escaped death or capture appeared to have made capitulation by the Syracusans almost inevitable. They discontinued their efforts to prevent the Athenians completing the southern

---

[1] Cf. F. E. Adcock, *The Greek and Macedonian Art of War* (1957), 86, 'it is a fair judgment of him that he was swift in action but slow to make up his mind'.

section of the wall stretching down from Epipolae. The Athenian fleet sailed into the Great Harbour and established a base in the north-western corner, where it could co-operate with the army. Abundant supplies were reaching the Athenians from Italy, and many of the Sicels who had hitherto hesitated to join them now sent military aid, confident that Syracuse was doomed (102.3–103.2). Inside the city the Syracusans seemed to have lost the will to resist. Their morale sank very low, and they began to distrust one another; they dismissed their generals, who included Hermocrates; there was talk of surrender and much unofficial negotiation with Nicias, presumably to elicit the terms on which he would be prepared to agree to an armistice.[1] Although no official decision was yet taken, the end appeared to be in sight (103. 3–4).

On the Athenian side, however, a slackening of military effort was already becoming marked. During the period between the death of Lamachus and the arrival of Gylippus at Syracuse not even the southern section of the Athenian wall was completed and apparently little further progress was made in building the northern section (7. 2. 4).[2] Thucydides does not expressly draw attention to the culpability of Nicias in failing to ensure that the builders pressed on with their work; but he leaves his readers in no doubt that Nicias could, and should, have taken prompter and more vigorous action to prevent Gylippus, who was known to be approaching, from reaching Sicily. At first Nicias did not even make any attempt to intercept the four ships of Gylippus, believing that nothing was to be expected from this small squadron more ambitious than raids on Athenian sea-communications with Italy, which was a major source of supplies (6. 104. 3).[3] Later, on learning that the Peloponnesians were at Locri, he did send four

---

[1] According to Plutarch (*Nic.* 18. 12) the Syracusans felt that terms should be settled before the Athenian blockading walls were completed. They doubtless wished to avoid unconditional surrender, remembering the fate of Melos.

[2] The length of this period is not determinable, since Thucydides, though as careful as ever to arrange the events of the summer in chronological sequence, does not indicate the intervals of time between them.

[3] Such is surely what is meant by the contemptuous phrase ληστικώτερον ἔδοξε παρεσκευασμένους πλεῖν.

Athenian ships to intercept them in the straits of Messana. It was probably an error to send so few when his main fleet was in no immediate danger of being attacked in the Great Harbour, but in any case he acted too late, since Gylippus had already passed through the straits before the Athenians arrived there (7. 1. 2).[1]

The Syracusans were about to hold an assembly to discuss capitulation when a single ship arrived bringing the Corinthian Gongylus, who by assuring them that help would very soon reach them persuaded them to abandon any thought of making peace (2. 1). The initial successes of Gylippus—how after marching from Himera he made contact with the Syracusans on Epipolae, and how he eventually broke the Athenian land-blockade—will be discussed in a later chapter, where attention will be drawn to the implied contrast between his leadership and that of Nicias.[2] In the first encounter with Gylippus Nicias is seen to have lost an opportunity by failing to attack when the Syracusan forces had fallen into disorder (3. 3, ἡσύχαзε); a little later he and the Athenians took the offensive, it seems, only because they felt impelled to do so by the seriousness of their position (6. 1). Even before Gylippus had secured a decisive advantage on Epipolae by driving the third Syracusan counter-wall beyond the line of the Athenian wall (6. 4), Nicias had already turned his attention to the occupation and fortification of Plemmyrium, a headland narrowing the mouth of the Great Harbour on the south just as Ortygia narrowed it on the north (4. 4). Whether the diversion of Athenian effort to this project affected the outcome of the vital struggle on Epipolae is a debatable question. It is the sort of question on which Thucydides is careful not to commit himself unless he is very confident that he knows the right answer. The motives attributed to Nicias in occupying Plemmyrium are reasonable enough: he wished to safeguard the passage of supply ships entering the Great

---

[1] Afterwards he sent twenty ships to intercept a Corinthian squadron of twelve sailing to Syracuse. There is no suggestion that in this instance he acted tardily, but the enemy successfully avoided interception (4. 7; 7. 1).

[2] See below, 281.

Harbour and to provide his warships with an anchorage from which they could operate more conveniently than from their present one if the Syracusans should challenge them at sea (4. 4). Thucydides adds, however, that Nicias 'already began to pay more attention to naval warfare, seeing that the prospects on land were now less promising for the Athenians since Gylippus arrived' (*ibid.*). This reaction to recent developments in the military situation betrays a defensive, almost defeatist, mentality. Naval action alone, however effective it might be, could never be an adequate substitute for the establishment of a blockade on land. Evidently Nicias no longer had in mind the reduction of Syracuse but was seeking rather to safeguard his forces against the development of a Syracusan offensive. It is made very clear that he had, almost deliberately, surrendered the initiative. Thucydides points out that the new base at Plemmyrium had a serious disadvantage which caused the crews of the Athenian ships to deteriorate for the first time: to obtain adequate supplies of water and firewood they had to go out into the country beyond their fortifications, where they were vulnerable to attacks by the Syracusan cavalry (4. 6, cf. 13. 2). The personal responsibility of Nicias for the decline of Athenian fortunes is heavily stressed.

Towards the end of the summer he became convinced that his position at Syracuse was a perilous one and that the Athenian assembly must decide without delay either to abandon the whole enterprise and recall his forces from Sicily or to send out large reinforcements (8. 1). Because he considered the needs of the situation to be so urgent, he adopted a procedure which was evidently unusual: in addition to sending messengers to make a verbal report, he also composed a written dispatch, which was to be read in full to the assembly (8. 2–3). While awaiting a reply, which he could not hope to receive until the winter was far advanced, he was content to remain on the defensive (8. 3). The responsibility for making decisions had been passed to others.[1]

---

[1] As στρατηγὸς αὐτοκράτωρ (6. 8. 2; 26. 1) Nicias possessed the authority to withdraw the expeditionary force from Sicily without consulting the assembly if

The Thucydidean version of this letter from Nicias to the assembly (11–15) is certainly not a copy of the original or even an abstract of its salient points. In introducing it Thucydides uses τοιάδε (10), as is his normal practice in the case of speeches, whereas documents reproduced verbatim are introduced by τάδε.[1] Its language and style are thoroughly Thucydidean,[2] as is much of its reasoning.[3] The general tenor of the letter was doubtless known to him, and he may conceivably have seen a copy of it; but he has chosen to present to his readers his own version of it, which is designed to perform the same function as his speeches, where he has himself supplied τὰ δέοντα. It is as instructive and revealing as any speech; nowhere are his own views on the leadership of Nicias more plainly traceable.

Nicias begins by explaining how the arrival of Gylippus with reinforcements has balked the plan of the Athenians to reduce Syracuse by blockade. Because they are now outnumbered, they cannot hope to restore the situation with their present forces; hence, on land at least, they have become no longer the besiegers but the besieged (11). The enemy are appealing for more troops from the Peloponnese and from Sicily and intend to launch simultaneous attacks by land and sea. They can now hope to challenge Athenian naval supremacy, knowing that the Athenian ships and crews have deteriorated through having been on active service so long. The Athenians in their open anchorage have no facilities for keeping their vessels in a serviceable condition, and every available trireme is needed to protect their supply ships from attack when entering the Great Harbour (12. 1–13. 1). The

he thought fit; but to have taken this step would have demanded from any general a high degree of moral courage (cf. Ferguson, *C.A.H.* v, 299). Thucydides creates the impression that Nicias was above all eager on this occasion (as he certainly was later, 7. 48. 3–4) to avoid making a decision for which he might be censured.

[1] Steup, n. *ad loc.*

[2] The prevalence of parentheses (11. 3; 13. 2; 14. 2) constitutes one example.

[3] The inclusion of generalisations (14. 1–2; 14. 4), which is a feature of Thucydidean speeches, is not wholly appropriate to what purports to be a factual report.

progressive deterioration of the crews is very serious. Many sailors have been killed by the Syracusan cavalry while in quest of firewood and water outside the defences of Plemmyrium, and the servants are deserting in large numbers. Non-Athenians conscripted as sailors, who have hitherto welcomed their remunerative employment, do not relish the unforeseen prospect of having to go into action against the Syracusans and are melting away. Some sailors have prevailed upon the trierarchs to accept untrained slaves from Hyccara as substitutes for themselves. All these adverse factors are combining to hasten the decline of naval efficiency, which is notoriously difficult to maintain at a high level even in the best conditions (13. 2–14. 1). Nicias acknowledges that he is powerless to halt this decay. Unlike the enemy, he has already exhausted all available sources from which he might make good his losses in manpower, and if the cities in Italy from which he obtains supplies desert the flagging Athenian cause, the Syracusans will have won without having to strike a blow (14. 2–3).[1] After declaring that he has chosen to be absolutely frank in order that the assembly may consider the situation with a full knowledge of the unpalatable facts, Nicias denies that the soldiers or their leaders are to blame. They virtually achieved the objective of the expedition when opposed by the Syracusans alone; now, with all Sicily united against them and further aid for the enemy expected from the Peloponnese, they are no longer strong enough to meet their present difficulties, which will soon be much intensified. Therefore the Athenians at home must come to a decision at once and act upon it as soon as the spring begins: they must either recall their expeditionary force or send another equally powerful together with large sums of money. Nicias asks to be relieved of his responsibilities as commander-in-chief because illness has made him unfit to discharge them; he claims indulgence

---

[1] From the phrase ἐκπολιορκηθέντων ἡμῶν (14. 3) Nicias could be deemed to have already envisaged that the Athenians might be forced to surrender. This verb, however, does not necessarily imply that beleaguered persons become prisoners but only that the place where they are beleaguered is lost, cf. 75. 5. In 15. 1 (cf. 8. 1) Nicias seems to assume that the Athenians can withdraw at will.

on the ground that he has a long record of distinguished service as a leader while still in good health (14. 4–15. 2).

Whatever knowledge Thucydides had about the content of the dispatch has been adapted with masterly skill to provide his readers with instruction and guidance. The original text, had it been preserved, might have supplied more detailed information; it could hardly have presented a more penetrating analysis of the situation at Syracuse and of the dangers threatening the Athenians there, and it could certainly not have thrown so much light upon the leadership of Nicias. As in some speeches, Thucydides tends to foreshadow future developments, while avoiding actual anachronism. It is for this reason that the dispatch makes the position of the Athenians appear to be considerably more desperate than the preceding narrative, in which the events since the arrival of Gylippus are recorded, would seem to warrant.[1] Doubtless the chronic pessimism of Nicias, as well as his eagerness to impress upon the assembly how serious was the plight of his forces, influenced what he wrote; but the Thucydidean version presents the situation rather as it became in the spring of 413 than as it was in the late summer of 414. It is hard to reconcile the case made by Nicias about the position at sea with the record of subsequent events. The Athenians are alleged to have been compelled to keep every available ship in operation in 414 because of the imminent danger of enemy attack on a large scale (12. 4–13. 1). Yet in the following spring the Syracusans were still uneasy about the prospects of a naval offensive and needed strong encouragement from Gylippus and Hermocrates before they would commit themselves (21. 2–4). The tone of the dispatch suggests that, when it was written, the naval efficiency of the Athenians was already disintegrating, but shortly before the arrival of Demosthenes in the middle of the following summer they were still capable of putting into operation the skilled manœuvres for which they were famous (36. 3–6). Thucydides has in his version of the dispatch taken the opportunity to focus attention upon sources of Athenian weak-

---

[1] Dover, n. on 10–15, makes this point.

ness, which were more easily appreciated in retrospect. Thus the reader is prepared in advance for the fall of Plemmyrium and the gradual emergence of Syracusan supremacy at sea.

The picture of Nicias presented here is almost wholly unfavourable. He is, as always, conscientious, and he shows frankness, which may be deemed commendable, in refusing to gloss over disagreeable truths (14. 4). In addition, he has taken pains to keep himself well informed about the actions and intentions of the enemy (12. 1–2; 15. 2). There is here no hint of his capacity for dogged and inspiring courage to which Thucydides later gives much prominence. His many failings appear to be only to a very limited degree attributed to the handicap of his physical condition (15. 1). There are significant omissions in the report. Nicias does not explain why he did not exploit the overwhelming advantage gained by the Athenians in the spring and early summer, or why he failed to intercept the army of Gylippus before it could establish contact with the Syracusans. He apparently attributes the victory of Gylippus on Epipolae to superior numbers (11. 2), whereas the preceding narrative shows that it was due rather to superior leadership.[1] He argues rather lamely that without substantial reinforcements he cannot even contemplate attempting to destroy the Syracusan counter-wall and thereby regain the initiative (11. 3). He refers to the efforts of the enemy to obtain more troops (12. 1); he has evidently made none himself, though Italy was a potential source of manpower, as Demosthenes was to show.[2] He is somewhat more convincing when he explains why his ships and crews have deteriorated. Some deterioration was doubtless inevitable because of their long absence from home bases, but it was evidently intensified by his decision to occupy Plemmyrium, which, as pointed out above, Thucydides seems to have regarded as an error of judgement. It is evident that an energetic leader with some capacity for enforcing his authority and main-

---

[1] See below, 279–81. The reinforcements brought by Gylippus cannot have amounted to more than about 3,500 men (1. 5).

[2] See below, 266–8.

taining the spirit of the men under his command could at least have checked the process of decline. Nicias confesses himself unable to do this, pleading that the Athenians are not naturally amenable to discipline (14. 2). His criticism of the trierarchs for having permitted the substitution of Hyccaran slaves for trained sailors (13. 2) betrays a neglect of duty on his own part. He must have failed to impress upon them that, even at times when the prospect of a Syracusan offensive at sea seemed remote, it was imperative to preserve a high level of naval efficiency. Here as elsewhere in the dispatch he blames anyone except himself.[1]

Thucydides uses the dispatch, as has already been noted, in the same way as he uses speeches. In a few of his speeches, most obviously that of Athenagoras in the Syracusan assembly (6. 36–40),[2] he deliberately creates an unfavourable impression of the speaker. His version of the dispatch is designed largely to reinforce the conclusions suggested in his narrative. It makes even more abundantly clear his conviction that the leadership of Nicias since the death of Lamachus had lacked vigour and firmness and was a major factor in bringing about the transformation of the military position.

The Athenian reaction to the dispatch is recorded very briefly. Thucydides gives a mere summary of decisions: there is no hint that public opinion was divided and no reference to a debate in the assembly (16. 1–2). He may be intentionally contrasting the Athenians with Nicias by showing that they at least had no difficulty in making decisions, whether right or wrong. He later implies that their refusal to relieve Nicias of his command was an act of folly, since after the arrival of Demosthenes and Eurymedon with the second expedition the indecision of Nicias proved ultimately disastrous.[3] The views of Thucydides on the crucial

---

[1] Dover, n. on 10–15.   [2] Cf. *Ryl. Bull.* XLI (1958), 249.

[3] The promotion of Menander and Euthydemus, who were already in Sicily, to share his responsibilities does not seem to have had the effect of producing more vigorous leadership or of halting the deterioration of the Athenian forces. Neither is mentioned again by Thucydides before the second expedition arrived (43. 2; 69. 4). According to Plutarch (*Nic.* 20. 5–8) they compelled

decision to send this second expedition are nowhere revealed.[1] He mentions, and probably shared, the astonished admiration of others for the boldness of the Athenians in refusing to be deterred by the occupation of Decelea (28. 3; 42. 2). Whether he considered them to have acted wisely or unwisely is a thorny problem which is not relevant here. In sending Eurymedon to Sicily at once with ten ships the Athenians were not, so far as is known, responding to any specific request by Nicias, except that this squadron carried a sum of money. They took this action out of consideration for their forces at Syracuse, whose spirits would be raised by the news that the second expedition was being prepared (16. 2). It is strange that Eurymedon was not ordered to stay at Syracuse, where his experience and authority might have proved valuable. The gravity of the situation there does not seem to have been even yet fully understood at home. Attention was concentrated upon efforts to make the second expedition strong enough to win the war in Sicily; this war could well have been lost before its arrival.

Little is heard of Nicias during the first half of 413, while the Syracusans exploited the advantages won in the previous summer because of his shortcomings as a leader. The loss of Plemmyrium was very damaging to the morale of the Athenians (24. 3), and their position became more and more serious. The few references to Nicias suggest that he was still virtually in sole command despite the promotion of Menander and Euthydemus and that occasionally at least he acted with unexpected energy and resourcefulness. He succeeded in persuading his Sicel allies in the interior to ambush a detachment of troops marching to Syracuse to reinforce the enemy. Heavy casualties were inflicted, and this

---

Nicias against his better judgement to commit the Athenian fleet to action when Demosthenes was known to be approaching, their motive being to win personal credit while the opportunity offered itself. This story may have some foundation, but it is not easily reconcilable with the narrative of Thucydides (36–41), which suggests rather that the Athenians had to fight because they were attacked and had no alternative.

[1] Unfortunately his celebrated judgement in 2. 65. 11 gives no hint of his opinion on this point, cf. *C.Q.* VIII (1958), 109.

action won a valuable respite for the Athenians, since it caused the Syracusans to defer their intention to deliver a general attack upon them (32–33. 3). Later, during the series of naval engagements just before the arrival of Demosthenes, Nicias 'compelled' trierarchs whose ships had suffered damage to have them repaired (38. 2), an incident showing that he was not always so lax in his relations with subordinates as might be inferred from a passage in his dispatch (13. 2). On the same day he had merchantmen moored at intervals in front of his naval base to serve as a protective screen behind which his triremes could find shelter if hard pressed (38. 2–3). This device proved its worth during the major battle fought on the following day when it saved the Athenians from a crushing defeat (41. 2–3). They were, however, now in desperate straits and could not hope to stave off disaster much longer without the support of the second expeditionary force.

5. *From the arrival of Demosthenes to the last sea battle*

In the narrative covering this phase of the campaign the personality of Nicias is again prominent, and his influence, though largely negative, is seen to have deeply affected the development of the military situation. He is contrasted with Demosthenes, whose views were often in conflict with his. It was largely because he shrank from the ordeal of having to face the anger of the Athenian assembly that he withheld his consent so long to the proposal of Demosthenes to withdraw from Syracuse, and his obstinate indecision turned what could have been no more than an inglorious failure into a catastrophe. It is, on the other hand, during the same period that there begins to emerge a quality of which there has hitherto been little trace, namely his fortitude in striving to buoy up the spirits of his men by exhortation and personal example.

The views on the military situation expressed by Demosthenes after the arrival of the second expeditionary force and his efforts to regain the initiative will be discussed in a later chapter.[1]

---

[1] See below, 269–71.

Nicias was persuaded by Demosthenes to agree to the plan for a night attack on Epipolae,[1] though he did not himself take part in it, doubtless because of his physical weakness (43. 1–2). When this attack was repelled with heavy loss, the generals held a conference: they were conscious that the troops, depressed by the deterioration of their prospects and by the prevalence of sickness in the camp, wished to leave Syracuse as soon as possible (47. 1–2). Thucydides gives a detailed account of this conference, and his treatment of the part played by Nicias is especially illuminating (47. 3–49. 4).

Demosthenes with characteristic bluntness called for an immediate withdrawal from Sicily while it could still be carried out without difficulty, and he produced some sensible reasons for believing that to continue the expedition would be harmful to Athenian interests (47. 3–4). Thucydides next reports not what Nicias said but what he felt and did not say: that he too took a gloomy view of the situation but wished to prevent an open vote being recorded in favour of withdrawal through fear that Athenian intentions might be betrayed to the enemy (48. 1).[2] This summary of his private and undisclosed feelings is followed by a summary of his largely private and undisclosed views about the weakness of the Syracusans, which Thucydides believes to have been well-founded because they were based on communications from traitors inside the city (48. 2, cf. 49. 1). No other passage provides a clearer indication that Thucydides was able to consult

---

[1] Thucydides (43. 1) does not state whether Nicias raised any objections. According to Plutarch (*Nic.* 21. 3–6) he opposed this plan, which he condemned for its rashness (cf. 22. 1), at a conference of the generals and was compelled to yield only when his colleagues supported Demosthenes. It is, however, evident that Plutarch, or his source, has taken liberties with the facts, presumably to accentuate the contrast between Nicias and Demosthenes, by transferring to this conference part of the report by Thucydides on the conference held after the failure of the attack on Epipolae (cf. *C.Q.* xxxv [1941], 64 n. 2).

[2] The phrase μετὰ πολλῶν is scarcely intelligible, since this conference is not a public meeting even if, as is likely enough, some subordinate officers were present. Krüger is probably right in believing that the words are a gloss on ἐμφανῶς. The Syracusans, apart from a few traitors (48. 2), did not in fact learn until some weeks later that the Athenians contemplated evacuation (51. 1).

someone in whom Nicias had confided: he cannot be guessing. He makes the implicit claim to know what was unknown to Demosthenes and Eurymedon (cf. 49. 4), and there is every reason to believe him. He goes on to state explicitly that Nicias was in fact still undecided on the problem of withdrawal, whereas in his speech he categorically rejected the proposal of Demosthenes (48. 3). Thucydides reports two arguments upon which Nicias based his case against this proposal. First, if the generals decided to withdraw from Sicily on their own initiative and without the sanction of the assembly, they would be condemned to death for neglect of duty, and he for his part would prefer to run the risk of an honourable death in battle (48. 3-4). Secondly, the Syracusans were in an even worse plight than the Athenians, being on the verge of collapse because of their crippling expenditure on the prosecution of the war (48. 5). This second argument is a reply to Demosthenes, who had maintained that to continue the campaign would involve a useless waste of money (47. 4). Thucydides insists that Nicias was accurately informed about the financial difficulties of the Syracusans (49. 1); to this extent, but only to this extent, he is defending Nicias.[1] On the implications of the first argument he refrains from comment. His readers might thus appear to be left to draw their own conclusions from his account. Many have concluded that Nicias was guilty of unpardonable selfishness in subordinating the vital interests of Athens to his own desire to avoid personal dishonour. This is surely the conclusion that Thucydides intends to draw.[2] It is at least arguable that his implied criticism of Nicias is somewhat harsh.

Demosthenes persisted in urging withdrawal but suggested, in order to meet the objections of Nicias against returning to Greece, that the Athenians should make Thapsus or Catana their base,

---

[1] Cf. de Romilly (Budé), VI-VII, *note complémentaire* on 47-50 (p. 170).

[2] It is true that ancient and modern points of view may differ on questions involving personal honour; but this passage—and indeed the whole account of the conference—seems to me to be one of many in which Thucydides, while not openly expressing any opinion, is indirectly suggesting to his readers what opinion they should form.

from which both fleet and army could operate to better advantage than from their present position (49. 2–3). Although Eurymedon supported Demosthenes, Nicias continued to object. He could presumably have been outvoted, just as he was outvoted by Alcibiades and Lamachus at Rhegium, but his colleagues, it appears, allowed the conference to end without a decision, believing that his unwonted assurance must be founded upon secret information which he was not prepared to disclose even to them.[1] Thucydides skilfully recreates in a few words the atmosphere of uncertainty and indecision at the Athenian headquarters.[2]

Within a very few weeks after this conference the arrival of strong reinforcements for the Syracusans and a further spread of sickness in the Athenian camp caused even Nicias to relinquish his opposition to the proposal to withdraw from Syracuse (50. 3). It is a little surprising to learn that his obstinacy was overcome before the Athenians suffered another defeat by land or sea, so that Thucydides may have somewhat overstressed the extent of disagreement between the generals at their recent conference. Nicias now insisted only that an open vote should not be taken. It may be noted that, as well as being a safeguard against detection by the enemy, the absence of an open vote would hamper the prosecution if, after returning to Athens, any of the generals were impeached there. When secret preparations for evacuation were

---

[1] Such is the natural interpretation of 49. 3–4 (and also of 50. 3), but the status of Menander and Euthydemus at this time is uncertain (Dover, n. on 49. 3). If they were entitled to vote and if they sided with Nicias, his view must have commanded a majority; and it is possible that Menander, who may perhaps have supplied Thucydides with information (see above, 175 n. 1), was reluctant to admit that he had voted against withdrawal. It is also possible that Demosthenes and Eurymedon did not press the issue to a vote because they were sure that Menander and Euthydemus would support Nicias. Diodorus (13. 12. 3) states that of those attending the conference some agreed with Demosthenes and others with Nicias, but there is no reason to believe that his statement is based on evidence independent of Thucydides. It seems most probable that no vote was taken.

[2] With his use of ὄκνος . . . μέλλησις . . . ὑπόνοια in 49. 4 may be compared his accumulation of abstract nouns when he describes the delays of Archidamus in 431 (2. 18. 3–4; see above, 128).

complete, there occurred the famous eclipse of the moon—the date was 27 August—which caused most of the Athenians to urge the generals to postpone the implementation of their decision. Nicias, sharing the superstitious view of the majority, refused even to hold further consultations about withdrawal until the period of twenty-seven days prescribed by the seers had elapsed (50. 4). At this point Thucydides inserts a parenthesis criticising with unusual frankness the addiction of Nicias to superstition (*ibid.* ἦν γάρ τι καὶ ἄγαν θειασμῷ τε καὶ τῷ τοιούτῳ προσκείμενος).[1] Like other intellectuals of the time, Thucydides despised all forms of superstition,[2] and he evidently felt that, if Nicias had not adopted a superstitious attitude towards the eclipse, the fears of the troops could have been allayed and the withdrawal could have been accomplished with every prospect of success while the enemy was not yet forewarned (cf. 51. 1; 56. 1).[3] Here Thucydides calls attention to a characteristic of Nicias which is a personal one and must normally have been discernible only in private life. He does so because its consequences were so momentous.[4]

After this opportunity had been so ill-advisedly wasted, the position of the Athenians deteriorated rapidly. They were defeated in a sea battle in which Eurymedon was killed (52), and the Syracusans now planned to block the mouth of the Great Harbour (56. 1). The Athenian generals held another conference: it was attended also by the taxiarchs, whose presence is presumably mentioned because it was exceptional (60. 2). On this occasion there seems to have been no serious disagreement between the generals. It was decided that, after concentrating

[1] See above, 11.
[2] Finley, 310–11 (2. 21. 3 and 8. 1. 1 could be added to his collection of relevant passages).
[3] Dover, n. on 50. 4, is surely right in maintaining that the point of the criticism of Nicias by Thucydides 'is not that he was more superstitious than the men whom he commanded, but that an educated man in a responsible position should have been much *less* superstitious' (his italics).
[4] The picture presented by Plutarch (*Nic.* 24. 1) of Nicias devoting all his time to sacrifice and divination may reflect Syracusan propaganda reproduced by Philistus.

their forces in a more confined space, they should commit all their resources to an effort to escape by sea; if they failed in this, they would fight their way to safety overland (60. 2–3).

When the struggle was about to begin, Nicias observed that the Athenians were depressed by their unusual experience of having been defeated at sea; he therefore called them together and addressed them (60. 5) in a speech of which Thucydides gives a summary (61–4).[1] It is at this point that Nicias begins to appear in a different light. Hitherto he has been shown to have been largely answerable, by his dilatory and irresolute leadership, for the desperate situation in which the Athenians found themselves. From now onwards he becomes, somewhat unexpectedly, an almost heroic figure. Undaunted by his own physical weakness, he made a supreme effort to encourage his troops and was never satisfied that he had exerted himself enough on their behalf.

His speech on this occasion, as summarised by Thucydides, reproduces the normal features of a παρακέλευσις and cannot be said to be particularly distinctive. Part of it describes the tactics and technical devices being adopted by the Athenians to counter-act those of the enemy (62). Addressing each section of his audience—hoplites and sailors, Athenians and allies—he impresses upon them how much is at stake and how vital it is to their interests, and to the interests of those at home, that the battle should be won. He encourages them to believe that, despite their past defeats and the seriousness of their present plight, they can achieve victory if they strive to give of their best. Though con-ventional,[2] it is a sincere and courageous speech. It forms an antilogy with the speech attributed to 'the generals of the Syrac-usans and Gylippus' (66–8),[3] and the main purpose of Thucydides is, in accordance with his practice in antilogies before battles, to outline the standpoint of each side and to weigh up their prospects

---

[1] Luschnat, 85–94, analyses this speech, cf. de Romilly (2), 156–8.

[2] Cf. especially 61. 3 with its references to the fortunes of war. These sentiments are, however, charasteristic of Nicias and resemble those of his speech before the retreat (77. 2–4).

[3] See below, 283.

as a prelude to the battle itself. The personal qualities of Nicias become more prominent when Thucydides describes how, when the fleet was on the point of going into action, he felt dissatisfied with the efforts which he had already made and appealed again to the trierarchs, calling upon each of them in turn to be worthy of their ancestors and their fatherland. He did not seek to avoid commonplaces, appreciating their effectiveness in situations of extreme peril such as this (69. 2-3).[1] The emotional tone of this passage prepares for the emotional account of the ensuing battle (70-1).

6. The retreat and the final disaster

After the Syracusan victory Nicias gave his support to the proposal of Demosthenes that one more effort should be made to break out through the mouth of the Great Harbour; but the sailors, convinced that they could not redeem their defeat, refused to obey orders (72. 3-4).[2] Thereupon Nicias showed that, if their spirit was broken, his was not. Hereafter his fortitude in adversity is frequently given prominence. It may have been partly through emotional stress that he allowed himself to be deceived by the stratagem whereby Hermocrates deterred the Athenians from setting out by land during the night after the battle (73. 1-74. 1). When, however, the march was at last about to begin, he once more made most vigorous efforts to cheer his despondent men as he passed from group to group. These efforts are described in vivid terms (76, βοῇ τε χρώμενος ἔτι μᾶλλον ἑκάστοις καθ' οὓς γίγνοιτο ὑπὸ προθυμίας καὶ βουλόμενος ὡς ἐπὶ πλεῖστον γεγωνίσκων ὠφελεῖν τι), and the speech reporting the substance of his exhortations (77) reflects his character and his personal beliefs[3] more distinctively than his speech before the final sea battle. He points

---

[1] Luschnat, 99-100, points out that nowhere else in the History is a supplement in oratio obliqua added after a general's speech reported in oratio recta, and he attributes it to the interest of Thucydides in the character of Nicias.

[2] There is no reason to accept the version of Diodorus (13. 18. 2) that Nicias at this point favoured retreat by land in preference to the plan of Demosthenes.

[3] Luschnat, 101-3, draws attention to the personal element in this speech.

out that he, who has always had a reputation for good fortune,[1] is now exposed to the same dangers as the humblest of his hearers; and he claims that, especially as he has lived an unimpeachable life in his relations with gods and men, he can expect a reversal of his present misfortunes whereby his long-standing good fortune will be maintained (77. 2–3). He develops this line of thought, with more piety than logic, by arguing that the enemy have already been granted sufficient success and that, if the Athenians have incurred divine displeasure, they have received enough punishment and now deserve pity rather than jealousy from the gods (77. 3–4). These ideas about the relation between god and man, which resemble those of Pindar and Herodotus, were already old-fashioned in the late fifth century; they were no longer acceptable to the intellectual movement of that period by which Thucydides was so profoundly influenced. He was, however, evidently prepared to admit that the code of behaviour associated with these ideas had some value (cf. 86. 5) and that it was to a large extent the source from which Nicias derived the qualities displayed in the last stages of the campaign. In the rest of his speech Nicias urges his men to be resolute, drawing confidence from the size and excellence of their army; to maintain strict discipline so that the plans of the generals for their safety may have the best chance of accomplishment; to appreciate how vitally the fortunes of Athens depend on their success or failure (77. 4–7).

The efforts of Nicias on this occasion were not confined to exhortation. While Demosthenes led the Athenian rearguard, which was likely to have to bear the brunt of Syracusan attacks during the retreat, Nicias assumed command of the leading division, amounting to slightly less than half of the whole force (78. 2; 80. 4). Responsibility for directing this division on the march might have been entrusted to a commander physically

---

[1] Cf. 5. 16. 1 and 6. 17. 1 (where this reputation is mentioned with contempt by Alcibiades). Plutarch refers frequently to the εὐτυχία of Nicias (*Nic.* 2. 5; 9. 4; 18. 10; 20. 1; 27. 5).

sounder than Nicias,[1] but he evidently chose, because the situation was so critical, to resume active duties after a long interval, and his determination seems to have overcome his bodily weakness.[2] It is noteworthy that the division of Nicias maintained cohesion on the march better than that of Demosthenes during a stage when neither was under attack (80. 4; 81. 2), and that at the last Nicias seems to have remained the cooler.[3]

On the fifth night after leaving Syracuse the Athenians tried to elude the enemy by stealing away under cover of darkness in a direction different from that of their previous route. Thucydides mentions only that Nicias and Demosthenes agreed to adopt this expedient (80. 1); he does not disclose which, if either, was the originator of it. During the march by night there was some panic and disorder, especially in the rearguard under Demosthenes, so that in the morning Nicias and his men were several miles ahead (80. 3–4; 81. 3). Nicias is reported to have felt that the best prospect of escape lay in pressing on with all speed and stopping to fight only if compelled to do so (81. 3). By hurrying forward he might appear to have been doing a disservice to the rearguard, and even to the whole army, which could surely have resisted attack more effectively if united. Thucydides, however, neither expresses nor implies disapproval of his decision and seems rather to be critical of Demosthenes.[4]

When Nicias was informed by the Syracusans that Demosthenes and the rearguard had surrendered, he refused to credit the report (83. 1), evidently believing that it was a ruse designed to cause him to abandon his efforts to lead his own division to safety. On learning that the news was true, he made a very remarkable proposal to Gylippus and the Syracusans. He offered, in the name of the Athenian state, to defray the whole of the expenditure

---

[1] Menander, who survived the expedition (see above, 175 n. 1), must have been available. Euthydemus may have been killed in the final sea battle (Dover, n. on 16. 1).

[2] Cf. Plut. *Nic.* 26. 4–5, whose picture is perhaps founded exclusively upon the account of Thucydides.

[3] See below, 274.   [4] See below, 273–4.

incurred by the Syracusans in the course of the war if they would allow his force to withdraw without further loss; as a guarantee of good faith one Athenian for each talent of the total debt was to be left behind in Syracusan custody (83. 2). It is strange, and indeed regrettable, that Thucydides has recorded these negotiations so briefly: he merely states the terms proposed by Nicias and adds that they were not accepted by the Syracusans and Gylippus (83. 3). He seems to have felt unable, or unwilling, to explain the reasons why Nicias took this action or to suggest to his readers, directly or indirectly, what conclusions they should draw from the incident.[1] The motive of Nicias cannot have been solely to save the remainder of the force under his command from being massacred, since he could apparently have achieved this object by other, and indeed surer, means. When the Syracusans informed him that Demosthenes had surrendered, they urged him to do likewise, and presumably he could have obtained similar terms,[2] namely that none of the prisoners was to be put to death either by execution or through maltreatment or starvation while in captivity (82. 2). Nicias could not have foreseen that the Syracusans would play false and would subject the prisoners to the horrors of the stone-quarries (87. 1–3, cf. 77. 4). His offer to reimburse the victors, though made under conditions of emotional stress, can hardly have been the outcome of a sudden impulse, because its terms seem to have been carefully thought out. He must have realised that, if the enemy accepted his proposal, he himself would inevitably be exposed to the fury of the Athenian assembly, a situation that he had earlier sought to avoid at all costs (48. 4, cf. 14. 4). He could doubtless, like Alcibiades, have escaped execution

---

[1] Modern scholars have shown more inclination to paraphrase than to comment on the report of Thucydides. Freeman, 390, maintains that Nicias 'had no authority to bind the Athenian people to any terms', which is by no means certain since the powers of the Athenian generals in Sicily were exceptionally wide.

[2] The Syracusan soldiers would certainly have welcomed an end to the fighting. Even before the capitulation of Demosthenes they had shown some disinclination to risk their lives when total victory was assured (81. 5).

by going into exile. He was, however, virtually condemning himself, if not to death, at least to banishment by making his offer on behalf of the Athenian people, and in this respect he deserves credit for having acted unselfishly. Whether the proposed agreement, if accepted, would have proved on balance beneficial to Athenian interests is a question impossible to answer with any confidence. Some weeks earlier Nicias had himself estimated Syracusan war expenditure at 2,000 talents, excluding borrowings (48. 5), and the sum required from the Athenian treasury to implement the terms of his proposal would have been enormous. A crippling burden would have been inflicted upon Athenian finances, and prospects of recovery from the effects of the disaster in Sicily would have been seriously damaged. On the other hand, Nicias is insistent in each of his last two speeches that Athens could not hope to survive unless the Athenians serving in Sicily contrived to return home (64. 1; 77. 7). He appreciated that trained manpower, of which there had been a shortage at Athens at least since the plague, was an indispensable weapon of war (cf. 13. 2). It may have been his conviction that, if he could purchase freedom for a substantial body of troops, who could help to defend Athens instead of remaining immobilised in captivity, no price was too high to pay. He might well have been right.

When the Syracusans and Gylippus rejected his proposal, he did not attempt on that day to continue the march because the Athenians were so exhausted. During the night, doubtless on his orders, they tried to steal away unobserved, but the Syracusans were not to be deceived a second time by the same stratagem, and the plan was abandoned before it had been put into operation (83. 4–5). On the following day the Athenians struggled on to the Assinarus and were being massacred in the river bed when Nicias surrendered himself to Gylippus. Thucydides records the surrender of Nicias as briefly as that of Demosthenes, but he strikes a far more personal note: Nicias chose to give himself up to Gylippus because he trusted him more than the Syracusans, and he urged Gylippus and the Spartans 'to treat him in whatever way they liked but to stop slaughtering the soldiers' (85. 1). Although the second point provides further evidence of his unselfish devotion to the men under his command, which has been so prominent in the preceding narrative and speeches, the motive attributed to him in choosing to surrender to Gylippus is somewhat less creditable. This motive is more fully explained a little later where his main reason for confidence in Gylippus is stated to have been that he was conscious of being in favour with the Spartans because he had promoted the restoration of the prisoners captured on Sphacteria by persuading the Athenians to make peace (86. 3–4). That he tried to seize a possible chance of saving his own life when his death could not benefit the Athenians would be judged by many to be a pardonable, even sensible, action. Had he lived, he would surely have made efforts to persuade the Syracusans to mitigate their inhuman treatment of the Athenian prisoners. Nevertheless, the reference by Thucydides to his motive in surrendering to Gylippus might be, and apparently has been,[1] interpreted unfavourably. When the fate of the Athenian generals was debated, Gylippus did in fact, as Nicias had anticipated, try to save their lives; but his reasons, according to Thucydides, for opposing their execution (86. 2) were less creditable than those attributed to him in advance by Nicias (86. 4).

Thucydides is not content to record that Nicias and Demosthenes were executed; he goes on to consider why despite the opposition of Gylippus sentence of death was passed on them (86. 3–5). Because some factors which probably contributed to this verdict could not be disclosed in public, the real reasons for it were difficult to establish,[2] and Thucydides expresses some mis-

---

[1] Plutarch, *Comp. Nic. et Crass.* 5. 4, probably has this passage in mind when he charges Nicias with having made a shameful attempt to save his own life, though he is also doubtless influenced by the views of Philistus (*F. Gr. Hist.* 556 F 53), as may be seen from *Nic.* 27. 2.

[2] The influence of contemporary and later propaganda is discernible in the account of Plutarch (*Nic.* 28. 2–5), though much of his material is doubtless authentic, and also in that of Diodorus (13. 19. 4–33. 1), which is almost worthless.

givings about the trustworthiness of information supplied to him
(86. 4, ὡς ἐλέγετο; 86. 5, τοιαύτη ἢ ὅτι ἐγγύτατα τούτων αἰτία
ἐτεθνήκει). Yet the question evidently seemed to him to be sufficiently important and interesting to demand some discussion. The
execution of generals who had surrendered was an act raising
legal and moral issues of a kind which in the first half of the
History tends to evoke investigation and debate.[1] Here, however,
the discussion is concerned almost exclusively with the personal
lot of Nicias and leads on to the famous judgement on his life and
death (86. 5), which will be considered below. Thucydides implies that the fate of the generals, as well as that of the whole
captured army, was decided by a mass meeting of the Syracusans
and all their allies, though his account is somewhat lacking in
precision on this point.[2] He suggests that, had the Spartans been
in a position to impose their will upon the meeting, they would
have caused Nicias to be spared in recognition of his services to
them dating back to the Sphacteria episode. It was this consideration, as has already been mentioned, that led Nicias to surrender
to Gylippus. Two groups, however, were most insistent in
demanding that Nicias should be sentenced to immediate execution. Certain Syracusans who had been in treasonable communication with him feared that he might under torture disclose their
guilt, while others, above all the Corinthians, were afraid that
he might use his great wealth to procure his escape and might
then cause them further damage.[3] This allusion to his wealth is
noteworthy: Alcibiades seems to be the only other contemporary

---

[1] See below, 274, on the question whether the execution of Demosthenes was a
violation of the terms agreed with him when he surrendered.

[2] Cf. Plut. *Nic.* 28. 1, ἐκκλησίας δὲ πανδήμου Συρακοσίων καὶ τῶν συμμάχων
γενομένης.

[3] Both groups are concerned about the possible consequences if Nicias were not
executed at once. They seem to be countering proposals, possibly by moderates, to defer a decision for a time and meanwhile to try to extract valuable
information from him by torture. The debate offers obvious opportunities for
dramatic presentation (as is illustrated so deplorably by Diod. 13. 19. 4–33. 1),
but Thucydides has not chosen to avail himself of them, perhaps because
Nicias is no longer an actor but a victim.

Greek whose financial circumstances are mentioned by Thucydides (6. 15. 2–3).[1]

There remains to be considered the final reference to Nicias in the *History*, the brief but celebrated tribute to him which has given rise to much discussion in modern times.[2] ἥκιστα δὴ ἄξιος ὢν τῶν γε ἐπ᾽ ἐμοῦ Ἑλλήνων ἐς τοῦτο δυστυχίας ἀφικέσθαι διὰ τὴν πᾶσαν ἐς ἀρετὴν νενομισμένην ἐπιτήδευσιν (7. 86. 5). The last few words, which have been interpreted in many different ways, may be translated: 'because of his principles of conduct[3] which he had invariably practised in accordance with goodness'.[4] In this context ἀρετή is essentially a moral term (cf. 2. 40. 4; 5. 105. 4); it denotes the uprightness shown by Nicias throughout his life both as a private citizen and as a political and military leader; it includes moderation and stability, which Alcibiades so conspicuously lacked.[5] Although elsewhere, as in the well-known assessment of Antiphon (8. 68. 1),[6] ἀρετή may denote ability, here it does not.

It would be a mistake to read too much into this brief tribute to the character of Nicias. It cannot legitimately be described as an obituary,[7] a term inappropriate even to the long passage on

---

[1] 4. 105. 1, where he draws attention to his own possession of mining rights in Thrace, might perhaps be added. On 2. 13. 1, which implies that the property of Pericles in Attica was considerable, see above, 31.

[2] A recent and valuable survey is provided by H. A. Murray, *B.I.C.S.* VIII (1961), 33–6 and 41–6.

[3] ἐπιτήδευσις here has the same meaning as in 2. 36. 4, where it denotes 'the principles underlying Athenian life public and private' (Gomme, n. *ad loc.*). It embraces the basic beliefs on which a man's way of life, ἐπιτηδεύματα (cf. 6. 15. 4 and 28. 2 on Alcibiades), was founded.

[4] I share the conviction of many scholars, including Stahl, Schwartz 354–5, and Dover, that both πᾶσαν and νενομισμένην agree with ἐπιτήδευσιν and not with ἀρετήν: One reason for rejecting the strange view, favoured by J. B. Bury, *Ancient Greek Historians* (1909), 119–20, and others, that the whole phrase is ironical is that νενομισμένην would have to be taken with ἀρετήν: this is unnatural. Other reasons for rejecting this view are that there seems to be no parallel in the *History* for the use of irony in a similar way and that Thucydides is hardly likely to have chosen an ironical comment as his final reference to a man whose heroism in adversity he has depicted with so much sympathy.

[5] Finley, 246.

[6] See above, 9–10.

[7] Murray, *B.I.C.S.* VIII, 44, uses this term.

Pericles discussed in an earlier chapter.[1] Even Thucydides could not compress an obituary into twenty words. He is not here attempting a general assessment of Nicias but is focusing attention upon a single, though important, quality. There is no reason to believe that he is by implication denying Nicias qualities which he does not mention. In two passages in which he credits persons with ἀρετή, using the word in much the same sense as here, he couples it with ξύνεσις: the persons are Brasidas (4. 81. 2) and the Peisistratidae (6. 54. 5). It should not, as some scholars maintain,[2] be inferred from comparison with these passages that Thucydides intends his readers to notice the omission of ξύνεσις when he credits Nicias with ἀρετή and to draw conclusions from it. Neither he himself nor his readers could be expected to know the *History* by heart. In any case the qualities in which he found Nicias wanting were boldness, enterprise and energy; there seems to be no suggestion in the account of the Sicilian expedition that he believed Nicias to have been lacking in intelligence.

If this tribute to the uprightness of Nicias had occurred in the work of any other historian, it would probably have evoked very little discussion. It is startling only because nowhere else does the *History* contain sentiments of the same kind. Thucydides seldom comments on the deaths of leading individuals, and only here is his comment concerned with moral standards; but, if this judgement is unique, so also are the circumstances which prompted it. Nicias is the most tragic character in the *History*. He directed with a high sense of duty an enterprise of which he disapproved, for some months without colleagues to share his responsibilities and latterly under the handicap of severe illness. In the closing stages of the campaign he displayed heroic devotion. The good fortune which had carried him through the Archidamian war deserted him, and he died a miserable death. It is not the practice of Thucydides to be indulgent towards incompetent leadership, and,

---

[1] See above, 40.

[2] G. F. Bender, *Der Begriff des Staatsmannes bei Thukydides* (1938), 49-51 with n. 139; Murray, *B.I.C.S.* VIII, 35-6 and 45.

as has been seen in the present chapter, he shows no indulgence towards the shortcomings of Nicias. For a moment, however, he abandons his normal dispassionateness because his emotions have been stirred by the tragedy of a good man who involved himself and thousands of others in disaster. This goodness was of a kind that Thucydides admired and believed to be a very important ingredient of good leadership (cf. 2. 60. 5). Thucydides pays this tribute to Nicias partly through sympathy for his cruel fate and partly through a desire to do him justice.

CHAPTER XII

ALCIBIADES

N
O major figure in Athenian history was so colourful or so
unconventional as Alcibiades. All the surviving evidence,
including the varied assortment of material assembled in
the *Alcibiades* of Plutarch, stamps him as an individualist. Thucydides would, one imagines, have been compelled to treat him
rather differently from other leaders if his career had belonged to
the period covered by the first half of the *History*, mainly because
he ignored to a large extent the conventional separation between
public and private life which was accepted by almost all his
contemporaries. Nevertheless, even when every allowance has
been made for the abnormal characteristics of Alcibiades, the
presentation of him by Thucydides does illustrate very strikingly
the differences in the treatment of individuals between the two
halves of the *History*.

1. *Advocacy of Athenian friendship with Argos*

The passage in which Alcibiades is mentioned for the first time is
remarkable for its exceptionally personal tone (5. 43. 2–3). In the
first half of the *History* Thucydides includes hardly any personal
detail and seems to have deliberately excluded it, even where it
might have been relevant, except in excursuses when writing
about persons long dead such as Pausanias and Themistocles.
Here he makes the point that Alcibiades was still young when he
first sought political leadership (43. 2).[1] It is very seldom that
Thucydides supplies information about the age of individuals,[2]

---

[1] Cf. the references to his youth in the debate on the Sicilian expedition (6. 12. 2;
17. 1; 18. 6).

[2] He does mention that in 427 Pausanias was still a minor in order to explain
why his uncle deputised for him in conducting the invasion of Attica in that

though there are instances in which it might have been instructive. To have learned, for example, how old Brasidas or Demosthenes was when each first became prominent would have been valuable; and indeed the *History* provides no evidence that Pericles was an old man when he died, except that he had held a military command almost a quarter of a century earlier (1. 111. 2). Besides mentioning the age of Alcibiades, Thucydides also refers to the eminence of the family to which he belonged and to its former associations with Sparta. These personal details are certainly not irrelevant. They help to explain the political standing of Alcibiades in 420 and the reasons why he chose to advocate a policy of friendship with the Argives and hostility towards the Spartans. The latter had offended him by negotiating the recently concluded peace treaty through Nicias and Laches and by ignoring him despite their close relationship with his family in the past and his own attempts to renew it (cf. 6. 89. 2). He is stated to have been convinced that Athenian interests would best be served by allying with Argos, but it is perfectly clear that, to Thucydides at any rate, he was influenced to a much greater extent by personal considerations.[1]

When in the spring of 420 a series of disagreements between Athens and Sparta caused their relations to become strained, Alcibiades saw an opportunity to implement his policy of alliance with Argos. He privately induced the Argives and their allies to send envoys to invite Athens to join their coalition (5. 43. 3). The Spartans, alarmed by this development, also sent an embassy to Athens, and it was upon this embassy that Alcibiades played his famous and very characteristic trick. By promising the Spartan ambassadors that he would obtain for them the satis-

year (3. 26. 2, cf. 1. 107. 2 on a similar situation in the Pentecontaetia). References to youth often have a political flavour, since young aristocrats were traditionally prone to violence when they saw opportunities to overthrow democracies (6. 28. 1; 38. 5; 39. 2; 8. 65. 2; 69. 4; 92. 6).

[1] Cf. de Romilly (1), 196. In 5. 43. 3 Thucydides states that Alcibiades had from the outset opposed the conclusion of peace with Sparta πανταχόθεν νομίζων ἐλασσοῦσθαι.

faction of their claims, he persuaded them not to acknowledge in the assembly, as they had already acknowledged at a meeting of the Boule, that they had come with full powers to conclude a settlement. When they denied in the assembly that they had full powers, he denounced them for inconsistency and dishonesty, thus bringing upon them the indignation of the Athenians, who were on the point of consenting without further ado to ally with the Argives when an earthquake interrupted the debate (44. 3-45. 4). On the next day, as has already been seen,[1] Nicias, who is presented as the personal rival of Alcibiades, persuaded the assembly to defer a decision on the question of the Argive alliance until further efforts had been made to bring about a reconciliation with Sparta. After these had proved abortive, the Athenians had no longer any hesitation in accepting the recommendations of Alcibiades to join the Argive coalition (46). His wits had won success for him in the first major political conflict of his career.

Thucydides describes this episode with a wealth of vivid detail. He also reports the motives and feelings of Alcibiades (43. 2-3; 45. 1 and 3) with so much confidence as to suggest that he had indisputable evidence about them, though they are mostly such that even Alcibiades is unlikely to have wished them to be widely publicised. Thucydides is not on the whole well-informed about events at Athens during the years immediately after his own banishment, but in this instance he may, by some happy chance or because he made searching enquiries, have possessed abundant information from a reliable source, some of it known only to a few. There are, however, in his account some obscurities and incongruities which may have arisen because he has somewhat exaggerated both the role of Alcibiades in the consultations at Athens and the influence of the trick played on the Spartan envoys in determining the outcome.[2] If so, the reason is perfectly clear.

[1] See above, 170.
[2] The discussion of the episode by Brunt, 65-9, is, in my opinion, largely convincing, the explanation by Hatzfeld, 89-93, almost wholly without foundation.

He wished to focus attention upon Alcibiades at his first appearance as a man whose personality and personal ambitions were to exert a profound influence upon the course of history. He may also have overstressed the personal rivalry between Alcibiades and Nicias at this stage,[1] as well as the contrast between their characters, because he had in mind an occasion a few years later when their rivalry was to have far more momentous consequences. The stratagem whereby Alcibiades tricked the Spartan envoys, though not perhaps of a kind that Pericles would have practised, resembles that of Themistocles in 478, of which Thucydides seems to have approved (1. 90–3). He certainly does not condemn the unscrupulous cleverness shown by Alcibiades on this occasion; he only gives prominence to it, perhaps excessive prominence, as an essential feature of Alcibiades and therefore historically important.

After this almost sensational entry Alcibiades becomes for a time a relatively dim figure, though he evidently continued, as always, his restless activity. Thucydides mentions him frequently when describing the tangled relations between Athens and the Peloponnesian powers during the years from 419 to 416, but these references present a bare record of his actions. They provide hardly any indication of his motives and throw no light upon his personality. Thucydides adopts his most severely annalistic manner when writing about the part played by Alcibiades in this period. In 419 he led a small Athenian force to the Peloponnese, where, in association with the Argives and other allies, he marched into Achaea, apparently intending to win control over the entrance to the Corinthian Gulf (5. 52. 2). At the same time he seems to have been the instigator of a plan—it is not expressly attributed to him—to compel Epidaurus to join the Argive coalition, thus improving communications between Athens and Argos

---

[1] One of the motives attributed to Alcibiades in holding his secret conversation with the Spartan envoys is that he wished to destroy their association with Nicias (45. 3). This point calls for explanation which it does not receive. It is difficult to imagine that Alcibiades could have devised anything more likely to bring the envoys closer to Nicias than his own deception of them.

(53). It was also probably through his influence that the Athenians convened a conference at Mantinea,[1] but, whatever its purpose may have been, it failed to produce agreement (55. 1-2). When the Argives resumed hostilities against Epidaurus, Sparta reacted by sending an army in the direction of the Argolid, and the Athenians in their turn sent troops under Alcibiades to support the Argives against the threatened invasion. The Spartans did not move beyond their borders, and the force under Alcibiades thereupon withdrew (55. 2-4). He must have been under orders, which were presumably the result of pressure by Athenians opposed to his Peloponnesian policy, not to take any action unless Argos itself was in danger. Later, when the Argives complained of Athenian inertia, Alcibiades secured acceptance of their demand that the Athenians should transport helots to Pylos to make plundering raids on the Spartans (56. 2-3). In the following summer (418) during the campaign leading to the battle of Mantinea he was again in the Peloponnese acting as an envoy at Argos, where he had a difficult task in trying to patch up disagreements between the allies and to secure united action against Sparta (61. 2-3). He was still at Argos, or had returned thither, in the following winter, when he unsuccessfully opposed the oligarchs there who secured the acceptance of peace terms offered by the Spartans (76. 3). Finally, in the spring of 416 he was sent with a small fleet to Argos and took into custody some Argives suspected of sympathy with Sparta (84. 1). This action was evidently intended to strengthen the position of the Argive democrats, who were again in control,[2] and to provide a practical demonstration of Athenian good will.

It is remarkable that Thucydides has devoted so much attention to the first step taken by Alcibiades to implement his policy of

[1] Hatzfeld, 101.

[2] Alcibiades may well have had a hand in planning the democratic uprising against the oligarchs who had negotiated the Argive reconciliation with Sparta (82. 2-3) and also in renewing the defensive alliance between Athens and Argos (82. 5, cf. S.E.G. x, 104); but Thucydides does not mention that he was implicated.

intervention in the Peloponnese and so little attention to its later stages. To account satisfactorily for this disparity of treatment is not at all easy; it could be due to some factor of which no trace has survived. Modern scholars have attempted to explain why Thucydides has dealt so briefly with the efforts of Alcibiades to weaken Sparta by supporting Argos, but their explanations are not altogether convincing. It is most improbable that his brevity is due to his own disapproval of this policy.[1] The theory that brevity in Thucydides denotes personal disapproval is a highly questionable one; brevity indicates rather that the event or topic with which he is dealing is of no great importance, or has little relevance to the history of the war, or does not illustrate any general principle on which he wishes to focus attention. It is also difficult to understand why, if disapproval of Athenian intervention in the Peloponnese caused Thucydides to deal so summarily with its development in 419/16, he did not adopt the same method of showing his disapproval when reporting its initiation in 420. A totally different approach to the problem is to maintain that much of the fifth book is unrevised and that the sections on the Peloponnesian policy of Alcibiades in 419/16 are only a draft designed for subsequent expansion.[2] It is true that the narrative of these years, apart from the full report on the campaign ending in the battle of Mantinea (57–75), is on a small scale, being less detailed than that of 420. There is, however, no cogent reason for believing that Thucydides had any intention of expanding it. The events described belong to a period of nominal peace, and though some of them were by no means peaceful, they were to a large extent inconclusive and had not much influence upon subsequent developments. Some events in the Archidamian war are described no less summarily and with no more explanation.[3]

---

[1] This is the view of de Romilly (1), 195–200. It is not by any means clear, in my opinion, that he did disapprove of the policy of Alcibiades or that he has underrated its effectiveness.　　[2] Brunt, 69–70.

[3] For example, the Athenian seaborne raids on the Peloponnese in the first two summers of the war, cf. my views in *C.Q.* xxxix (1945), 75–84 modified in *Historia*, ix (1960), 390 n. 4.

The theory, once widely accepted, that most of the fifth book (25–116) is a hasty and incomplete link, written when Thucydides realised the unity of the Peloponnesian war, is one that has lost much ground in the last quarter of a century and deserves to lose more.

Neither of these explanations appears to be wholly satisfactory. The following third explanation, which may perhaps be preferable to either of them, suggests itself, though it is always a risky undertaking to try to read the thoughts of Thucydides. He doubtless felt himself impelled to lay great emphasis upon the striking personality of Alcibiades when introducing him, because it had a profound influence upon subsequent events. Even Alcibiades, however, is not kept continuously in the foreground from his first appearance until the end of the *History*: he is mentioned only once (7. 18. 1) between the winter of 415/14, when he made his speech at Sparta (6. 93. 1), and the winter of 413/12, when he played a part in the negotiations leading to the revolt of Athenian allies in Asia (8. 6. 3). It is hardly credible that he remained entirely passive during this period; but his efforts to exert his influence were either entirely abortive or without far-reaching consequences.[1] Similarly, though his policy of attempting to isolate Sparta during the years of nominal peace by close association with Argos was obviously of sufficient importance to be recorded, it did not produce any very striking results. Thucydides probably felt that it was neither a success nor a failure:[2] it did not prevent Sparta from remaining an obstacle to the imperialistic ambitions of such Athenians as Alcibiades himself, but it did hamper the efforts of the Spartans to restore their authority in the Peloponnese. Accordingly, Thucydides was content with a bare annalistic record of events. It is probably for the same reason that, after stressing the personal rivalry between Alcibiades and Nicias in

---

[1] Cf. *J.H.S.* LVIII (1938), 31–40, where I made some speculative suggestions about his activities during this period.

[2] Alcibiades himself naturally claimed that he achieved a personal success in spite of the defeat at Mantinea (6. 16. 6).

420, he does not refer to it again until he reports the debate on the Sicilian expedition. That their rivalry continued in the meanwhile is attested by secondary authorities.[1] Nicias retained his influence, and his opposition to the Peloponnesian schemes of Alcibiades was largely responsible for the vacillations of Athenian policy. The ostracism of 417 was, it seems, held to end the deadlock arising from their rivalry, but by a temporary and secret coalition they successfully thwarted its purpose and caused Hyperbolus to be ostracised.[2] Thucydides has not chosen to mention this celebrated incident here,[3] though he could have used it to illustrate once more the unscrupulous cleverness of Alcibiades.

2. *The expedition to Sicily*

The account of the debate in the Athenian assembly on the Sicilian expedition once more brings into prominence both the personality of Alcibiades and his rivalry with Nicias. The report of his speech is preceded by a celebrated passage providing a very revealing picture of him. It defines his motives in promoting the expedition and explains how the extravagant wildness of his private life and his pursuit of personal ambitions so alarmed most of the Athenians that they later ruined their own cause by discarding him and depriving themselves of his outstanding leadership (6. 15. 2–4).[4] The tone of this passage is strikingly personal: he was eager to rebut the strictures of his enemy Nicias, and he planned to augment his private wealth and private reputation by

---

[1] Cf. Plut. *Nic.* 11. 1–3.

[2] Plut. *Nic.* 11. 1–5; *Alcib.* 13. 4–7. There is some doubt whether 417 was the year in which Hyperbolus was ostracised, but the question is not relevant here.

[3] He does refer to it in 8. 73. 3, when recording the death of Hyperbolus, but without any indication that Alcibiades and Nicias were involved.

[4] See above, 9–10, and also 15, where it is pointed out that the latter part of the passage was very probably added by Thucydides long after he had written the main narrative of the Sicilian expedition (Adcock, 132–5, distinguishes two successive additions). The first part of the passage, however, namely 15. 2 and the beginning of 15. 3, which does not seem to belong to the late insertion, is no less personal than the rest.

leading an expedition which would conquer not only Sicily but also Carthage. His excessive expenditure on keeping a racing stable and on other costly pursuits is also mentioned. Thucydides has chosen to insert a second introduction of Alcibiades at the point where his influence was largely responsible for persuading the Athenians to undertake the expedition to Sicily. It throws more light upon the personality of Alcibiades than the passage in which he is first mentioned (5. 43. 2–3).

The speech of Alcibiades at the meeting of the assembly, as reported by Thucydides (6. 16–18), is largely a study of character. However closely Thucydides may have reproduced the substance of what was actually said by any speaker, he evidently adapted each speech to suit his own purposes in including it, and in this instance his main purpose is perfectly clear. Alcibiades begins, as in his speech at Sparta (89. 1), on a personal note. He defends himself against the personal attack made on him by Nicias,[1] who had argued that his extravagant way of life and his youth ought to have disqualified him from being appointed to command the expedition. He claims that his lavish displays of wealth, such as his *tour de force* at Olympia, brought honour and fame to Athens as well as to himself; that in public life his policy of intervention in the Peloponnese had benefited Athenian interests (16–17. 1). The prospects of success in the west were, he declares, favourable because the Sicilians lacked political stability and because their military resources had been exaggerated (17. 2–5). The situation at home ought not to deter the Athenians from undertaking the expedition, since they enjoyed naval supremacy (17. 6–8). They were under an obligation to answer appeals from their allies, and they must continue their imperialistic policy, as in the past, or they would lose their empire. Victory in Sicily would probably make them masters of all Greece, and they were secure from any risk of disaster in the west because their naval superiority would

---

[1] It is characteristic of Alcibiades that he has no hesitation in referring to his opponent by name (16. 1; 17. 1; 18. 6) whereas Nicias had only referred to him indirectly (12. 2–13. 1, cf. 10. 2).

enable them to withdraw at any time if they so wished (18. 1–5). They must reject the inertia of Nicias and resist his attempt to stir up animosity between young and old: men of all ages must work together with the vigour and enterprise traditionally associated with Athens (18. 6–7).

The keynote of this speech is youthful ambition. It is the speech of a brilliant and self-assured man whose judgement does not match his enthusiasm. His eagerness to win personal fame and fortune causes him to be too sanguine about the prospects of the expedition and to underrate its dangers. If the attitude of Nicias towards it is excessively cautious, that of Alcibiades is almost reckless. Readers of his speech are made to feel that to put much trust in him would be very unwise. Its effect, however, was to make the Athenians even more intent upon undertaking the expedition (19. 1). Such was the power of his personality, for good or ill.

While preparations for the expedition were being completed, two sensational domestic scandals came to light, the mutilation of the Hermae and the profanation of the Mysteries. Thucydides includes a surprisingly detailed account of these scandals (27–9; 53. 1–2; 60–1). It is not his normal practice to dwell upon the internal history of Athens or of any other state, unless it influenced the course of the war. He evidently considered these scandals to have been important partly because they affected public feeling before and after the sailing of the fleet, intensifying the atmosphere of tension which he describes so graphically. His principal reason, however, for being interested in them and for discussing them in some detail, even though much remained obscure (27. 2; 60. 2), was that Alcibiades was implicated and that the charges brought against him[1] caused him to be recalled from Sicily and

---

[1] Although his enemies tried to create prejudice against him by linking his name with both scandals (28. 2), he was formally accused only of having profaned the Mysteries (28. 1; 61. 1). If, as is very probable, the mutilation of the Hermae was intended to cause the abandonment or postponement of the Sicilian expedition, it is almost inconceivable that Alcibiades can have played any part in it, cf. Hatzfeld, 178 n. 1; D. MacDowell, *Andokides on the Mysteries* (1962), 192–3.

to become an exile. It is improbable that when Thucydides wrote his sixth and seventh books he had as yet come to regard the recall of Alcibiades as an error of judgement fatal to Athenian prospects in Sicily.[1] Nevertheless, the sudden removal of his dynamic personality was bound to affect the planning and execution of the whole enterprise and to upset the balance between the generals, leaving the strategy of the campaign largely in the hands of Nicias.[2] The presentation of this episode thus prepares the reader for developments which did in fact take place. The position of Alcibiades in political life at Athens is also very skilfully portrayed. Nowhere, except perhaps in the eighth book when describing the rise and fall of the Four Hundred, does Thucydides throw more light on the conflict between rival politicians at Athens. The brilliance of Alcibiades had enabled him to outstrip lesser men with similar aspirations,[3] who were now delighted to have an opportunity of rousing popular feeling against him (cf. 89. 5); they hoped thereby to oust and supplant him. Because his personal ambition was notorious, these jealous rivals easily gained credence for charges that he was plotting to overthrow the democracy (28. 2; 60. 1; 61. 1 and 4). When he demanded an immediate trial, they were successful in securing its postponement, and their motives in this manœuvre are carefully defined (29). The personality of Alcibiades occupies the foreground throughout most of the report on this episode.

There is no further mention of him until the Athenians have reached Rhegium and the three generals hold their conference there. It was suggested in the previous chapter that the presenta-

---

[1] *C.Q.* VIII (1958), 107–9, where I have maintained that when he wrote 2. 65. 11 (which belongs to a passage added at or after the end of the war) he had formed this opinion in consequence of the outstanding military gifts shown by Alcibiades between 411 and 407.

[2] Cf. Plut. *Nic.* 15. 1–4 and *Alcib.* 21. 8–9, whose conclusions are probably inferences from the narrative of Thucydides and not derived from an independent source.

[3] They are not named here because all the emphasis is on Alcibiades, but 8. 65. 2 shows that the most important of them was Androcles. Others were Peisander and Charicles (MacDowell, *Andokides*, 193).

tion of this conference by Thucydides tends to overstress the disagreements between the generals and that their main concern was to devise the means to keep their forces supplied during the next few months.[1] The proposal of Alcibiades was that they should try to win over as many Sicilian cities as possible by diplomacy: to gain Messana was especially desirable because it would prove an ideal base for their fleet. When they had ascertained who would support them, they should attack Syracuse and Selinus unless these cities yielded to their demands (48). This plan, as described by Thucydides, is thoroughly characteristic of Alcibiades. It recommends that Athenian efforts should be concentrated largely upon diplomacy, the sphere in which he himself had most claims to be a master—his military talents were as yet unrecognised even by himself—so that he could expect to play the leading role. He may not, however, have intended this diplomatic offensive to last very long, and Thucydides, in order to present a neat antithesis with the plans of the other generals, has probably laid rather too much emphasis upon it and too little upon the subsequent military action envisaged in his plan. To achieve some success as soon as possible was important to him in view of the charges hanging over him, and his ambitious schemes of western conquest (15. 2; 90. 2) demanded that the whole of Sicily should be reduced with the least possible delay. He doubtless appreciated, however, that the prospect of capturing Syracuse at the first assault was very remote and that the Syracusans would not necessarily commit their forces at once to battle outside their walls. If the Athenians found themselves encamped near Syracuse without a victory to their credit and without the support of allies from whom they could obtain supplies,[2] they might soon be in desperate straits. Thucydides, who unmistakably implies a preference for the proposals of Lamachus, has perhaps underrated the astuteness of Alcibiades on this occasion, partly because his plan

---

[1] See above, 174–7.
[2] The dependence of the Athenians upon the assistance of allies is mentioned in the speech of Euphemus at Camarina, 86. 3 and 5.

had met with little success when he was recalled and partly from a desire to underline the contrast between him and his colleagues.

When his plan had been accepted, he first crossed to Messana, but his overtures there were rebuffed. The Athenians then sailed with part of their fleet to Naxos, where they were welcomed, and on to Catana, which refused them entry. After a demonstration and reconnaissance at Syracuse, where they issued a proclamation demanding the restoration of the Leontines, they returned to Catana. Here the generals were invited to address the assembly, but while Alcibiades was speaking, some Athenian troops found their way into the market place, apparently by a lucky chance, and their presence swayed the vote of the assembly in favour of an accord with Athens (50–1). Thucydides does not report, even in a few words, the speech of Alcibiades to the assembly, the reason doubtless being that the decision to support the Athenian cause was secured mainly by force and not by persuasion. Catana was a valuable acquisition and became the Athenian base for operations against Syracuse. After a fruitless attempt to win Camarina combined with another demonstration at Syracuse, Alcibiades found orders awaiting him to return home to stand trial (52–3). Because of fears that troops sympathetic towards him might mutiny if he were arrested, he was allowed to sail in his own ship. Thus he and others accused with him were able to go into hiding at Thurii and to escape their escort; later he crossed from Italy to the Peloponnese (61. 4–7). Before he left Sicily, he found an opportunity to balk part of his own plan to secure allies there. At the time of his recall he was engaged in intrigues designed to win Messana with the aid of a faction favouring the Athenians, but he now disclosed this plot to the opposing party. The result was that, when in the following winter his colleagues took a force to Messana in the expectation that the city would be betrayed to them,[1] their hopes were unfulfilled (74). This incident, which Thucydides mentions almost casually, is of considerable significance because it suggests that, if Alcibiades had remained in Sicily for even a few

[1] Alcibiades would, one imagines, have taken action at Messana much earlier.

more weeks, his plan might well have achieved a greater measure of success. He probably had in hand similar intrigues elsewhere. When after his recall a second attempt was made to win the support of Camarina (75. 3; 88. 2), public feeling there was well disposed towards Athens (88. 1). If Alcibiades instead of the unknown spokesman Euphemus had conducted the negotiations, he might well have devised some means of bringing about a result more favourable to the Athenians.

3. *Assistance to Sparta (first phase)*

His arrival in the Peloponnese was very timely for the Spartan government. Not long after he landed at Cyllene in Elis an embassy from Syracuse reached Corinth and proceeded thence to Sparta accompanied by Corinthian envoys, who were instructed to reinforce the Syracusan plea for Spartan aid. It was doubtless because the Spartans expected this appeal but had not yet decided what their response should be that Alcibiades received an official invitation to go to Sparta, which included a guarantee of his personal safety (88. 7–9). Most Spartans must have distrusted him and must have felt hostility towards him because of his Peloponnesian policy during the period after the Peace of Nicias. There were, however, obvious advantages in being able to consult a man who possessed an intimate knowledge both of Athenian policies in Greece and of Athenian aims in the west (cf. 93. 1); they were perfectly free to reject any advice that he might offer and to disbelieve any information that he might give. A meeting of the assembly was held at which the Syracusans, the Corinthians and Alcibiades all tried to rouse the Spartans to action (88. 10). Thucydides has chosen to report only what Alcibiades said (89–92).

The speech of Alcibiades at Sparta is among the most remarkable and most brilliant of Thucydidean speeches. It is, in a sense, the antithesis of the Funeral Speech; whereas the Funeral Speech portrays the way of life and the ideals of a whole city, this speech portrays the personality of an individual. A considerable part of it is devoted to self-justification, which is here virtually equivalent to self-revelation. Alcibiades embarks at once, without any formal introduction, upon an attempt to allay the suspicion to which his political record at Athens naturally exposed him when addressing a Spartan audience. His policy of trying to weaken Spartan authority in the Peloponnese had, he argues, been forced upon him by the Spartans themselves, who had slighted him by rejecting his offers of help and by negotiating with his enemies (89. 1–3). He also claims that his audience ought not to be prejudiced against him because he had been a democratic leader. His family had attained the leadership of the democracy through opposing tyranny. Neither he nor they were demagogues; they did not subscribe to the principles of democracy, about which they had no illusions, but had sought advancement under a democratic constitution because it was firmly established and could not safely be altered while Athens was threatened by enemies (89. 3–6). His frankness, though doubtless deliberately disarming, is very striking: he assumes that it was natural for a politician to subordinate his principles, and even the interests of his own city, to the pursuit of personal ambition.

Almost more striking is the effrontery of his self-defence, in a celebrated passage towards the end of the speech (92. 2–4), against the charge, which would inevitably be brought against him, that in offering advice and assistance to Sparta he was guilty of betraying his native city. It must have drawn a gasp from such Spartans as were able to understand it. Using the methods of argument practised in the intellectual circles at Athens to which he had belonged, he defines as a true patriot 'not the man who, when unjustly deprived of his country, does not attack it but the man who because of his longing for it tries by every means to regain it' (92. 4). The upshot of his outrageous reasoning is that, because the Athenians had wronged him and caused him to become an exile, he was fully justified in making every effort to injure them and aid their enemies. In the actual speech of which

Thucydides here gives a summary, Alcibiades must certainly have sought to allay Spartan mistrust by a defence of his past and present conduct. If, however, Thucydides had been interested only in the effect of the speech on Spartan policy, he could have reproduced the substance of this self-defence in a few words or omitted it altogether. He may have chosen to dwell upon it partly because it illustrates the decay of moral standards, which was a consequence of the war, and the perversions of language to which this decay gave rise,[1] a subject in which he shows much interest in the first half of the *History*. His principal reason, however, must surely have been that this self-defence throws so much light upon the personality of Alcibiades, whose novel and characteristically self-interested attitude towards his own exile suddenly began to influence the situation in Sicily and in Greece.

The central part of the speech contains what the audience must have been most eager to hear. Alcibiades first describes Athenian plans for conquest in the west and subsequently in Greece (90. 2–91. 1). He goes on to declare that the Siceliots could prevail if united, but that Syracuse could not survive alone and that, if it fell, all Sicily, and soon afterwards Italy as well, would be lost (91. 2–3). He then recommends measures designed to thwart the Athenians, namely direct intervention by Sparta in Sicily by sending both military aid and, more important, a commander-in-chief, as well as diversionary action at home by openly attacking the Athenians and occupying Decelea (91. 4–7). Even in this part of the speech, which is less concerned with Alcibiades himself, almost every sentence bears the distinctive stamp of his personality. He stresses his special qualifications to give full and accurate information (90. 1; 91. 1) and also declares his confidence that his recommendations are feasible (92. 1). His outline of Athenian aims, though doubtless he makes the most of them in order to reinforce his plea for Spartan action, reproduces his own very sanguine assessment of what the Athenians might expect to gain

---

[1] Finley, 229–32, who cites 3. 82. 4. Much of the third book is concerned with the deterioration of accepted standards, cf. Gomme (1), II, 385–6.

by undertaking the expedition to Sicily (cf. 15. 2; 18. 4) and ignores the views of his opponents.[1]

The report of Thucydides on these consultations at Sparta has been criticised by some modern scholars, who have accused him of representing the speech of Alcibiades as more original in its recommendations and more effective in evoking Spartan action than it actually was.[2] This criticism is perhaps a natural reaction to his tendency in the second half of his *History* to attach so much importance to the influence of leading individuals; but there is no reason to find him guilty of serious misrepresentation here.[3] It is true that the Syracusan and Corinthian envoys, whose speeches are not recorded, undoubtedly appealed to Sparta for aid in Sicily (88. 10) and may perhaps have pleaded almost as persuasively and effectively as Alcibiades. It is, however, nowhere attested, and indeed not very likely, that anyone except himself proposed that a leading Spartan should be sent out to organise the defence of Sicily;[4] and the arrival of Gylippus undoubtedly proved a turning point in the situation there. It is also true that the permanent occupation of a fortified base in Attica had been mooted long ago (1. 122. 1; 5. 17. 2) and that the Spartans did not seize Decelea at once but more than a year later (7. 19. 1), after the Athenians had meanwhile provided a *casus belli* by openly attacking Laconia (6. 105. 2). Here the most valuable contribution made by Alcibiades probably lay in specifying Decelea, in preference to any other position in the mountains of Attica, as the most

---

[1] He is not being strictly truthful when he states (91. 1) that his former colleagues in Sicily were committed to the execution of his programme, cf. Hatzfeld, 210, with n. 1.

[2] Brunt, 71–2; Hatzfeld, 211–13.

[3] This case seems to me to be totally different from that of the passage describing the negotiations in the Athenian assembly in 420, where there are grounds for believing that he has exaggerated the influence of Alcibiades (see above, 214–15).

[4] The Syracusan envoys were probably reluctant to admit the need for a commander-in-chief from Greece, while the Corinthians may have felt that, because of their links with Syracuse, anyone sent out to take command ought to be a Corinthian. The Spartans themselves can hardly have been sufficiently well-informed to appreciate the deficiencies of organisation in Siceliot resistance to the Athenians.

suitable site for the establishment of an ἐπιτειχισμός. It is most unlikely that the Spartans had reached even a provisional decision on the location of their projected base, and the advice of a former Athenian general, who had taken part in secret discussions at Athens about defensive strategy, must have been particularly welcome. The length of the interval between the debate at Sparta in the winter of 415/14 and the occupation of Decelea in the spring of 413 appears at first sight to suggest that the account of Thucydides is inaccurate in one respect. If the Spartans seized Decelea because of the advice of Alcibiades offered immediately after his arrival, they acted with quite remarkable slowness, even by Spartan standards. It is indeed conceivable that he did not recommend the occupation of Decelea at his first appearance before the Spartan assembly, and that Thucydides, who naturally wished to avoid including more than one speech by Alcibiades at Sparta, has incorporated in his summary one piece of advice given at various later dates (cf. 7. 18. 1).[1] Although some Thucydidean speeches may well reproduce the substance of what a speaker said on several separate occasions, it is unnecessary to suppose that this is one of them. There is a simpler and more convincing explanation of the apparent difficulty. Thucydides does not state that the Spartans accepted at once the advice of Alcibiades to occupy Decelea, but only that 'they now began to direct their attention' towards this project (6. 93. 2). It was indeed a formidable undertaking upon which they could not, and did not, embark lightly.[2] They had no experience of operating an ἐπιτειχισμός, and many of them must have doubted whether it would prove effective. It demanded long preparation and substantial effort (7. 18. 4), involving much expense and the need to secure the co-operation of the Boeotians and other allies. It could be attempted only in conjunction with an invasion of Attica, which required a general levy of contingents from all the members of the Peloponnesian

---

[1] This is the explanation of Wilamowitz, *Hermes*, LX (1925), 299–300, cf. de Romilly (Budé), VI–VII, *Notice* xxxiv and (2) 67.

[2] F. E. Adcock, *C.R.* LXI (1947), 3–4, draws attention to the difficulties of the operation.

League, and the Spartans had discovered long ago that to mobilise the League army at any time of year other than the spring presented very great difficulties (3. 15. 1–16. 2). Even if they were willing to commit themselves to an open breach with Athens, it was very doubtful whether they could complete their preparation in time to establish an ἐπιτειχισμός in the spring of 414, and their next opportunity was in the following spring. Hence it is likely that Alcibiades did, immediately after his arrival at Sparta, urge the Spartans to occupy Decelea and that they were impressed and influenced by his recommendation, but that because of practical difficulties they were for a long time unable to implement it.

For all these reasons the account of Thucydides may be accepted as substantially true. The speech of Alcibiades at Sparta was crucial, and Thucydides has not exaggerated its influence upon the course of events in Sicily and in Greece. Before Alcibiades spoke, the Spartans were inclined to send an embassy to Sicily to dissuade the Syracusans from coming to terms with the Athenians, but were disinclined to send aid (6. 88. 10); they were also contemplating an invasion of Attica but seem to have had no real intention of putting this plan into operation (93. 1). After he spoke, their attitude was fundamentally altered (93. 2).[1] They were converted largely because he was obviously so well qualified to offer them good advice (93. 1). Thereafter he continued his efforts to encourage them to take action (7. 18. 1), and he must also have occupied himself, as always, in intrigues designed to promote his own interests. It is not, however, until after the Athenian disaster in Sicily that his diplomatic activities receive further mention from Thucydides.

---

[1] Thucydides does not apparently intend to draw a distinction between the views of 'the ephors and officials' (88. 10) and those of 'the Lacedaemonians' (93. 1). If any such distinction had been intended, it would surely have been more clearly marked.

4. *Assistance to Sparta (second phase)*

The eighth book of Thucydides is packed with reports of secret negotiations and intrigues. He seems to have wished to suggest that their influence upon the course of the war was at least as great as that of military operations, which were mostly on a small scale or inconclusive. In many of these diplomatic exchanges Alcibiades played a part; in some he was the leading figure. Full and circumstantial accounts are given in most instances; they prompt the reader to feel that Thucydides has been remarkably fortunate in having obtained so much information about details known at the time only to the few persons who were present. For this reason some scholars have suggested that parts of the eighth book are based upon information derived directly from Alcibiades.[1] There are chronological objections to the suggestion that Alcibiades was himself the informant of Thucydides: the eighth book, which is so clearly an unrevised draft, was very probably written soon after the events recorded in it, and the two men are not likely to have met while Alcibiades was serving Athens as general and Thucydides was an exile.[2] On the other

[1] The idea is certainly not much less than a century old and may well be older. T. Fellner, *Forschung und Darstellungsweise des Thukydides* (*Untersuchungen aus der alten Geschichte*, II, Wien, 1880), 67–74, maintains that Thucydides derived from Alcibiades some information contained in the eighth book, including the substance of 45–6 and 56. M. Büdinger, *Poesie und Urkunde bei Thukydides* (*Denkschrift d. Wiener Akad. d. Wissenschaften*, Phil.-Hist. Cl. XXXIX, 1891, 3), 10–15, goes further and suggests that Thucydides was able to consult Alcibiades in Thrace in the closing years of the war. See also T. R. Glover, *From Pericles to Philip* (1919), 69 n. 5. Brunt, 65–96, who maintains that Alcibiades was the informant of Thucydides for all the episodes in which he was involved, including those in the fifth and sixth books, makes out a good case, but wisely does not claim that it is conclusive. Delebecque, 73–241, tries to prove much the same thesis by minute analysis of the narrative, but this attempt, though most ingenious, is not altogether convincing, cf. my review in *C.R.* XVII (1967), 24–6.

[2] Cf A. Andrewes, *Historia*, X (1961), 11 n. 28. Adcock, 85–8, believes that Thucydides finished the eighth book not later than 410 when too close to the events to have had a clear view of them; he considers that a meeting with Alcibiades could well have taken place by 410.

hand, Thucydides may well have had an opportunity, soon after 411, of consulting someone who had been closely associated with Alcibiades and had enjoyed his confidence. When Alcibiades was recalled from Sicily in 415 to stand his trial, an unspecified number of Athenians, doubtless including some who were on intimate terms with him, were also recalled for trial and accompanied him to Sparta.[1] At least some of these were apparently still with him in Asia in 411 (8. 97. 3); but they did not necessarily remain with him throughout his period of service as general until 406, especially as they were no longer outlaws (*ibid.*). If Thucydides obtained information from one, or more than one, of them, it would inevitably give prominence to Alcibiades and reflect his point of view. It is not the practice of Thucydides to disclose his sources, and his method of composition is such that any attempt to identify them is necessarily speculative. In the eighth book, however, because the process of integrating his material is so obviously incomplete, such attempts are perhaps somewhat less hazardous than elsewhere. There are good reasons for believing in the existence of what will hereafter be called his Alcibiadean source, though to define exactly which passages are, and which passages are not, based upon it does not seem to be feasible.

While Thucydides probably had the good fortune to obtain full and reliable information about negotiations in which Alcibiades was involved, the eighth book does not appear to exaggerate his achievements or his influence upon the course of events, except perhaps here and there to a very limited degree. It is certainly not the habit of Thucydides merely to echo the judgements of his informants; he forms his own judgements on the basis of evidence supplied to him. Alcibiades is not in the foreground throughout the eighth book, and his failures are not

[1] 6. 53. 1; 61. 4-7; 88. 9. Among these were probably Axiochus, his uncle, and Adeimantus, a fellow demesman, who were denounced with him (Andoc. 1. 16); unfortunately there is no evidence that either served in Sicily. When communicating with the Athenian base at Samos (8. 47. 2; 50. 4; 51. 1-2), Alcibiades may well have made use of Athenian exiles with him at the court of Tissaphernes.

disguised or excused. At some points information is lacking about his relations with others, which may well have been known to Thucydides, and his actions are attributed to self-interest to an extent that even he would hardly have acknowledged. It is true that he displayed unusual qualities of intellect and imagination, qualities of a kind that Thucydides found absorbingly interesting. There is, however, every reason to believe that he is prominent in the eighth book because he did in fact play a vitally important role.

Among the secret negotiations and intrigues described in detail by Thucydides are those leading to the first revolts in the Athenian empire shortly after the disaster in Sicily (8. 5–14). Alcibiades, reappearing in the *History* after a long interval, very soon becomes a leading figure in a complex series of developments. The first appeals for Spartan aid in support of Athenian allies wishing to revolt came from Euboea and Lesbos and were addressed to Agis at Decelea (5. 1–3). Envoys from Chios and Erythrae made a similar appeal not to Agis but direct to Sparta, and they were accompanied by a representative from Tissaphernes, who promised financial subsidies (5. 4–5). There also arrived at Sparta two Greek exiles sent by Pharnabazus to urge the Spartans to support revolts in the Hellespont (6. 1). It was through the agency of Alcibiades, who had the advantage of close friendship with Endius, one of the ephors, that the Spartans accepted the proposals of the Chians and Tissaphernes. The influence of Alcibiades seems to have been the decisive factor (6. 3). His motives, though not explained at this point, become clear from the subsequent narrative, as will be seen below. Later a meeting of the allies at Corinth resolved to mobilise a Peloponnesian fleet and send it to Chios, but, presumably in deference to the feelings of Agis and of the other applicants for assistance, the fleet was to sail on from Chios to Lesbos and thence to the Hellespont (8. 2).[1] Implementation of this plan was delayed by a series of setbacks, most of them avoidable, which suggest that the Peloponnesians were guilty of

---

[1] This decision is consistent with the optimistic feeling throughout the Greek world that Athenian power would at once collapse (2. 1–4).

gross incompetence (6. 5; 8. 3–11. 3). Most of the fleet destined for Ionia was blockaded by the Athenians near the Isthmus, and the Spartans were so disheartened that they were inclined to abandon the whole enterprise; but they were dissuaded by the arguments of Alcibiades, who induced them to send Chalcideus and himself with the small Spartan contingent of five ships to Ionia, where he confidently expected to cause widespread revolts (11. 3–12. 1). He also appealed in a private conversation to the self-interest of his friend Endius: if the expedition brought about the revolt of Ionia and won Persia as an ally, the credit for these achievements would be reaped by Endius himself and not by Agis. Thucydides adds that there was enmity at this time between Alcibiades and Agis (12. 2, ἐτύγχανε γὰρ τῷ Ἄγιδι αὐτὸς διάφορος ὤν).[1]

At this point the personal aims of Alcibiades begin to emerge, and they become clearer as the narrative proceeds (cf. 17. 2). He saw in this situation an opportunity to regain his lost status as an influential figure in the Greek world, and he was determined to seize it. He was in contact with prominent Milesians some time before Miletus revolted (17. 2), and there is some evidence that he had long-standing ties with Ionian aristocracies.[2] It was thus probably at his instigation that the envoys from Ionia, unlike those from Lesbos, were sent to Sparta and not to Agis at Decelea. Thucydides defines with unusual emphasis the extent of the personal power and independent authority exercised by Agis (5. 3). Even when it was agreed to give precedence to the appeal from Ionia (8. 2) the allied fleet assembled at the Isthmus remained under his control (9. 1; 11. 2), and he evidently intended that whatever success it might attain in Asia should be credited mainly to himself (12. 2). Alcibiades must have felt that, if his enemy were to be the principal sponsor and organiser of the attempt to destroy the Athenian empire, he himself had no hope of being allowed to play any part whatever in the execution of this design. If, on the

---

[1] The subject of this parenthesis is undoubtedly Alcibiades (cf. 45. 1) and not Endius (as is maintained by Steup, n. *ad loc.*).

[2] H. Schaefer, *Würzb. Jahrb.* IV (1949/50), 287–96.

other hand, he could convince the ephors that he, with his flair for diplomacy and his unrivalled knowledge of the Athenian empire (12. 1), was admirably qualified to promote their interests in Asia, he might hope to make himself the virtual director of the whole enterprise. Although it was an unforeseen stroke of good fortune for him that the Peloponnesian ships were blockaded at the Isthmus, he played his hand with great skill, and his private approach to Endius was a characteristically adroit move.[1] Thucydides does not record this series of events from the viewpoint of Alcibiades, since he is not writing biography; nor does he dwell upon the personal aspirations of Alcibiades. He evidently felt, however, that he must draw attention to them because he believed, with good reason, that they constituted an important factor in the development of the war at this stage.

The success of Alcibiades and Chalcideus in instigating revolt at Chios, and soon afterwards at Erythrae and Clazomenae, must be counted a remarkable achievement, especially as they were handicapped by having brought with them only an insignificant number of ships and apparently no financial aid. Their plans were skilfully prepared and executed. Their voyage across the Aegean was completed with speed and secrecy, and before they reached Chios they conferred with some Chian conspirators at a point on the mainland (12. 3; 14. 1). The mass of the population was taken aback and thoroughly bewildered by their unexpected arrival, but they had arranged with oligarchs in league with them that the Boule should be assembling for a meeting, and they both addressed it. The Chians were told that a large fleet was coming from Greece but not that most of it was blockaded at the Isthmus (14. 2). Chalcideus was evidently no Brasidas, and his function on this mission seems to have been almost wholly military;[2] diplom-

---

[1] Cf. my discussion of these developments in *J.H.S.* LVIII (1938), 38–9.

[2] Cf. 16. 1; 19. 2; 24. 1. His name, and not that of Alcibiades, is associated with the first treaty between Sparta and Persia (17. 4; 36. 2; 43. 3) because Alcibiades cannot have been invested with official authority to conclude an agreement in the name of the Spartan state. The difference in status between Chalcideus and Alcibiades is clear from 11. 3.

atic activities must have been largely in the hands of Alcibiades, who was a tried expert in this field. Thucydides surely intends his readers to infer that the bluff and deception required to bolster up a rather weak case were supplied by Alcibiades. The Chians were convinced; indeed they threw themselves with great enthusiasm into the struggle for the liberation of Ionia, encouraging others to follow their lead (19. 1; 22. 1). Thucydides later defends them against charges of foolhardiness to which they were evidently subjected when they were on the verge of having to surrender. In this passage (24. 5), which is a remarkable one, he seems to mean that their decision, though it proved to be an error of judgement, was justifiable on the basis of the evidence at their disposal.

For a time the cause of the rebels made good progress. Teos revolted (16), and then Chalcideus and Alcibiades gained another striking success by winning Miletus (17. 1-3). Again there is evidence of careful planning and of swift and secret action whereby Athenian efforts to prevent the revolt were narrowly forestalled. At this point Thucydides makes a most revealing though somewhat clumsy statement about the aims of Alcibiades, which helps to explain his earlier policy. He is reported to have been eager to gain Miletus before the arrival of the large fleet soon expected from the Peloponnese, his intention being 'to secure for the Chians and himself and Chalcideus and Endius, who had sent him out, in accordance with his promise the prestige for having caused as many cities as possible to revolt supported only by the Chian forces and Chalcideus' (17. 2). If he was afraid that the Peloponnesian fleet would receive its orders from Agis, his fears proved groundless: there is no evidence that Agis exerted any influence upon the direction of the war outside Attica after the first revolts in Asia (cf. 60. 2). It was, however, vital to the interests of Alcibiades that Astyochus, who was being sent from Sparta as *nauarchos* to assume command of the Peloponnesian and allied forces in Asia (20. 1), should not be allowed to steal all the credit for winning Ionia for the Peloponnesian cause. It was for this reason that no time must be lost in securing the revolt of

Miletus. An almost more impressive success achieved while Chalcideus and Alcibiades were still in charge of Spartan interests in Asia was the conclusion of the first treaty between Sparta and Persia, which was negotiated with Tissaphernes (17. 4–18).

Thereafter the situation began to deteriorate. More revolts took place through the efforts of the Chians, but that of Lesbos (22) was at once crushed by swift and vigorous action on the part of the Athenians, who also recovered Clazomenae (23). Chalcideus was killed in a skirmish, and Chios, as has already been mentioned, was so hard pressed that it was almost reduced to surrender (24). Finally Athenian forces won a victory outside Miletus and were preparing to build a blockading wall there when the long-awaited Peloponnesian fleet, which amounted to fifty-nine ships including a squadron from Sicily, sailed into the nearby Gulf of Iasus (25–6). Alcibiades, who had fought in the battle, rode out to report to the commanders of the fleet the dangerous situation arising from the defeat at Miletus, and he urged them to hasten thither to rescue the city from being blockaded (26. 3).

There is no suggestion in the account of this episode that Alcibiades had as yet incurred any suspicion of disloyalty to the Peloponnesians. He seems, on the contrary, to have made most strenuous efforts in their interests, even though his own status was likely to be adversely affected by the arrival of their fleet. When, however, he next appears in the *History*, Thucydides mentions that he was 'suspected by the Peloponnesians after the death of Chalcideus and the battle at Miletus' and that a dispatch was sent to Astyochus from Sparta instructing him to put Alcibiades to death (45. 1). Astyochus, however, does not appear to have been at Miletus when this order was issued;[1] he had sailed to Asia with a small squadron before the main fleet was ready, but he

[1] His arrival there is reported in 36. 1, but 45. 1 shows that there is a chronological overlap between the account of the negotiations at the court of Tissaphernes, which begins at that point, and the preceding narrative, which is concerned mainly with the development of the military situation. The problems arising from the peculiar structure of the eighth book cannot be discussed here.

proceeded first to Chios (23. 1), where he was detained by a series of events which will be discussed in a later chapter,[1] and he was very probably still there at this time. It was doubtless for that reason that Alcibiades was forewarned of the order for his execution[2] and was able to escape to the court of Tissaphernes. Thucydides does not specify the charges against Alcibiades, much less express any opinion about their validity. He does, however, make clear that it was Peloponnesians serving in Asia who became suspicious of Alcibiades and that their complaints evoked the order sent to Astyochus.[3] A parenthesis—ἦν γὰρ καὶ τῷ Ἄγιδι ἐχθρὸς καὶ ἄλλως ἄπιστος ἐφαίνετο—explains why the reaction from Sparta to these complaints was so drastic.[4] Peloponnesians on both sides of the Aegean must have been bitterly disappointed that their efforts to bring about the collapse of Athenian power had not made more progress. They were doubtless very willing to find a scapegoat in Alcibiades, who had, they could argue, misled them by exaggerating Athenian weakness and underestimating the difficulties of their task (cf. 12. 1).

There is, on the other hand, some reason to believe that their suspicions of Alcibiades were not without foundation. The statement of Thucydides that he was suspected 'after the death of Chalcideus and the battle at Miletus' should be linked with an earlier statement, which has already been discussed, that he wished to gain as much credit as possible for himself and his collaborators before the Peloponnesian fleet arrived (17. 2). Deprived of his partner

[1] See below, 292–5.
[2] According to Plutarch (*Alcib.* 24. 4), he took good care, while still collaborating with the Spartans, not to put himself in their hands because he had learned of this order. Hence he seems for some time to have been playing a double game.
[3] Cf. Hatzfeld, 225 n. 7, whose interpretation of τοῖς Πελοποννησίοις and ἀπ' αὐτῶν in 45. 1 is convincing.
[4] A new board of ephors was now in office, and its members may have been unsympathetic towards Alcibiades. Endius, who had been largely responsible for sending him to Ionia (see above, 234) can hardly have been one of them, since it is most unlikely that anyone was permitted to serve as ephor in two consecutive years, cf. U. Kahrstedt, *Griech. Staatsrecht*, I (1922), 162. Some Spartans may have already felt that the treaty concluded with Tissaphernes had made excessive concesssions to Persia (36. 2, cf. 43. 3–4).

Chalcideus, he could not hope to influence to the same extent the newly arrived commanders, to whom he was not likely to be *persona grata*, and he might soon find himself relegated to a subordinate position or discarded altogether. Accordingly he may well have turned his thoughts in another direction where he saw better prospects of serving his own interests. When eventually he fled to the court of Tissaphernes, he must have been confident that he would find security there and would not be handed over to the Peloponnesians; he could surely, if necessary, have found some other refuge. There is no evidence of contact between him and Tissaphernes before the battle at Miletus (26. 3), but it is likely that they met somewhat earlier when the first treaty with Persia was being negotiated (17. 4). Tissaphernes doubtless welcomed opportunities to consult a man who had a flair for intrigue equal to his own and also an expert knowledge of Greek politics. Alcibiades probably saw the potential advantages to himself offered by this contact and may well have visited Tissaphernes several times, ostensibly as the agent of the Peloponnesians. Hence he may already have been paving the way for a closer association between himself and Tissaphernes, thereby evoking from the Peloponnesians justifiable suspicions that he was playing them false.[1]

It is strange that Thucydides does not state more explicitly the reasons for the breach between Alcibiades and the Peloponnesians and for his flight to Tissaphernes. Possibly he was unable to obtain trustworthy evidence, but this explanation is not easily reconcilable with the fact that he is so remarkably well-informed about the intricate series of negotiations which began immediately after the flight of Alcibiades. Perhaps Thucydides chose to regard this breach with the Peloponnesians as a personal matter, the outcome of solicitude on the part of Alcibiades for his own

---

[1] It could have been in collusion with Alcibiades that Tissaphernes persuaded (28. 2, πείθει) the Peloponnesians to use their forces against the Persian rebel Amorges at Iasus. Although the capture of Iasus was financially profitable to them (cf. 36. 1), some of them may have considered this expedition to have involved a waste of time and effort (28. 2–4).

interests and his own safety, whereas the diplomatic activities in which Tissaphernes was involved materially influenced the course of the war.

5. At the court of Tissaphernes

The account of the ensuing diplomatic moves and of their consequences is dominated by Alcibiades to an extent that is very exceptional.[1] It begins with a long passage of *oratio obliqua* giving the substance of his recommendations to Tissaphernes on relations with the Greeks generally (45. 2–46. 4). This passage, like others in the eighth book, is somewhat clumsy and lacking in clarity. The main theme is interrupted by a report of what Alcibiades, acting on behalf of Tissaphernes, said to representatives of Greek cities asking for money (45. 4–6); but this reply to their requests is consistent with his advice to Tissaphernes and helps to explain it. Financial economy is the leading motive of the policy which he urges the satrap to adopt. It appears that, at any rate by Persian standards, Tissaphernes was genuinely in some financial embarrassment (5. 5; 45. 6): the Persian monarchy still regarded the Greeks as a potential source of revenue and had not yet learned to use its wealth to bring political pressure to bear on them. There is, however, at least some hint that Tissaphernes was inclined to be miserly and that Alcibiades was acute enough to detect this weakness and exploit it for his own advantage.[2] He urged Tissaphernes to reduce the subsidy paid to the Peloponnesian crews, bribing their officers in order to stifle protests (45. 2–3). He insisted that it was contrary to the interests of the Persians to help either Sparta or Athens to gain a quick victory, because in that event they would find themselves involved in a costly and dangerous conflict against the victor; a cheaper and safer policy

---

[1] Details of secret consultations described so fully in 45–56 can have been obtained, directly or indirectly, only from a person, or persons, who attended them. This part of the eighth book is more likely than any other to be dependent on information derived from Alcibiades himself or someone closely associated with him.

[2] Delebecque, 83.

would be to allow the two combatants to exhaust one another (46. 1–2). He then advanced some shrewd arguments showing why it would be more profitable to the Persians to co-operate, to the limited extent which he had explained, with the Athenians than with the Peloponnesians (46. 3–4).

Tissaphernes was evidently too wily to divulge his real feelings about this advice. Thucydides does not claim to possess reliable evidence about them but infers that they were mainly favourable from the actions of the satrap, who by his increasing reluctance to aid the Peloponnesians began to undermine the efficiency of their naval forces (46. 5). On the other hand, the real aims of Alcibiades, who certainly cannot have disclosed them in his conversations with Tissaphernes, are fully known to Thucydides and are defined without any reservation. The main purpose of his recommendations was to pave the way for his own return to Athens, and he believed that his best prospect of attaining this end was by showing that he had enough influence with Tissaphernes to persuade him to support the Athenians (47. 1–2). He had no confidence at this stage that the Athenian democracy would consent to his return even as a recompense for securing Persian aid.[1] He was, however, as well-informed as ever about the secret plans of others, and he had learned that some Athenian officers at Samos belonging to the upper classes were plotting to overthrow the democracy. He entered into negotiations with these conspirators and provided them with a powerful incentive to put their scheme into operation by leading them to believe that, if an oligarchy were to be established and he were to be restored, he could gain for them the support first of Tissaphernes and then of the Persian king (47. 2–48. 2). Even the Athenian rank and file at Samos, though disapproving of proposals involving constitutional change, took no steps to scotch the conspiracy at the outset because the prospect of Persian subsidies was so attractive. Vigorous opposition came only from Phrynichus, one of the

[1] The initial reaction of the assembly reported in 53. 2 (cf. 54. 1) suggests that he was right.

Athenian generals, who tried to convince the promoters of the scheme that the proposals of Alcibiades would not benefit Athens at all.

The substance of the objections put forward by Phrynichus is reported by Thucydides in a passage of *oratio obliqua* (48. 4–6) consisting mainly of arguments designed to refute those used by Alcibiades at the court of Tissaphernes. This speech of Phrynichus may thus be deemed to form an antilogy with that of Alcibiades, since the pair of speeches, though not delivered at the same time or place, is used to elucidate a complicated situation by presenting the reader with opposing points of view. Thucydides would not, it seems, have written extended versions of these speeches if he had revised the eighth book: he normally reports conferences between a few persons in *oratio obliqua*,[1] confining his use of *oratio recta* mostly to public debates.[2] It is, however, clear that he welcomes the opportunity to contrast two leading individuals pursuing basically contrary policies; this is a feature of his working method which is especially marked in the second half of the *History*. To him Phrynichus, whom he credits elsewhere with shrewdness of judgement (27. 5) and steadfastness in the face of danger (68. 3), certainly seemed a worthy opponent for Alcibiades. He explicitly endorses the first and most important point in the speech of Phrynichus,[3] namely that it was immaterial to Alcibiades whether Athens was governed by an oligarchy or a democracy and that his sole object in inciting revolution was to secure his own return. Phrynichus goes on to assert that Athens must at all costs avoid internal dissension, and he denies that it would be more beneficial for the Persians to give support to the Athenians than to the Peloponnesians (48. 4). He concludes by forecasting the reaction of the allied cities in the Athenian empire, claiming that he had entirely reliable knowledge of their views. What they wanted was freedom; they would be even more dis-

---

[1] Cf. the discussions among the Athenian generals in Sicily, 6. 47–9 and 7. 47–9.

[2] One exception is the brief speech of the Elean Teutiaplus at a meeting of trierarchs (3. 30; see above, 143).

[3] 48. 4, ὅπερ καὶ ἦν, cf. 47. 1.

trustful of an oligarchy than they were of democracy, and their disloyalty towards Athens was likely to be intensified by the establishment of an oligarchy (48. 5–7). That Thucydides believed Phrynichus to have been proved right about the reaction of the allies is confirmed by a later passage in which, writing of the period when the oligarchy was in power, he expresses much the same sentiments as his own opinion (64. 5, δοκεῖν δέ μοι). It is noteworthy that Thucydides implies, and even expresses, approval of the opinions voiced by Phrynichus in this speech. In a section of his work where the influence of Alcibiades is more plainly traceable than anywhere else, Thucydides shows himself to be as independent as ever in forming his own judgements, which he is at pains to convey to the reader; he follows his normal practice of refusing to reproduce uncritically the viewpoint of his informants.

Although the arguments of Phrynichus impressed Thucydides, they failed to deter the Athenian oligarchs at Samos from proceeding with their scheme. A mission led by Peisander was sent to Athens charged with the task of trying to win the support of Tissaphernes by securing the recall of Alcibiades and the overthrow of the democracy (49). Phrynichus, however, did not abandon his efforts. Alarmed by the prospect that the envoys from Samos would persuade the Athenians to recall Alcibiades, he embarked on a remarkably bold plan, which led to the following series of secret moves (50–1). He sent a message to the Spartan admiral Astyochus to inform him that Alcibiades was attempting to negotiate an agreement between Tissaphernes and the Athenians. Thereupon Astyochus went in person to confer with Tissaphernes and Alcibiades at Magnesia, where he disclosed to them the substance of the message from Phrynichus. Alcibiades at once informed the Athenians at Samos, demanding the execution of Phrynichus for treason (50. 2–4). The next move by Phrynichus was to communicate again with Astyochus reproaching him for his breach of confidence but now offering to betray to him the Athenian base at Samos with all the forces stationed there.

Astyochus acted as before and passed on this message also to Alcibiades (50. 5). Learning that Alcibiades was on the point of again communicating to the Athenians at Samos information received from Astyochus, Phrynichus forestalled him by announcing to them that, according to irrefutable reports in his possession, the Peloponnesians intended to attack their base at Samos while it remained unfortified. He gave orders for the fortifications to be completed with all speed and for preparations to be made to meet an attack (51. 1). The consequence was that, when a second message from Alcibiades reached Samos accusing Phrynichus of trying to betray the Athenian base there, this further charge of treason was dismissed as a calumny concocted by Alcibiades in order to ruin a personal enemy. The announcement by Phrynichus that an enemy attack was expected was believed to have been confirmed (51. 2–3).

In his account of this episode, which verges on melodrama, Thucydides continues to give the personal rivalry between Alcibiades and Phrynichus as much prominence as in the preceding chapters, where he creates an antilogy from their opposing points of view. The episode is presented as a battle of wits between two practised intriguers playing for high stakes and pursuing their private interests with relentless determination and infinite subtlety.[1] While the aim of Alcibiades was doubtless purely selfish, namely to remove every obstacle likely to hinder his recall, the motives of Phrynichus were not, it seems, so exclusively personal as they would appear at first sight to have been. Three factors have caused the personal element underlying the manœuvres of Phrynichus to be overstressed. In the first place, it was essential for him, if his plan were to succeed, to convince Astyochus that he was prepared to betray the Athenians because of the personal danger in which he found himself. Hence in both messages to Astyochus, as reported by Thucydides, he seeks to justify treasonable action on grounds of self-interest (50. 2 and 5). Secondly, information about the course of these intrigues, which

---

[1] I have examined the episode in some detail in *J.H.S.* LXXVI (1956), 99–104.

cannot have been widely known, must surely have been communicated to Thucydides either by Alcibiades himself or by some associate who was present with him at Magnesia when Astyochus visited Tissaphernes there;[1] and it was natural for Alcibiades to interpret the actions of Phrynichus in the worst possible light. The third and most important factor is that Thucydides, as has been already mentioned, is evidently disposed to underline the personal rivalry between Alcibiades and Phrynichus.

It is clear that, if Astyochus on receiving the first message from Phrynichus had taken action against Alcibiades for betraying Spartan interests, the whole elaborate scheme, so vigorously opposed by Phrynichus, in which Alcibiades was to act as the link between the Athenian oligarchs and Tissaphernes, would have been irreparably ruined.[2] Hence it is at least arguable that the principal aim of Phrynichus was not so much to get rid of Alcibiades, though this prospect undoubtedly attracted him, but rather to benefit the Athenians by frustrating a plan which, in his opinion, would be disastrous to their interests. His first message proved abortive because of his ignorance that Alcibiades had fled to Tissaphernes and was no longer in reach of Astyochus, who had in fact received an order from Sparta to put him to death (45. 1).[3] The object of Phrynichus in sending his second message is more obscure, but it is difficult to believe that he really intended to betray the Athenian base at Samos. If his sole concern at this stage was for his own safety, as Thucydides seems to imply (50. 5), he could have adopted the more normal course of fleeing into exile. An attempt to win Spartan favour by betraying his fellow-citizens was bound to be a most hazardous undertaking for him, and the recent breach between Alcibiades and the Spartans, which

[1] See above, 240 n. 1 (cf. Brunt, 77).
[2] Cf. 53. 3, where Peisander, addressing the Athenian assembly, declares that Alcibiades is the only person in the world (μόνος τῶν νῦν) who can bring about the conclusion of an agreement with the Persians.
[3] That Phrynichus mistakenly believed Alcibiades to be still at Miletus is not explicitly stated by Thucydides, but may be inferred from 50. 3.

was now known to him, was hardly likely to improve its prospects. His real aim may well have been not only to clear himself from the charge of communicating with the enemy but also to secure military advantages for the Athenians. If Astyochus, who had hitherto shown somewhat excessive caution, could be lured into attacking the Athenians in the belief that he would take them by surprise when in fact they were fully prepared, the Peloponnesians might well be crushingly defeated. Hence here again Phrynichus probably had Athenian interests at heart.

Since Astyochus did not choose to take the offensive against Samos and since Phrynichus was successful in evading suspicion, this strange episode does not appear to have had much effect upon the situation in Asia. It may, however, have had an important result which even the subtle Phrynichus can hardly have planned, a result not mentioned in the narrative of Thucydides, perhaps because the attention of the reader is directed almost entirely to the personal duel between Phrynichus and Alcibiades.[1] Tissaphernes must have realised from what Astyochus told him that Alcibiades had gone further than the actual circumstances warranted in leading the Athenian oligarchs to imagine that he could obtain Persian support for them. This discovery must surely have caused Tissaphernes some uneasiness, and his ultimate decision to reject the Athenian overtures (56. 3) may well have been influenced by it.[2] At all events, the account of this episode by Thucydides is probably one in which his habit of stressing, even overstressing, the contrast between opposing leaders has tended to

[1] 68. 3 provides a further indication that Thucydides has somewhat exaggerated the importance of their rivalry. In this passage the decision of Phrynichus to support the Four Hundred is attributed to his fear of Alcibiades, who knew of his intrigues with Astyochus but was unlikely to be recalled while an oligarchy was in power. Phrynichus must surely have had additional reasons for his decision: among them was doubtless one which influenced many prominent Athenians at the time, namely that for anyone unwilling to pay at least lip-service to oligarchy there seemed to be no prospect of enjoying any political influence in Athens in the immediate future (cf. 66. 5).

[2] I made this suggestion in *J.H.S.* LXXVI (1956), 103–4.

create a slightly misleading impression on points of some importance.[1]

After recording this sensational episode Thucydides resumes his account of the efforts made by Alcibiades to influence Persian relations with the Greeks by persuading Tissaphernes to follow his advice (52). Because Tissaphernes was far too shrewd to allow himself to surrender to the personal charm of his guest, this task was an arduous one. Alcibiades applied himself strenuously and continuously to it, knowing how much was at stake (ἅτε περὶ μεγάλων ἀγωνιζόμενος), especially for himself, since his future seemed to be wholly dependent on the outcome. He now urged Tissaphernes, much more openly and emphatically than before, to establish friendly relations with the Athenians. According to Thucydides, Tissaphernes was disposed to adopt this proposal but was afraid of the Peloponnesian fleet because of its numerical superiority (cf. 56. 2). His principal fear was, as is explained in a later passage (57. 1), that, if he committed himself irretrievably to a breach with the Peloponnesians, they might plunder his satrapy, which was almost defenceless,[2] in order to provide themselves with funds for paying their crews. While the anxiety attributed to Tissaphernes in regard to the reaction of the Peloponnesians seems to be authentic enough, there is some reason to doubt whether he genuinely desired an entente with the Athenians. Thucydides here refers to the feelings of Tissaphernes without

---

[1] Since the publication of my paper in *J.H.S.* LXXVI, Delebecque, 86-8, 96-8, has independently concluded that the motives of Phrynichus in communicating with Astyochus were not entirely personal. His treatment of the episode is, in my opinion, mistaken on two points. He accepts unreservedly the charge mentioned in very guarded terms by Thucydides (50. 3, cf. 83. 3) that Astyochus took bribes from Tissaphernes (see below, 304-7). He also interprets the phrase δόξας ὁ Ἀλκιβιάδης οὐ πιστὸς εἶναι in 51. 3 very broadly as though it referred to a general loss of confidence in Alcibiades by the Athenian oligarchs negotiating with him (88 with n. 1, cf. 90-1). The context shows that the words denote only disbelief in the charge of treason made against Phrynichus in the second message from Alcibiades. From 53. 1 and 3 and 54 it is clear that the oligarchs lost confidence in Alcibiades only when their negotiations with Tissaphernes broke down (56. 5).

[2] Hatzfeld, 240.

any of the cautious reservations found in some similar passages (46. 5; 56. 3; 87. 4), but his information must surely owe its origin to his Alcibiadean source, and Alcibiades doubtless wished to create the impression that his efforts to persuade Tissaphernes, though ultimately unavailing, very nearly succeeded.[1] Thucydides, though fully aware that Alcibiades was in the habit of exaggerating his influence with Tissaphernes (cf. 81. 2), has perhaps been insufficiently guarded in this instance. At all events, when very soon afterwards a delegation led by Peisander arrived from Athens to open negotiations, Alcibiades had already had to abandon any hope of inducing Tissaphernes to conclude an agreement with Athens. He had now to find some way of extricating himself from a predicament which might well have proved disastrous to his personal fortunes.

The negotiations with Peisander are described very largely from the viewpoint of Alcibiades (56. 2–4), and the narrative seems to bear the imprint of his influence; it does not appear to contain any information based on reports by the Athenian envoys. Alcibiades must in his own interests contrive to avoid having to acknowledge his failure to convince Tissaphernes; at all costs he must maintain the current illusion, which he fostered so carefully, that he was able virtually to dictate Persian policy towards the Greeks. Responsibility for the breakdown of the negotiations must be made to lie, not with him, but with the Athenian delegation. Accordingly he adopted the very characteristic stratagem of making exorbitant demands on behalf of Tissaphernes as the price of Persian friendship. The envoys were prepared to make great concessions, but when finally they could yield no more, they withdrew in anger believing that Alcibiades had deceived them (56. 4).[2] It is noteworthy that his crucial

---

[1] Cf. his claims in 6. 16. 6 for his Peloponnesian policy during the years after the Peace of Nicias.

[2] A later passage (63. 4) makes clear that they considered themselves to have been deceived not because Alcibiades had exaggerated his influence with Tissaphernes but because he did not himself wish the negotiations to succeed (ἐπειδήπερ οὐ βούλεται).

failure to persuade Tissaphernes is first mentioned in somewhat oblique and apologetic terms (56. 2, οὐ γὰρ αὐτῷ πάνυ τὰ ἀπὸ Τισσαφέρνους βέβαια ἦν).[1] More prominence is given to his purely negative accomplishment, which doubtless gave him considerable satisfaction, in suppressing the fact that his influence with Tissaphernes was very limited. The narrative thus seems to reflect his own version of the conference. There is, however, no justification for regarding the success of his subterfuge as unimportant or even as merely providing further evidence of his resourcefulness. It did have repercussions on the development of the complex situation in Asia. His estrangement from the Athenian oligarchs was, it is true, complete and irrevocable (63. 4; 68. 3; 70. 1); and Tissaphernes promptly resumed consultations with the Peloponnesians and negotiated the third of the treaties between them and Persia (57–8). Nevertheless, so long as Alcibiades retained his one trump card, namely his alleged power to influence Persian policy, his eclipse might be only temporary, and there was some prospect that he might have an opportunity of playing a leading role once more. This opportunity in fact presented itself within a few weeks.

When the Athenian forces at Samos finally decided to break with the oligarchy at home and elected as their generals men known to be loyal to the democracy (76. 1–2), it was necessary for them to take stock of their position. Thucydides presents the substance of their debate in a long passage of *oratio obliqua* (76. 3–7). Speakers sought to encourage their fellows by pointing to the advantages of the situation in which they now found themselves, and one of the views expressed was that, if they were prepared to recall Alcibiades, he would gladly secure for them the support of Persia (76. 7). Several of the speakers may have voiced this opinion, but it may be inferred from a later passage (81. 1) that among them was Thrasybulus, now one of the generals, who at a subsequent meeting eventually secured a majority vote in

---

[1] More precise language is used in the following sentence (56. 3).

favour of his proposal. He is stated to have believed that, only if Tissaphernes could be persuaded to change sides and support the Athenians, would their cause be saved, the same view as had been earlier attributed to Peisander and the oligarchs. Thrasybulus then went to the court of Tissaphernes and brought Alcibiades back with him to Samos (81. 1). Thus, according to Thucydides, it was the democratic leaders at Samos who took the initiative in bringing about this important development; there is no hint of any overtures made by Alcibiades. He was, however, as on other occasions, doubtless well-informed about a situation which might be turned to his own advantage, and the alacrity with which he responded to the invitation conveyed by Thrasybulus suggests that it may not have been wholly unexpected. Thucydides gives a detailed account of the democratic reaction at Samos against the Four Hundred from its inception (73. 1), and he was evidently able to obtain reliable reports from eye-witnesses. At this stage his narrative does not appear to be dependent upon his Alcibiadean source.[1]

6. *In Athenian service once more*

The first contacts between Alcibiades and the Athenian forces at Samos are described in a conspicuously skilful and instructive passage (81. 2–82). He delivers a speech in which he is at pains to inspire his hearers with confidence in their future. Characteristically, however, the keynote of his speech is his own indispensability: he insists upon his personal influence with Tissaphernes, who has undertaken to put at the disposal of the Athenians both financial resources, including even his private property, and also the Phoenician fleet now at Aspendus, but is not prepared to trust them unless Alcibiades himself is restored and can act as a guarantee of their good faith (81. 3). Thucydides inserts judgements of his own in his report of this speech as well as references

---

[1] Delebecque, 131–55 and 163–9, does not seem to me to have established his view that 63. 3–77 and 81–2 are founded upon information derived from Alcibiades.

to the motives of the speaker. Alcibiades, he observes, greatly exaggerated the extent of his influence with Tissaphernes,[1] and his motives were threefold: he wished to make the Athenian oligarchs afraid of him, to win greater esteem for himself from the troops at Samos, thus raising their morale, and to poison relations between the Peloponnesians and Tissaphernes as much as possible.[2] His speech evidently impressed the Athenian troops, who promptly elected him general, in theory on a basis of equality with Thrasybulus and other colleagues but in practice as supreme commander. His hearers were so inspired with confidence and felt so contemptuous of their enemies in Asia that many of them were ready to sail home to overthrow the Four Hundred. He opposed this suggestion and left Samos immediately after the meeting to visit Tissaphernes, saying that he wished to confer with him about the direction of the war. Thucydides again claims knowledge of his motive: it was to enhance his own prestige with the Athenians at Samos and with Tissaphernes. He intended the former to believe that there was close co-operation between Tissaphernes and himself, and he wished to impress upon Tissaphernes that, being now general and no longer a fugitive, he was in a position to benefit or injure him as he pleased. Thucydides comments that Alcibiades was using Tissaphernes to alarm the Athenians and the Athenians to alarm Tissaphernes (82. 3).

Readers of this passage are left in no doubt that the fortunes of the Athenians at Samos, as well as those of Alcibiades, though outwardly improved, rested on very brittle foundations. There is an air of instability, almost of make-believe. The impact of his personality upon their minds was all the greater because their anxieties made them unusually impressionable. Although he inspired them with confidence, indeed with overconfidence, they were in fact his dupes: the sole basis of his pose as their saviour was his claim to be able to win for them the support of Tissaphernes, who was in fact most unlikely to show towards them

---

[1] 81. 2, ὑπερβάλλων ἐμεγάλυνε, cf. 81. 3, μέγιστα ἐπικομπῶν.
[2] 83. 1 provides evidence of his success in this respect.

greater favour than he had shown towards the oligarchs. Alcibiades is also seen, especially in the penetrating analysis of his motives in visiting Tissaphernes (82. 3),[1] to have devoted himself almost exclusively to the advancement of his own interests. There is no suggestion that his rapprochement with his fellow-citizens had the effect of kindling in him any feelings of loyalty towards Athens. This rapprochement, it is true, marks the beginning of a period during which the renewed partnership between him and the Athenians was conspicuously successful. Here, however, Thucydides evidently wishes to underline the dangers of relying upon him. The next scene is, as will be shown below, designed to give a totally different impression.

What Alcibiades accomplished in his consultations with Tissaphernes is not recorded, but there is no reason to infer from the silence of Thucydides that the visit was entirely fruitless.[2] The Peloponnesians remained bitterly hostile towards Tissaphernes on the grounds that he was openly assisting the Athenians (87. 1); and it may be that Alcibiades secured on this occasion a promise, or a half-promise, from Tissaphernes not to use the Phoenician ships at Aspendus in support of the Peloponnesian fleet (88). Thucydides confines himself to mentioning that Alcibiades had already returned to Samos when a deputation from the Athenian oligarchs arrived there (85. 4–86. 1). These envoys were at first denied a hearing and threatened with violence by the Athenian troops. When they were eventually allowed to speak, their defence of the policies adopted by the oligarchy was rejected out of hand. There was a renewed and evidently much more violent demand that the fleet should sail to attack the Piraeus; Alcibiades spared no effort in seeking to dissuade the meeting from adopting this suicidal plan, which he condemned in the strongest terms, and eventually he was successful (86. 2–5). In a celebrated but much disputed comment Thucydides expresses the view that 'Alcibiades seems then for the first time

---

[1] The ironical ἵνα δή (an almost certain emendation of ἵνα δέ) should be noted.
[2] As Delebecque, 175, suggests.

(πρῶτον) and more than anyone else to have benefited the city' (86. 4)[1] and that Ionia and the Hellespont would at once have fallen into the hands of the enemy if the Athenian fleet had left Samos. He also insists that nobody except Alcibiades would have been able to restrain the mob at that moment (86. 5). After the conclusion of this meeting Alcibiades sent the envoys away carrying a personal message to the oligarchs at home.[2] He had no objection, he said, to the Five Thousand being in control of the state, but he demanded the deposition of the Four Hundred and the restoration of the democratic Boule; he urged the oligarchs not to yield to the enemy, declaring that, if they stood firm but only if they stood firm, there was a good prospect of an ultimate reconciliation between themselves and the armed forces at Samos (86. 6–7).

This passage is as graphic as the account of the earlier debate at Samos and is equally instructive in supplying the reader with guidance in assessing the qualities of leadership shown by Alcibiades at this time. Since, however, another side of him is presented here, the assessment suggested is a totally different one. The contrast in tone in the presentation of these two scenes is surely intentional;[3] it accounts to some extent for the unusually

---

[1] πρῶτον, the reading of B, which most scholars rightly prefer to πρῶτος, does not mean that, in the opinion of Thucydides, Alcibiades now benefited Athens for the first time in his life but only for the first time in the present series of events. I suggested this interpretation in C.Q. VIII (1958), 109 n. 1. Neither in his abortive negotiations with Peisander and the oligarchs nor immediately after his arrival at Samos (81–2, where, as pointed out above, the tone is unsympathetic towards him) did he render outstanding service to Athens; now, for the first time, he did.

[2] That it was a message from himself alone, conveying his own views and not those of the Athenian troops, shows how successful he had been in establishing his personal authority; cf. Busolt, 1499, 'wie ein Souverän entliess er die Gesandten'. A similar impression is created by his treatment of some Argive envoys whom he sent away, apparently on his own initiative, after thanking them for their offer of help (86. 8).

[3] Some scholars, including Schwartz, 78, have maintained that Thucydides has inadvertently included two accounts of the same debate at Samos. There are many reasons for rejecting this view, but among the most cogent is the fact that the two accounts give fundamentally different pictures of Alcibiades.

emphatic and explicit language with which Thucydides draws attention to the services of Alcibiades to Athens in dissuading his troops from sailing against the Piraeus. On this occasion it was they who were actuated by personal motives (86. 5, ἰδίᾳ), namely their anxiety about the treatment of their families by the oligarchs (74. 3), and this anxiety would have led them to commit an error of judgement which would have been disastrous to Athenian interests. The conclusion to be drawn from these two contrasted scenes is that, despite the selfishness of Alcibiades and his love of intrigue and double-dealing, such were his powers of persuasion and his personal magnetism that he could perform services in the public interest which were beyond the capacity of any of his contemporaries. His message to the Athenian oligarchs provides further evidence of his diplomatic subtlety, as may be inferred from the account of its effect when it was received at Athens (89. 1). It is seen to have been not so much a reasonable plea for restraint and reconciliation, as it would appear at first sight to have been, but rather a very shrewd device to disrupt the oligarchy by encouraging the moderates, such as Theramenes, and driving a wedge between them and the extremists. Thucydides evidently expects more observant readers to draw this conclusion.

It was not long before Alcibiades was called upon to demonstrate the extent of his influence upon the policy of Tissaphernes towards the Greeks. His exaggeration of this influence was a potential source of weakness which could have undermined his authority over the troops at Samos. If it were to be exposed, he might well lose their confidence as swiftly as he had gained it.

Tissaphernes now left for Aspendus, announcing that he would bring the Phoenician fleet back with him to Ionia. He gave the impression (ὡς ἐδόκει δή) that his motive was to conciliate the Peloponnesians, whose resentment against him had become more intense than ever before (87. 1).[1] Why he went to Aspendus and yet did not bring the ships to Ionia remained a mystery, and

---

[1] Cf. 78 on the scepticism of the Peloponnesian crews at Miletus about the Phoenician fleet.

Thucydides confesses that he was unable to obtain authentic information on this point. After adopting the Herodotean practice of quoting three conjectural explanations current at the time, Thucydides adds his own view. It was his conviction that Tissaphernes, being unwilling to give either the Peloponnesians or the Athenians the overwhelming advantage which would have resulted from the support of the Phoenician fleet, clung to his policy of exhausting both sides and reducing their efficiency; there was every prospect that this deterioration would continue if he were to sail to Aspendus and linger there inactive. The reason which he alleged for not bringing the ships was, Thucydides declares, palpably a mere pretext (87. 2–6).

The problem of the Phoenician fleet is relevant here only in so far as it concerns Alcibiades, whose reactions throw light upon his relations both with Tissaphernes and with the Athenians. When he learned that Tissaphernes had left for Aspendus, he sailed from Samos to Caunus and Phaselis with a small squadron, promising the Athenians that he would either bring the Phoenician fleet to their aid or at least prevent it being put at the disposal of the Peloponnesians (88). Thucydides makes clear that this promise contained a considerable element of deception; for he states categorically that Alcibiades had known for some time that it was not the intention of Tissaphernes to move the Phoenician ships to Ionian waters.[1] Hence Alcibiades must have been fully aware that there was no hope of fulfilling the first part of his promise, while the second part would be fulfilled in any event without any need for action on his part. He evidently did not proceed beyond Phaselis, so that on this occasion he had no

---

[1] In 88, εἰδώς, ὡς εἰκός, ἐκ πλέονος τὴν Τισσαφέρνους γνώμην ὅτι οὐκ ἄξειν ἔμελλε (sc. τὰς Φοινίσσας ναῦς), Thucydides is not confessing uncertainty and giving the probable reason why Alcibiades made his promise to the Athenians. In Hermes, LXXXVI (1958), 447–52, I have tried to establish that in all the passages in which Thucydides uses ὡς εἰκός, the meaning is not 'probably' but 'as was natural'. On this occasion it was natural that Alcibiades, having lived at the court of Tissaphernes and having recently revisited him, was aware of his intentions. As suggested above, Alcibiades may well have obtained during his most recent visit some assurance from Tissaphernes about the Phoenician fleet.

personal contact with Tissaphernes. To have presented himself at Aspendus might indeed have been hazardous, since the Spartan Lichas had accompanied Tissaphernes thither (87. 1) and was later joined by another Spartan with two ships (87. 6; 99). Such a visit was also unnecessary. The aim of Alcibiades was, according to Thucydides, to make the Peloponnesians distrust Tissaphernes by leading them to believe that Alcibiades himself and the Athenians were on cordial terms with him; greater pressure could thus be brought to bear upon Tissaphernes to commit himself to supporting the Athenians (88). Alcibiades evidently calculated that he had a good prospect of achieving what he planned by stationing himself at Phaselis, which was within easy reach of Aspendus.

When eventually he returned to Samos, he claimed credit for having denied to the Peloponnesians the support of the Phoenician fleet and for having caused Tissaphernes to become more friendly than before towards the Athenians (108. 1). The first of these claims was fraudulent, as has been pointed out above, and the second was justifiable only in the negative sense that the Peloponnesians lost patience with Tissaphernes and transferred their main fleet from Miletus to the Hellespont, where Pharnabazus offered to support them (99). The power of Alcibiades to influence Tissaphernes had in fact declined and not, as he had expected, increased since his appointment to a position of authority at Samos, and he never succeeded in obtaining any Persian assistance, financial or military, for the Athenians. His prestige with the Athenian forces was founded upon a myth,[1] and despite his remarkable flair for bluff he could hardly have concealed his deception of them much longer. It was fortunate for him that relations with Tissaphernes soon ceased to be of much import-

[1] It was perhaps largely for this reason that, when he received news while at Phaselis that the Five Thousand had granted him permission to return home (97. 3), he chose to remain in Asia for the present. He must have felt the necessity of having some positive and tangible successes to his credit which would counterbalance all the harm that he had done to Athens (cf. Plut. *Alcib.* 27. 1).

ance[1] and that he himself began to show unsuspected gifts of military leadership which raised his reputation higher than ever before. These developments, however, are not recorded by Thucydides because the *History* ends before he reaches them. Alcibiades is mentioned for the last time taking unspectacular but prudent action at Halicarnassus and Cos evidently designed to ensure that the Athenians did not sustain any further losses in the south while the main conflict with the Peloponnesians was being conducted in the north (108. 2).

The *History* of Thucydides is doubly incomplete. It breaks off abruptly on reaching the autumn of 411, six and a half years before the war ended; and the eighth book patently lacks revision with the result that it tends to be deficient in some distinctively Thucydidean qualities. Both kinds of incompleteness have caused the portrayal of Alcibiades to fall short of what it might have been. It is regrettable that the *History*, as handed down to posterity, contains no account of the period after 411 when for the first time he displayed military ability of very high quality and won the only notable victories of his career. Even though the Athenian democracy, restored to power in 410, refused him its wholehearted support, he succeeded in regaining and retaining the initiative for Athens during the long struggle in the Hellespont. Xenophon, who supplies a tolerably clear and reliable account of this period at the beginning of the *Hellenica*, seems to have been barely conscious that Alcibiades possessed gifts marking him as outstanding among his contemporaries.[2] In the famous passage assessing the personal qualities of Alcibiades, written at or after the end of the war, Thucydides refers briefly to the excellence of his military leadership (6. 15. 4, δημοσίᾳ κράτιστα διαθέντι τὰ τοῦ πολέμου), which undoubtedly applies to his services as commander

---

[1] In the course of his next visit to Tissaphernes he was arrested and thrown into prison; but when he escaped and eventually rejoined the Athenians in the Hellespont, he does not seem to have suffered any loss of prestige (Xen. *Hell.* 1. 1. 9–11; Plut. *Alcib.* 27. 6–28. 2).

[2] *Ryl. Bull.* XLIX (1966), 269.

of the Athenian forces from 411 and 407. The same passage also contains brief references to the reasons why the Athenians discarded him in 406 and to the damage which they inflicted thereby upon their own cause (*ibid.*). These judgements suggest that Thucydides had made some progress in collecting and sifting information on the closing phases of the war.[1] It would have been most instructive to have had his account of the circumstances leading to the virtual dismissal of Alcibiades together with some comment on it, since the treatment of generals by the Athenian democracy was, not unnaturally, a subject on which he felt strongly (cf. 4. 65. 4). He might also have included, at the point where the public career of Alcibiades ended, some discussion of his contribution to the history of the war.[2]

There is also reason to regret that the section of the *History* where Alcibiades is most continuously in the foreground is the eighth book, which suffers from some imperfections arising from lack of revision. Thucydides has assembled in this book a mass of detailed information, but he has not completed, and in some respects hardly begun, the process of refining his raw material. Some characteristic features of his technique are much less prominent here than they are elsewhere. These include his practice of focusing attention upon a limited number of significant episodes while dismissing others very briefly; his consciousness of a duty to use the events which he describes as the basis for general conclusions about human behaviour in war and politics; and his capacity for guiding the judgement of the reader by various indirect and subtle means. While providing a full record of what was done and said, he does not indicate so firmly as in other parts of his work why the war developed as it did. The narrative tends to be clumsy and confused, and there is some lack of intensity. It

---

[1] Adcock, 103, maintains, on different grounds, that Thucydides continued his *History*, perhaps in an incomplete form, beyond the point at which the extant text ends.

[2] It is conceivable that Thucydides may have inserted in the sixth book his celebrated assessment of Alcibiades (6. 15. 3-4) when he realised that he would be unable to complete his *History*.

may well be that, if Thucydides had revised the eighth book, he would have discarded much of its detail, including some relating to Alcibiades. Revision would, however, certainly have improved the book and doubtless also the presentation of Alcibiades contained in it, which, skilful and vivid though it often is, does not bear comparison with the brilliant treatment of him in the sixth book.

Although the picture of Alcibiades is incomplete, it is strikingly personal throughout. It was not the purpose of Thucydides, though fascinated by his unstable genius, to produce a balanced and rounded sketch of his personality but rather to trace its influence upon the course of the war. This influence was subject to violent fluctuations, and in periods when it was, in the opinion of Thucydides, a factor of little or no importance Alcibiades himself is given little or no prominence in the *History*. Nevertheless, Thucydides has produced what is virtually a character study, so far at least as public life is concerned; and indeed Alcibiades, in spite of his notoriety among his contemporaries, would have remained an almost shadowy figure if the *History* had not been written. Light is thrown upon his character mainly, as has already been seen, by implied comparison with other leading personalities: with Nicias, who was so utterly different from him; to a limited extent with Agis; with Phrynichus, shrewd and without illusions, who showed himself to be a most resolute adversary; with Tissaphernes, who, ostensibly on intimate terms with him, refused to be exploited or to succumb to his charm and eventually proved a match for him in diplomatic intrigue. Although this concentration of attention upon the contacts and conflicts between leading individuals is so prominent in the second half of the *History*, Alcibiades occupies a very special place in it. His personal ambitions are shown to have had an unparalleled influence, for good or ill, upon the fortunes of the Athenians; whereas he might have been their saviour, he proved in fact to be their evil genius. At the same time Thucydides suggests that, while there was something unique in Alcibiades, he shared with the post-Periclean democracy most of its virtues, such as enterprise, energy, and quickness of intellect, and also most of its vices, such as instability, unwillingness to take into account the interests of others, and intolerance of restraint. Paradoxically, even though Alcibiades was inclined to express contempt for the democracy (6. 89. 3–6; 8. 47. 2) and was twice discarded by it, he was himself almost a personification of it.

NOTE: In a persuasively written paper which has come to my notice since this chapter was completed, M. F. McGregor, *Phoenix*, XIX (1965), 27–46, maintains that Alcibiades throughout his career planned each of his moves with a calculating farsightedness and subtlety which Thucydides failed to appreciate. In particular, when at the court of Tissaphernes, Alcibiades deliberately incited the Athenian oligarchs to overthrow the democracy, foreseeing that there would be a reaction against the oligarchy and that by organising the restoration of the democracy he would be able to secure his own recall. This thesis, which cannot be fully discussed here, is dependent on the assumption—it could become more than an assumption when the further investigation foreshadowed on p. 35 is published—that from the outset the oligarchic faction at Athens was implacably hostile towards Alcibiades. Furthermore, what is meant by the oligarchic faction needs to be precisely defined: there were different shades of oligarchy, and in this period of internal strife many Athenians changed their political affiliations in order to secure personal advantages. I prefer Thucydides to McGregor. I am convinced that Thucydides, possessing, as he did, abundant information about the intrigues of Alcibiades, also enjoyed considerable knowledge of his aims and motives. Thucydides is, I believe, right in imputing a grave miscalculation to Alcibiades in Asia, namely that with characteristic overconfidence in his own powers of persuasion he expected to be able to exert an almost unlimited influence over the policy of Tissaphernes. Yet with equally characteristic adroitness Alcibiades avoided the consequences of his error, which might have been disastrous, by successfully concealing from others the fact that Tissaphernes proved a match for him and was prepared to accept his advice only to a moderate degree. It seems to me that Thucydides has provided discerning readers with plenty of guidance to show why Alcibiades in spite of his outstanding qualities seldom achieved his major aims.

CHAPTER XIII

DEMOSTHENES *(cont.)*

THE distinctive qualities of Demosthenes, both good and bad, as a military commander are almost as conspicuous in the second half of the *History* as in the first, and the views of Thucydides on his powers of leadership do not seem to have altered appreciably. He is, however, rather differently presented in the second half, a difference comparable with the difference in the presentation of Nicias, though it is much less marked and in the reverse direction. In the first half he is the central figure in the episodes in which he appears, and prominence is given to his personal responsibility for planning and conducting military operations. In the second half, though there is perhaps less reluctance to grant him credit for his originality and enterprise, he normally plays a secondary role, except for a brief period immediately after his arrival at Syracuse. One reason for this difference may be that, as will be pointed out below, Thucydides was evidently not in a position to obtain much reliable information about his motives and feelings in the period covered by the second half of the *History*. A more cogent reason is that Thucydides has chosen to present Nicias as the protagonist in the tragedy of the Athenian disaster. The decision to use Demosthenes mainly as a foil is natural enough, not so much because he served for only a few weeks in Sicily as because he was in no way responsible for the situation which he found there.

Demosthenes makes a single fleeting appearance in the *History* between 421 and his appointment to lead the Athenian reinforcement sent to Sicily in 413. In the winter of 418/17 he was involved in an episode to which Thucydides seems to have attached little significance, since only just enough detail is included to make the narrative intelligible (5. 80. 3). After the Spartan victory at

Mantinea the defeated army was joined by a force of 1,000 Athenians, which had arrived too late for the battle, and also by the Elean contingent. It then marched to Epidaurus, where it began to build fortifications with the intention of reducing the city to surrender by blockade. Before these fortifications were completed, the main body dispersed leaving behind a skeleton force, as was the accepted practice of the time, to maintain the blockade (75. 5–6). When subsequently Argos came to terms with Sparta and honoured this agreement by calling upon the Athenians to withdraw their troops serving at Epidaurus (77. 2; 80. 1), Demosthenes was sent to bring them back to Athens. It was impossible for the Athenians to reject the Argive demand, because their garrison was outnumbered by the contingents of their allies (80. 3). It is noteworthy that the mission with which Demosthenes was entrusted did not carry with it any responsibility for conducting military operations. He may, however, have been entrusted to do whatever he could to preserve Athenian influence in the Peloponnese, for he was not content merely to lead the Athenian garrison home. On the pretext of holding gymnastic contests he lured the allied contingents from the fortified area and shut them out; he then handed it over to the Epidaurians in the name of the Athenians alone, after renewing Athenian friendship with Epidaurus, which had been, as an ally of Sparta, a party to the Peace of Nicias. He thus made the best of the limited opportunities which were offered to him by being entrusted with this minor duty.[1]

Many lesser historians, including Xenophon who ranked the contrivance of clever ruses among the hallmarks of a good leader, would have found this incident attractive and might well have described it in detail. To Thucydides, however, the stratagem of Demosthenes was evidently unimportant and not very interesting.

---

[1] *I.G.* I², 302. 2–15, provides evidence that in 418/17 Demosthenes was entrusted with two missions requiring financial expenditure, the second being certainly to the Peloponnese. Why the payment voted to the first of these missions was later revoked is not determinable: the explanation offered by A. B. West and B. P. McCarthy, *A.J.A.* XXXII (1928), 350–2, is highly conjectural.

At this point he has already reduced the scale of his narrative, presumably because after the allied defeat at Mantinea, of which he has given a very full account, the challenge to Spartan authority in the Peloponnese was irretrievably doomed, though it was fitfully revived during the next two years. The enforced withdrawal of the last Athenian troops remaining in the Peloponnese was noteworthy in that it marked virtually the end of Athenian intervention there so vigorously sponsored by Alcibiades. The mention of this withdrawal naturally leads to a brief reference to the part played in it by Demosthenes. His minor achievement at Epidaurus might well have received fuller treatment if it had caused his reinstatement in popular favour at Athens, but evidently it did not. He was passed over when the Athenians appointed the leaders of their expedition to Sicily in 415, and he had to wait two more years before his long period of eclipse ended.[1]

Although Thucydides reports in some detail the substance of the dispatch sent by Nicias from Syracuse in the autumn of 414 (7. 11–15), he does not give an account of its reception at Athens, where it must have been fully discussed in the assembly. He is content with a bald statement of Athenian decisions (16).[2] He does not explain, directly or indirectly, why Demosthenes and Eurymedon were chosen to serve as colleagues of Nicias in Sicily and to command the second expeditionary force. While each of them had much experience of military leadership in the middle years of the Archidamian war, both had fallen into disfavour when operations with which they were associated had failed, and neither had been entrusted with any major command since 424. Eurymedon had actually been fined when the Athenian fleet commanded by himself and two other generals returned from Sicily without having achieved what the assembly expected of it

---

[1] M. Treu, *Historia*, v (1956), 433–4, while somewhat exaggerating the achievement of Demosthenes at Epidaurus, makes the attractive suggestion that, when the expedition to Sicily was being planned, Alcibiades, appreciating his quality, deliberately kept him out of the limelight through fear of being outshone.

[2] See above, 194.

(4. 65. 3).[1] The Athenians may on the present occasion have been influenced only by the common tendency to turn to tried veterans at times of crisis. They probably felt, however, that the energy of Demosthenes and his readiness to take decisions would prove valuable assets at Syracuse and that his proneness to over-elaborate an over-optimistic strategy would be held in check by Nicias. Eurymedon, who seems to have been competent but uninspiring,[2] may have owed his appointment partly to his previous experience of service in Sicily.

At the end of 414 Eurymedon was sent to convey ten ships and a sum of money to Nicias at Syracuse. Demosthenes, who remained in Greece to organise the powerful expeditionary force, Athenian and allied, which was to sail in the spring (7. 16. 2–17. 1), evidently applied himself to this task with his customary vigour. By about the end of March he was at Aegina with most of his force awaiting the arrival of the remainder (20. 2–3).

The voyage of Demosthenes to Sicily is described with a much greater wealth of detail than that of Nicias and his colleagues two years earlier.[3] The narrative amounts, however, to little more than a catalogue of facts and figures. It does not explain the intentions underlying the actions of Demosthenes; it records only the bare results of negotiations with cities from which he tried to obtain assistance; it does not describe conferences held on the Athenian side; it does not contain any judgements on men or events, either expressed or even, it seems, implied. These distinctive features suggest that, while Thucydides was able to secure full and trustworthy reports from Athenians or others who sailed with the second expedition, his informants did not include anyone in close contact with Demosthenes during the voyage. This impression

[1] As has been pointed out above, 118, the view that Demosthenes was prosecuted after the Athenian defeat at Delium is almost certainly without foundation.

[2] Gomme (2), 147–8, cf. (1), III, 496, suggests that Thucydides criticises Eurymedon by implication on both occasions when he was called upon to deal with the stasis at Corcyra. Elsewhere he is colourless.

[3] It is also much more fully described than the efforts of the enemy to send aid from the Peloponnese to Syracuse in 413; of these only a sketchy and somewhat confused account is given.

receives some confirmation from the narrative of events after the arrival of the second expedition: there is plenty of information about the opinions expressed by Demosthenes at consultations with his colleagues, but his unexpressed feelings or motives are, unlike those of Nicias, seldom if ever reported. It is true that, as has been suggested above,[1] Thucydides intentionally gives less prominence to Demosthenes than to Nicias. On the other hand, because Athenian casualties in Sicily, in action and in captivity, were so heavy, he may well have had no opportunity to question any survivor of the expedition who had been closely associated with Demosthenes.

After sailing from Aegina Demosthenes proceeded to attack the Laconian coast, as he had been ordered (20. 2), in association with another force under Charicles. The two generals occupied and began to fortify a small area on the mainland opposite Cythera with the intention of establishing a permanent garrison there. It was similar in shape to Pylos and was designed to serve the same purpose (26. 1–2). Demosthenes was a pioneer in the development of ἐπιτειχισμός, but there is no justification for accusing him of having allowed his interest in operations of this kind to detain him in Laconia when he would have been better advised to have hastened on towards Sicily. The Athenians were now engaged in a double war, as Thucydides insists (18. 2; 28. 3), and could no longer devote all their attention to the struggle at Syracuse. The Spartans were sensitive about the establishment of enemy strongposts in their own territory. The occupation of Pylos had caused them to withdraw at once from Attica (4. 6. 1), and though this new threat could not be expected to produce a similar reaction since they had now had some experience of ἐπιτειχισμός, their war preparations would inevitably be hampered, including their efforts to send further aid from the Peloponnese to their allies in Sicily. Demosthenes evidently did not remain in Laconian waters longer than was absolutely necessary. As soon as the area where the garrison was to be established had been

---

[1] See above, 261.

occupied, he left to Charicles the task of fortifying it while he himself hurried on towards Corcyra in order that he might reach Sicily with all possible speed (7. 26. 3, εὐθὺς...ὅτι τάχιστα).

Thucydides provides a full, perhaps almost complete, list of the places where Demosthenes called before he reached Sicilian waters. He also reports on the reinforcements joining the Athenians in the course of the voyage: he gives details about the numbers of allied troops recruited in Italy, though not about those recruited in north-western Greece (31; 33. 3–6; 35). Demosthenes evidently made strenuous efforts to enlist as much support as he could from allies of Athens. The extent of his success in Italy, where he collected in all 700 hoplites, 750 javelin-throwers and two ships, is somewhat surprising.[1] The rapid deterioration of Athenian forces at Syracuse must have been almost as fully known to the Italiots as it was to the Siceliots, who at about the same time were at last rallying with enthusiasm to the aid of the Syracusans (33. 2), confident that Syracuse would be victorious. At Thurii, it is true, Demosthenes seems to have had a stroke of luck: he arrived shortly after an outbreak of violence when the faction favouring the Athenians had expelled its opponents and was apparently in no position to refuse him military aid (33. 5–6; 57. 11).[2]

This voyage began in haste but continued at leisure. Such, at least, is the impression created by the account of Thucydides, which raises a problem of some importance. Although the chronology of these months is not very clear, Demosthenes must surely have left the Laconian coast for Corcyra by about the middle of May and yet did not reach Syracuse until about the middle of July.[3] He evidently spent some time, perhaps a week or two, in north-western Greece and even longer in southern Italy. The

[1] The leaders of the first expedition had gained no support at all in Italy, though they do not seem to have made much effort to do so until they reached Rhegium, where they were rebuffed (6. 44. 2–3).

[2] Treu, *Historia*, v (1956), 436, suggests very tentatively that the rising at Thurii may have been pre-arranged so as to coincide with the approach of the Athenian fleet.   [3] Cf. K. J. Beloch, *Gr. Gesch.* II, 2 (1916), 239–40.

review of the troops held near Thurii and the subsequent march overland to the border of Crotoniate territory, together with calls at unnamed cities between Croton and the straits of Messana, must have involved considerable delays (33. 6; 35).[1] The question therefore arises whether Demosthenes may have acted unwisely in devoting so much time to the enlistment of reinforcements instead of hastening on to Syracuse to relieve the first expeditionary force, which was under severe pressure (36. 1; 41. 4) and might have been overwhelmed before he arrived. Did he secure from the addition of allied contingents to his force an advantage outweighing the obvious disadvantage of having to delay so long while recruiting them? Not all the allied troops can have been of high quality, and while the Acarnanians joined him with some enthusiasm (57. 10), the Thurians apparently did not (57. 11).

Demosthenes seems to have begun to give the recruitment of additional troops priority over the need for haste from about the time when he was joined off the coast of north-western Greece by Eurymedon, who informed him about the situation at Syracuse, including the loss of Plemmyrium (31. 3). This news might have been expected to have caused him to hurry rather than to linger. He evidently felt, however, that the prime duty of his expedition was to recapture Epipolae and restore the blockade of Syracuse in order to reduce the city to surrender; it was characteristic of him that he interpreted his mission offensively rather than defensively (cf. 42. 3–5). He seems to have been prepared to accept the risk, which he may have underrated, that he might not arrive in time to save the forces of Nicias from being destroyed, if only by enlisting substantial reinforcements he could improve his prospects of gaining his main objective. As an expert in the use of light-armed troops, he may originally have felt that they would be more effective than hoplites on the steep and broken terrain of Epipolae. He had been denied the services of 1,300 Thracian peltasts who had been engaged by the Athenians for the expedition, probably on his recommendation, but reached Athens too

[1] Cf. Treu, *Historia*, v (1956), 435–6.

late to sail with him (27. 1). It may have been because he had been deprived of these Thracians that he made a special effort to enlist light-armed troops during his voyage.[1] These factors suggest that the slowness of his progress was, to some extent at least, dictated by his views on the needs of the military situation and was not due to inertia, which would have been most uncharacteristic of him. There remains a suspicion, perhaps more than a suspicion, that his judgement was at fault in setting so much store by the enlistment of reinforcements when Nicias was falling into an increasingly dangerous position at Syracuse.[2]

The question whether or not Demosthenes acted unwisely is less relevant to the present work than the question whether or not Thucydides thought that he did. As has already been pointed out, it is the practice of Thucydides to guide the judgement of the reader by indirect methods of various kinds. He is, however, most punctilious in trying to ensure that the verdict suggested to the reader is a fair verdict based on evidence which he confidently believes to be trustworthy. In this instance he very probably lacked wholly trustworthy evidence, since he seems to have been able to obtain very little information about the plans and motives of Demosthenes during the Sicilian expedition except for those actually expressed at conferences with Nicias. Hence, though he does seem to give a slight hint that Demosthenes acted unwisely, he is content to leave this question virtually unanswered: probably he felt unable to give an authoritative verdict. The reader is thus presented with little more than a bare record of the facts and is left to make up his own mind, which is most unusual except in passages of highly condensed narrative. It may well have been his opinion that there was less need to give the reader guidance on this question than on many others, because despite the delays en route Demosthenes did arrive at Syracuse in time.[3]

---

[1] He visited some insignificant islands off Tarentum, where he hired a small detachment of 150 javelin-throwers from a Messapian chief (33. 4, cf. 57. 11).

[2] See above, 195–6.

[3] It might be argued that he has included details about the voyage of Demosthenes for another reason, namely that he was fascinated by the variety of the

The arrival of Demosthenes and his expeditionary force in the Great Harbour transformed the situation at Syracuse. The confidence of the Syracusans and their allies was shattered by this manifestation of Athenian power and resilience, and the morale of the Athenians belonging to the first expeditionary force was revived (42. 1-2). There is an abrupt change of tone in the narrative of Thucydides. For a time the Athenians again held the initiative, and there was an end of the indecision and hesitation which had been so prominent throughout the past year. Demosthenes at once sought to put into operation plans designed to exploit the effect produced by his arrival. His views about the military situation, past and present, are recorded in some detail (42. 3-5). The long parenthesis (42. 3) criticising the past strategy of Nicias, who is alone held responsible as though he had been in sole command throughout the expedition, has been discussed in an earlier chapter because this criticism almost certainly reflects the opinion of Thucydides.[1] There is, however, no doubt whatever that the parenthesis, although he does not use the accusative and infinitive construction, reproduces the views of Demosthenes, which are characteristically pungent. At first sight readers of the whole passage (42. 3-5) might infer from the verbs chosen by Thucydides (νομίσας. . . ἀνασκοπῶν. . . γιγνώσκων. . . ἐβούλετο . . . ἠπείγετο. . . ἡγεῖτο) that he is reporting the unexpressed feelings of Demosthenes. It is, however, much more probable that he is summarising what Demosthenes said at a conference held with the other generals, as is assumed by Plutarch.[2] Consultations must have been held immediately after the arrival of Demosthenes and Eurymedon, and it is unlikely that the former, whose uncompromising bluntness on other occasions is emphasised by Thucydides (cf. 47. 3-4; 49. 2-3), refrained from criticising the

forces assembled at Syracuse for the final struggle, as may be seen from his catalogue in 57-59. 1. There is, however, no likelihood that his account of the voyage was written in anticipation of the catalogue, to show how some of the allied contingents on the Athenian side came to be at Syracuse. The catalogue was probably written some years later than the rest of the narrative (Dover, n. on 57-59. 1).   [1] See above, 181-2.   [2] See above, 197 n. 1.

earlier leadership of Nicias through unwillingness to give offence to a colleague. The views of Demosthenes on the action which the Athenians ought to take in the present situation are thoroughly characteristic. It was, he felt, essential to regain the key positions on Epipolae from which the blockade of Syracuse could be restored and to get the better of the enemy forces occupying them. If this aim were achieved, Syracuse could be reduced to surrender; if it were not achieved, the only sensible course would be to withdraw from Sicily and abandon the expedition. The report of Thucydides, though perhaps exaggerating the extent to which Demosthenes oversimplified a complex situation, presents a vivid picture of his forthright realism and effectively contrasts his personality with that of Nicias.

Demosthenes made his first attempt to regain control of Epipolae by using siege-engines supported by infantry against the Syracusan counter-wall. When this method of attack proved unsuccessful, he prevailed upon his colleagues to agree to his plan to destroy the enemy defences on Epipolae by delivering a surprise attack at night from the western part of the plateau (43. 1–2). The account of this night-engagement is a masterpiece of graphic description (43. 3–44. 8), in which Thucydides makes most effective use of information derived from eyewitnesses on both sides (44. 1). The feature of the battle upon which he lays most emphasis is the confusion arising from the fact that it was fought at night.[1] He shows how the Athenians, after making good progress at first and overrunning the Syracusan counter-wall (43. 5), eventually suffered a heavy defeat because they fell into ever-increasing disorder, being unable in the moonlight to maintain their cohesion or to distinguish friend from foe. They failed to overcome the very great difficulties involved in launching an assault by night which demanded rapid movement by large forces over broken ground.[2] Did Thucydides believe that the

[1] Cf. de Romilly (2), 170–1.
[2] It is difficult to understand why the Athenians did not halt their attack when they had captured the Syracusan counter-wall, which was their principal

outcome was inevitable and ought to have been foreseen? He evidently considered that Demosthenes was exposing the Athenians to great dangers in choosing to attack by night, and to some extent he represents their defeat as the natural consequence of the circumstances in which the battle was fought (44. 2–6). He does not, however, seem to imply that Demosthenes was guilty of a palpable blunder in advocating a night attack. It was the conviction of Demosthenes that only by adopting his plan could the Athenians hope to regain control of Epipolae (43. 2). He doubtless appreciated the risks involved in committing his whole army, which was a large one, to a night operation, but he was evidently prepared to run these risks because he saw no prospect of winning a decisive success by any other expedient. He must also have felt that, if his plan failed, its failure would at least evoke from his colleagues a unanimous vote to withdraw from Sicily. Thucydides seems to have considered that this conception of the strategic problem was a not unreasonable one, though here, as in the first half of his *History*, he creates the impression that Demosthenes tended to indulge in over-elaborate and over-optimistic planning.

The conference held by the Athenian generals after this defeat has already been discussed at some length because the report of Thucydides on it throws so much light upon his attitude towards Nicias.[1] Demosthenes is treated as a character of secondary importance. At the outset he declared his intention to vote for immediate withdrawal from Sicily while there was still plenty of time to complete the voyage home before the winter began and while the Athenian fleet was still superior to that of the enemy. He argued that the Syracusans could not now be defeated without great difficulty and expense, and that the Athenian military resources now employed against them could be put to more

objective. The task of clearing the enemy from the rest of Epipolae west of Achradina could surely have been completed in daylight, when there would no longer be the same danger of falling into disorder. It may be that this was the intention of Demosthenes and that the leading Athenian troops, who pressed on enthusiastically to complete the rout of the enemy and thus fell into disorder (43. 7), were ill-advisedly acting on their own initiative.

[1] See above, 197–9.

profitable use against the Peloponnesians, who had established an outpost in Attica (47. 3–4). Later, after Nicias had spoken against his proposal, he suggested a compromise, namely that the Athenians should move from Syracuse to Thapsus or Catana, whence their army could maintain itself by plundering enemy territory and their fleet would no longer forfeit the advantages of its superior seamanship by having to operate in the confined space of the Great Harbour. He insisted that on no account must they linger any longer at Syracuse but must withdraw at once without any delay (49. 2–3).[1] While Eurymedon agreed with Demosthenes, Nicias persisted in his opposition, and the generals ended their discussion without reaching any decision (49. 4).[2]

The report of Thucydides on this conference leaves no room for doubt that, in his opinion, Demosthenes was right and Nicias wrong about the vital issue under debate. At the same time, readers of the report may feel, and probably Thucydides intended them to feel, that Demosthenes, though he did make a concession to the objections of Nicias, would have had a better prospect of converting him to his own viewpoint if he had adopted a somewhat more conciliatory attitude; that he aggravated the obstinacy of his senior colleague by his brusque insistence that withdrawal was the only sensible course of action. Patience was perhaps not a quality in which Demosthenes excelled.

In the narrative describing the final stages of the struggle at Syracuse the fortitude of Nicias in adversity becomes increasingly prominent, while Demosthenes, whose forthrightness has hitherto been contrasted with the hesitancy of Nicias, is allowed to recede into the background. Demosthenes, with Menander and Euthydemus, commanded the Athenian fleet in the last desperate battle in the Great Harbour (69. 4), and he must have been partly

---

[1] The last sentence (49. 3), which adds nothing new, seems to have been included in order to stress the vehemence with which he voiced his convictions.

[2] See above, 199 n. 1, where the problem arising from the omission by Thucydides to define the status of Menander and Euthydemus, who are not mentioned in the account of this conference, is discussed and the conclusion is reached that probably no vote was taken.

responsible for the plans agreed at a meeting of the generals and the taxiarchs held shortly before the battle (60. 2–4). There is, however, no reference to his contribution to these preparations; and, more significant, the speech of encouragement to the Athenian troops of which Thucydides gives a summary in accordance with his normal practice (61–4) is that of Nicias, whose efforts to sustain Athenian morale are given much prominence.[1] Thucydides does, however, mention that after the defeat of the Athenians Demosthenes approached Nicias with a proposal that they should make another effort at daybreak to force a passage through the mouth of the Great Harbour. Nicias agreed, but the Athenian sailors refused to obey their leaders (72. 3–4). The mention of this proposal by Demosthenes provides evidence that he too refused to be daunted by adversity.

The generals had now to undertake the task of trying to lead to safety a huge body of dispirited men by a long march through difficult country, where they would inevitably be harassed by an enemy much superior in mobility and organisation. Thucydides gives prominence to the efforts of Nicias to hearten the Athenians (76) and reports his speech in *oratio recta* (77). Demosthenes, who is merely stated to have made similar efforts and expressed similar views (78. 1), is made to play an even more subordinate role in the narrative describing the Athenian attempt to escape by land, though he was in command of the rearguard (78. 2) amounting to more than half of the whole force (80. 4). When the generals found themselves unable to make any further progress westwards and marched their men away by night in a southerly direction, his division fell into great confusion. At daybreak it was lagging far behind that of Nicias, which was able to press on rapidly because it had not become disorganised to the same extent (80. 3–81. 2). There is perhaps at this point an implied criticism of Demosthenes for having failed to check the spread of disorder so that the progress of his division was so much slower than that of Nicias (cf. 81. 2). Thucydides gives a more palpable indication

---

[1] Cf. the final exhortation of Nicias reported in *oratio obliqua* (69. 2–3).

that Demosthenes was at fault when, after being overtaken by the enemy, he lost time by drawing up his troops for battle instead of hurrying on: the result was that they were at once surrounded and became an easy target for enemy missiles when they were crowded together in an olive-grove enclosed by a low wall (81. 4). In this critical phase Demosthenes temporarily lost his nerve and became as panic-stricken as his troops (*ibid.* ἐν πολλῷ θορύβῳ αὐτός τε καὶ οἱ μετ' αὐτοῦ ἦσαν). He seems, however, to have recovered his composure later in the day sufficiently to negotiate the surrender of the Athenians in his division on terms guaranteeing that no prisoner should lose his life either by execution or by inhuman treatment in captivity (82. 2).

The passage in which Thucydides describes this surrender, though graphic and moderately detailed,[1] contains no information about the part played by Demosthenes.[2] Philistus is known to have reported that Demosthenes expressly excluded himself from the terms of capitulation and attempted to commit suicide.[3] The second item in this tradition is surely authentic, and the absence of any reference to it in the account of Thucydides affords striking evidence of his wish to focus attention upon Nicias as the protagonist of this final episode. Whether Demosthenes really concluded an agreement from which he was himself excluded is much more debatable. Philistus, who was himself a Syracusan, may well have reproduced an official fiction designed to clear the Syracusans from charges of having committed a breach of faith when they subsequently condemned Demosthenes to execution.[4]

---

[1] Points of interest are the meagreness of the response by the islanders to the proclamation offering them freedom (82. 1) and the filling of four shields with money handed over by the prisoners (82. 3).

[2] He does not even state explicitly that Demosthenes personally conducted the negotiations on the Athenian side, cf. 82. 2, πρὸς τοὺς ἄλλους ἅπαντας τοὺς μετὰ Δημοσθένους ὁμολογία γίγνεται.

[3] *F. Gr. Hist.* 556 F 53 (from Paus. I. 29. 12). Plutarch (*Nic.* 27. 2), evidently following the same tradition, adds that Demosthenes was forcibly prevented by the enemy from inflicting a fatal wound upon himself.

[4] Possibly he tried to commit suicide while parleying with the enemy during a truce but before the instrument of the surrender had been officially concluded

The death of Demosthenes evokes from Thucydides only a very brief comment. He makes the point that Demosthenes was the most hated enemy of the Spartans because of their disaster at Pylos, whereas Nicias was their best friend (86. 2–3). He then proceeds to explain why these feelings of goodwill did not save Nicias from being executed with his colleague (86. 4), and he adds his celebrated judgement, which has already been discussed,[1] that the miserable end of Nicias was unmerited (86. 5). He makes no corresponding pronouncement about the fate of Demosthenes, who is not mentioned again. Some modern scholars have felt that Demosthenes here suffers an injustice, since he was more deserving of sympathetic comment than Nicias.[2] This attitude appears at first sight to be entirely justifiable: Demosthenes had, after all, made vigorous efforts to retrieve an unfavourable situation for which Nicias was largely responsible, and when these efforts were unsuccessful, his sensible design to cut Athenian losses had been frustrated by the obstinacy of his colleague. It must, however, be remembered that the expression of opinion about the fate of Nicias, which is in no way concerned with the strategic direction of the campaign, is very exceptional, indeed in some respects unique. The absence of comment on the fate of Demosthenes is much more consistent with Thucydidean practice.[3] He was not sufficiently outstanding to demand special treatment, nor, though he died an honourable death in the service of his country, did his fate seem, to Thucydides at least, so exceptionally tragic as that of Nicias.

There remains something rather puzzling, indeed rather un-

by the exchange of oaths. This explanation would account for the fact that they were successful in preventing him from killing himself; they may then have claimed that by his action he had forfeited his personal right to be included in the agreement. It may be noted that suicide by defeated generals was traditionally Roman rather than Greek, but cf. 2. 92. 3 (the Spartan Timocrates in the battle off Naupactus).   [1] See above, 209–11.

[2] Freeman, 406; B. W. Henderson, *Great War between Athens and Sparta* (1927), 396.

[3] Gomme (1), II, 190 notes that 'Thucydides comments on the deaths of only three Athenians': these are Pericles, Cleon and Nicias. Antiphon might, as he suggests in a parenthesis, be added.

satisfactory, about the presentation of Demosthenes in the second half of the *History*, as in the first. He is an important figure whose actions and expressions of opinion are at some stages reported in detail. Readers must feel, however, that they are supplied with insufficient guidance to enable them to assess his quality with any confidence. Perhaps Thucydides has chosen to withhold such guidance because he was himself in two minds and wished to avoid any risk of being unfair. It may also be that, even when writing the second half of the *History*, he could never quite forgive Demosthenes for having so firmly rejected the principles of Periclean strategy.

CHAPTER XIV

GYLIPPUS

No military figure in the *History* of Thucydides was more consistently successful, or suffered fewer setbacks, than Gylippus. Because he played a prominent part in the defeat of the Athenians in Sicily, his contribution to the ultimate victory of the Peloponnesians could be held to have been greater than that of any Spartan except Lysander. He is not, however, ranked by Thucydides among the outstanding leaders of the Peloponnesian war, and it might be argued his leadership hardly receives the credit to which the records of his success might seem to entitle him. Nor does his personality, except in the narrative of his earliest achievements, make much impact upon readers of the *History*.[1] To Thucydides he was, it seems, neither a very great man nor a particularly interesting one, and this lukewarmness is reflected in the attitude of modern scholars, who have shown little inclination to study and assess his qualities. Dearth of evidence cannot have seriously restricted the treatment of him by Thucydides, whose knowledge of actions and plans on the Syracusan side becomes considerably fuller after his arrival: evidently plenty of information about him from trustworthy sources was available, including some about his motives. Thucydides might well have chosen to interpret the development of the struggle at Syracuse by contrasting the personal qualities of Gylippus with those of Nicias. At first indeed he does, but the contrast is not sustained beyond the end of 414, when the Athenian stranglehold on Syracuse was broken, and it is only at the close of his account that a little further light is briefly thrown upon the personality of Gylippus. That he has chosen to present

[1] Cf. the brilliant comment of de Romilly (Budé), VI–VII, *Notice* xvi, 'Gylippe reste toujours dans une demi-lumière'.

277

Gylippus in this way calls for some explanation, since it does not conform to his general attitude towards leading characters in the second half of his work. An explanation will be more readily found when his account of the part played by Gylippus has been examined and its distinctive features noted.

The Spartans sent Gylippus to Sicily in response to the recommendation of Alcibiades that they should appoint a Spartan officer to organise the forces already fighting the Athenians there and to bring pressure on others to lend support (6. 91. 4). He was instructed to assume command over the Syracusans[1] and to make every effort to provide assistance for them with all possible speed (93. 2). He is introduced simply as 'Gylippus the son of Cleandridas'. The absence of biographical detail about himself or his father, who had been prominent some thirty years earlier,[2] is consistent with Thucydidean practice, but it is perhaps a little surprising that no mention is made here, or indeed elsewhere, of any previous experience that he may have had in military leadership. At first the record of his actions, which is detailed and includes references to his views (104. 1; 7. 1. 1), leads the reader to form a very favourable opinion of his ability and personality.[3] It seems that Sparta has found, not perhaps another Brasidas, but at least a worthy successor to Brasidas.

While his fleet, which was mainly Corinthian, was assembling at Leucas, news from Syracuse exaggerating the progress of the Athenians in building their wall of circumvallation caused him to sail at once with only four ships instead of waiting for the rest, as he had evidently intended: while despairing of Sicily, he was

---

[1] The Syracusans presumably welcomed his appointment, partly in the expectation that it would help to allay the suspicions of potential allies still hesitating to commit themselves through fear of Syracusan imperialism (cf. 88. 1). Thucydides nowhere defines his legal status at Syracuse; it may well have been deliberately left unspecified, cf. *Camb. Hist. Journ.* vii (1942), 76.

[2] That Cleandridas had been granted citizenship at Thurii is mentioned where it becomes relevant (104. 2), but there is no reference to his banishment from Sparta (cf. Plut. *Nic.* 28. 4).

[3] Cf. the comment of W. S. Ferguson, *C.A.H.* v (1927), 296, that the case of Gylippus showed 'how much depended upon personality in warfare'.

determined to save Italy (6. 104. 1). He called first at Tarentum and then at Thurii, but a storm forced him to return to Tarentum and delayed him for some time (104. 2).[1] Eventually he reached Locri, where he learned that, contrary to earlier reports, Syracuse was not yet completely invested by land. Here he discussed with the Corinthian commander Pythen whether they should risk sailing straight for Syracuse or should proceed along the north coast of Sicily to Himera and, after collecting troops there, march overland to Syracuse (7. 1. 1). The report of this consultation, though very brief, is important for several reasons. It shows that Thucydides had information about a staff conference held by Gylippus before reaching Syracuse and was sufficiently interested in his strategic plans to mention an alternative which was considered but rejected. It also suggests that, at this stage at any rate, Gylippus acted with characteristically Spartan caution, since the plan chosen is seen to have been the less hazardous of the two.[2] A third point is that Gylippus is shown to have already appreciated the importance of pressing every available man into service against the Athenians in order to try to secure the advantage of superior numbers.[3] He recruited troops from Himera, Selinus, Gela and the Sicels and led them towards Syracuse. Thucydides mentions as one reason why the Sicels were willing to grant him support that he gave them the impression of having enthusiasm for his mission (1. 3–5).

When he approached Epipolae from the west, he set his troops in readiness for battle, but their ascent of the plateau was evidently unopposed, and he was able without difficulty to establish contact with the Syracusans, who had come to meet him (2. 3–4). Thucydides notes that his arrival marks a turning point in the struggle for

[1] He evidently visited Thurii in person, as is natural in view of its links with his father, and did not merely send an embassy.

[2] The Corinthian Gongylus, who with a single ship sailed direct to Syracuse, escaped interception (2. 1), as did twelve other ships which were to have joined Gylippus at Leucas (4. 7; 7. 1).

[3] It will be seen that not long after his arrival (7. 2) and again in the following summer (46) he left Syracuse to gather reinforcements from other parts of Sicily.

Syracuse (2. 4, παρὰ τοσοῦτον μὲν αἱ Συράκουσαι ἦλθον κινδύνου). His offer of a truce to the Athenians, if they would evacuate Sicily within five days, was doubtless made to stiffen morale on the Syracusan side and to provide both sides with evidence of his own self-confidence; he cannot have expected for a moment that the Athenians would accept (3. 1–2).[1] Thucydides presumably mentions this offer, even though nothing came of it, with the intention of showing that Gylippus knew how to conduct what would today be called psychological warfare. Two military moves which were halted before they could be developed are probably mentioned to draw attention to his appreciation of the dangers arising from the inferiority of the Syracusan troops in organisation and discipline. On the day of his arrival he withdrew his army without engaging the enemy when he saw the Syracusans falling into disorder (3. 3); and later he cancelled a night attack on a weak part of the Athenian wall when he realised that he had failed to secure the initial advantage of taking the Athenians by surprise (4. 2–3). He did, however, capture the enemy fort at Labdalum, partly through a diversionary threat to the main body of the Athenians entrenched behind their defences (3. 4). He was also now pressing on the construction of a cross-wall in a westerly direction across Epipolae; its purpose was to intersect the Athenian wall, which on the high ground of the plateau was not even nearing completion (4. 1; 5. 1). To achieve this aim it was necessary to dislodge the Athenians from their positions, and when he believed that the moment was ripe, he made a general attack. It was repelled with some loss (5. 1–3). He then addressed his troops in a speech briefly reported by Thucydides (5. 3–4). He blamed himself for their defeat: he had made the mistake of delivering his attack in the confined space between the fortifications, where he could not make use of his cavalry and javelin-throwers. This self-criticism may or may not have been valid, but there is no doubt that he assumed personal responsibility for the defeat in order that his troops might not attribute it to their own failings. He seized

[1] Freeman, 243.

the next favourable opportunity to resume the offensive, choosing his ground so as to have plenty of room in which to use the cavalry and javelin-throwers to advantage.[1] The Athenians were routed, and on the following night the Syracusan counter-wall was extended beyond the line of the Athenian wall. The danger that Syracuse might be completely blockaded by land was past (6. 2–4; 11. 2).

Thucydides believed, and wished his readers to believe, that Gylippus was almost entirely responsible for this vital success,[2] which in a few days transformed the military situation and won the initiative for the Syracusans.[3] There is a striking contrast between his leadership and that of Nicias. He is credited with determination, resourcefulness, military skill and a capacity for extracting good service from rather poor human material. If at times he acted cautiously, his caution is seen to have been justifiable. Here, one feels, is a military leader of high quality whose personality will continue to dominate the narrative of the war in Sicily so long as he remains in command. This expectation is not fulfilled, as will be seen below. His partial eclipse is only to a limited extent attributable to the ever-increasing importance of naval operations, in which he did not apparently play an active role. Thucydides seems to be no longer disposed to keep him in the foreground, though his achievements were by no means at an end.

Throughout the winter of 414/13 Gylippus was absent from Syracuse seeking aid from other parts of Sicily (7. 2; 21. 1). This

---

[1] The comment of Plutarch, Nic. 19. 7, ἔδειξεν ὁ Γύλιππος οἷόν ἐστιν ἐμπειρία, is probably an inference, by himself or some predecessor, from the account of Thucydides.

[2] As de Romilly (2), 78–9 (who analyses the whole episode in great detail) points out, the statement of Plutarch, Nic. 19. 6, that 'Thucydides says that the whole accomplishment was due to Gylippus' is not an error: although Thucydides nowhere expressly pronounces this judgement, it is implicit in his entire narrative. It is noteworthy that Plutarch makes this comment here and not later.

[3] Nicias had characteristically become pessimistic about Athenian prospects on land even before this Syracusan victory (4. 4; see above, 189).

quest for large reinforcements was based upon a sound appreciation of military needs, but Thucydides, who does not mention
the extent of its success, perhaps implies that the response was
disappointing.[1] When he returned to Syracuse in the spring, he
joined with Hermocrates and others in urging the Syracusans to
challenge the enemy at sea for the first time. His speech is reported
very briefly (21. 2), that of Hermocrates at greater length (21.
3–4). The plan for a simultaneous assault upon the Athenians by
sea and land may have been conceived by Gylippus, but he is not
expressly credited with it (22. 1). The value of his leadership in the
execution of the plan does receive recognition. He commanded
the land forces and delivered a surprise attack on the three
Athenian forts at Plemmyrium while the attention of the Athenians on shore was diverted by the struggle at sea, in which the
Syracusans were eventually defeated. All three forts were captured (23. 1–2), a most valuable success which much increased the
difficulties of the Athenians in bringing in supplies and contributed
to the deterioration of their morale (24. 3). The Syracusans now
believed that they might overwhelm the Athenians before the
reinforcement under Demosthenes could arrive. The efforts of the
Syracusans were directed mainly to naval operations, but another
attempt was made to throw the Athenians into confusion by
simultaneous attacks by land and sea. Gylippus led his army
against one side of the fortified Athenian camp, while troops from
the Olympieum threatened the opposite side. These attacks, however, were evidently diversionary and were not intended to
breach the Athenian defences; their aim was rather to provide the
Syracusan fleet with some prospect of taking the enemy by surprise (37. 1–38. 1).

The arrival of Demosthenes with his reinforcement plunged
the Syracusans into despair (42. 2) and temporarily restored the
initiative to the Athenians. The Syracusans took no action by land
or sea (42. 6). Gylippus may have felt confident in the defensive
strength of the Syracusan positions and have been content to

[1] Cf. Ferguson, *C.A.H.* v (1927), 299–300.

await an Athenian offensive, but his reaction to the new situation is not recorded. During the night battle on Epipolae he tried to stem the Athenian advance with Syracusan and Siceliot troops, but in vain; it was first halted and repelled by a Boeotian detachment (43. 6–7). Shortly after the defeat of this night attack he left Syracuse again to collect reinforcements, declaring that he now expected to storm the fortified camp of the Athenians (46). On this occasion he returned with substantial aid (50. 1). Later, during the naval battle in which Eurymedon was killed, he led a force along a sea-wall on the western side of the Great Harbour, his intention being to destroy the crews of Athenian ships forced ashore outside their own defences and to give the Syracusan sailors a better chance of towing these ships away. Here, however, his troops fell into disorder and were routed (53. 1–2).

Passages describing the increasing self-confidence of the Syracusans, as their grip on the enemy tightened, suggest that they were beginning to feel themselves less dependent upon external aid and external leadership. They envisaged the glory that would be theirs if the Athenian expeditionary force was destroyed (56. 2; 59. 2).[1] The account of the final battle in the Great Harbour is preceded, in accordance with Thucydidean practice, by reports of speeches by generals. On the Athenian side the speaker is Nicias, on the Syracusan side 'the generals of the Syracusans and Gylippus' (69. 1, cf. 65. 3). The latter speech (66–8) contains nothing distinctively Spartan or peculiarly appropriate to Gylippus, whereas some of the ideas expressed suggest that they are of Syracusan origin.[2] It is even less a speech by Gylippus than that of 'Cnemus and Brasidas and the other generals of the Peloponnesians', which precedes the account of the second battle against Phormio (2. 86. 6), is a speech by Cnemus. Largely formal references to Gylippus in conjunction with 'the Syracusans' occur in the description of the Athenian attempt to escape by land (7. 74. 2; 79. 4; 82. 1;

[1] Cf. 51. 1. In 59. 2 καὶ οἱ ξύμμαχοι, found only in B, is probably an error.
[2] Especially those of 68. 1–3. Freeman, 347–8, believes that the speech represents what a Syracusan general said. Luschnat, 94–9 (wrongly in my opinion), treats it as a speech of Gylippus.

83. 2). From the time of his arrival he normally led the Syracusan and allied land forces in person, and he was evidently in command of the army which harried the Athenians during their desperate retreat and finally forced the survivors to surrender. He is less prominent than might have been expected in the narrative of these operations, even though they are described mainly from the Athenian point of view. His personal contribution to their success is not determinable because it is not until they were virtually complete that any action or plan is attributed exclusively to him.

Thucydides does, however, include in his concluding pages on the war in Sicily three references to Gylippus which strike a more personal note and throw some light on his character. When the Athenians found that they could make no further progress in their attempts to reach Catana and succeeded in slipping away unobserved by night in a southerly direction, most of the Syracusan and allied troops blamed Gylippus, accusing him of having deliberately allowed the enemy to escape (81. 1). Thucydides supplies no details but seems to imply that the charge was false. The incident is interesting because it provides evidence of Syracusan antipathy towards Gylippus. While Thucydides does not discuss the origin or the extent of this feeling and does not allude to it elsewhere,[1] he is careful to draw attention to its existence and evidently believes it to be of more than merely biographical interest. The passage may supply a clue to the general attitude of Thucydides towards Gylippus and will be considered again below. When the Athenians were being butchered in the river bed of the Assinarus, Nicias surrendered to Gylippus personally 'because he trusted him more than the Syracusans'[2] and begged him to stop the massacre. Gylippus accepted his plea and gave orders for the first time that the Syracusans should take prisoners (85. 1-2). This passage reveals the character of Nicias rather than that of Gylip-

---

[1] The difference of opinion between Gylippus and the Syracusans on the treatment of Nicias and Demosthenes (86. 2, considered below) might be regarded as evidence of friction, but it occurred when hostilities had ceased and his mission was ended.

[2] The reason why Nicias took this view is explained in 86. 4.

pus.[1] There is, however, reason to believe that the latter was influenced by humanitarian feelings, since he could presumably have taken Nicias as his prize without agreeing to halt the slaughter of the Athenians. The third passage is less creditable to Gylippus. He objected to the decision to put Nicias and Demosthenes to death, but his opposition was evidently the outcome neither of compassion nor of a conviction that to execute them would be an act of injustice. His motive, according to Thucydides, was to add to his other achievements the distinction of taking his two principal adversaries home with him to Sparta (86. 2).[2] It is true that Thucydides realistically acknowledged the extent to which leading men were influenced by self-interest and that he did not find the pursuit of it necessarily reprehensible.[3] In this case, however, the question at issue had legal and moral aspects, and if the conscience of Gylippus allowed him to ignore them completely in the interests of personal aggrandisement, he can hardly be acquitted of callousness. Thucydides would not perhaps have referred at all to this protest by Gylippus—it had no effect upon the outcome—if he had not wished to mention its slightly disreputable motive.

The Syracusans did not choose to hail Gylippus as their saviour and liberator. They did not load him with distinctions comparable with those granted by the Amphipolitans to Brasidas or by a later generation of Syracusans to Timoleon. It is true that Greeks tended to honour the dead more lavishly than the living. It is also true that the relations between the Syracusans and Gylippus in the period between the execution of the Athenian generals and his return to Greece are not altogether clear.[4] Thucydides is silent, and the secondary authorities are a little suspect and also slightly

[1] See above, 206–7.

[2] καλὸν τὸ ἀγώνισμα ἐνόμιζέν οἱ εἶναι. The same phrase is twice used of the fame which the Syracusans hoped to win by destroying the Athenian expeditionary force (56. 2; 59. 2).

[3] See above, 95.

[4] 8. 13 implies that he returned with the Peloponnesian ships in the spring of 413 but does not exclude the possibility that he may have left Sicily earlier.

conflicting.[1] There is, however, no doubt that the Syracusans withheld from him such honours as would have been recognised throughout the Greek world as an acknowledgement that they owed their victory to his leadership.[2] They may well have done him less than justice, feeling that any recognition of his services might detract from their own prestige. A similar view, however, seems to have been taken at Sparta, where, so far as is known, he was granted neither honours nor advancement. Although it was not until more than seven years after his return from Sicily that he was convicted of misappropriating money, he was not entrusted with any major command during this period, and at the time of his disgrace and banishment he was serving as a subordinate to Lysander.[3] Rank and seniority tended to weigh more heavily than merit when the Spartan authorities made military appointments,[4] and Spartan leaders distinguishing themselves in distant areas might incur jealousy at home.[5] Nevertheless, experience of serving abroad and of leading contingents from other Greek states ought, one feels, to have been a strong recommendation when the war in Asia began, and an even stronger one when the defects of Spartan leadership there were revealed.

There is, therefore, some indication, though it does not amount

[1] Timaeus, who stated bluntly that they sent him away ἀκλεῶς καὶ ἀτίμως (F. Gr. Hist. 566 F 100 c), may be suspected of bias arising from a desire to represent the victory over the Athenians as a wholly Siceliot achievement. According to Diodorus (13. 34. 4) the Syracusans 'honoured with the spoils of war the Spartans whom Gylippus had commanded', a vague and superficial statement which does not necessarily presuppose the conferment of any honours upon Gylippus personally.

[2] Even Timaeus could hardly have used the phrase quoted in the previous note if Gylippus had received the not uncommon honour of citizenship (which was bestowed upon his father by the Thurians).

[3] The fullest version of this well-known story is that of Plutarch, Lys. 16. 1–17. 1, cf. Diod. 13. 106. 8–9. Thucydides probably wrote his sixth and seventh books in the years immediately after the end of the war in Sicily (see above, 15); if so, he cannot have known about the ultimate fall of Gylippus when he wrote these books.

[4] Gylippus is said to have been a mothax (Aelian, V.H. XII, 43), which could well have been a handicap.

[5] Cf. 4. 108. 6–7 on Brasidas.

to conclusive evidence, that a substantial body of opinion did not consider the mission of Gylippus to have been an unqualified personal success. Hence the lukewarmness of Thucydides in his overall treatment of Gylippus would probably not have surprised many contemporaries. On the other hand, it is impossible to believe that Thucydides was content to accept a current verdict uncritically. It was never his practice merely to reproduce public opinion or official judgements—as an intellectual, he tended to distrust both—but rather to draw his own conclusions from all the evidence available to him, which must normally have far exceeded the evidence presented to his readers. Here he does not explain what underlies the change in his attitude towards Gylippus, which completely alters the balance of his general assessment. He does not point to any defects in the leadership of Gylippus in the campaign of 413; he merely refrains from bringing him into the foreground, thus giving the impression that somehow his leadership failed to maintain its previous standards. He does, however, supply one hint, namely his reference to the outcry by the Syracusans against Gylippus during the Athenian retreat (81. 1), which suggests that friction had already developed. Fortunately this hint is clarified by evidence derived from the Sicilian tradition, which is not wholly dependent upon Thucydides and provides a certain amount of supplementary information, some of it probably authentic. Fragments of Timaeus attest that Gylippus had become unpopular with the Syracusans, who resented not only the severity with which he imposed discipline of the Spartan type but also his Spartan manners and his avarice.[1] At the outset Gylippus must have been enthusiastically acclaimed by the Syracusans, and although, as Thucydides shows, he recognised at once the need for improving their military discipline and organisation,

---

[1] Timaeus, *F. Gr. Hist.* 566F100a–c. Timaeus was certainly less trustworthy than Philistus, the originator of the Sicilian tradition, who was an eyewitness of the struggle at Syracuse (*F. Gr. Hist.* 556F56). It is possible that Timaeus gave an exaggerated picture of the rift between Gylippus and the Syracusans. That he antedated it is suggested by the charge of inconsistency made against him by Plutarch, *Nic.* 19. 5.

he seems to have handled them with tact and understanding. Doubtless they responded eagerly enough for a time to his efforts to remedy their defects, but, with their chronic intolerance of authority, they may well have shown some disinclination to submit to long and arduous training. If Gylippus then became increasingly exasperated and finally lost patience with them, his behaviour would have been typical of Spartan leaders except Brasidas, and he doubtless forfeited their favour, as well as that of Thucydides. This situation may well have developed during the spring of 413 after his return from his quest for reinforcements. If, while maintaining his energy and resourcefulness, he lost his capacity for handling sympathetically the strangely assorted forces under his command,[1] the quality of his leadership was no longer the same, and the impression created by the changed attitude of Thucydides towards him is fully justified.

Why then, if there was a decline in the leadership of Gylippus, does Thucydides omit to draw the attention of his readers unequivocally to it? The reason may be that it is a side-issue, which is extraneous to his main theme and to a certain extent conflicts with it. His account of the struggle in Sicily during the summer of 413 is designed to show how the Syracusans exploited the advantage gained in the previous autumn and, except for a brief period after the arrival of Demosthenes, continuously increased their pressure upon the Athenians until they finally destroyed them. Nicias is prominent throughout the narrative covering this period because the weakness of his leadership was to a large extent responsible for the Athenian disaster. It is the tragedy of Nicias no less than that of the Athenians, and his self-devotion heightens its tragic element. If there was a deterioration in the leadership of Gylippus, it did not affect the ultimate result and was a factor of secondary importance; whatever influence it may have had was in a direction contrary to the general trend of events. Hence Thucydides mentions Gylippus whenever he plays a prominent

[1] The Corinthian leaders, who were mainly responsible for organising the Syracusan naval effort, may have shown more understanding.

part in the struggle but no longer chooses to focus attention upon his ability or his personality.

There is perhaps one other factor that has influenced the attitude of Thucydides towards the contribution of Gylippus to the defeat of the Athenians. He had a profound admiration for Hermocrates, whom he pictures as a statesman of almost Periclean stature, endowed with outstanding qualities of intellect and character.[1] Hermocrates, like Pericles, excelled as a war leader in the broadest sense rather than as a commander of troops on the battlefield; indeed his brief period of office as general in 414 was one of continuous setbacks for the Syracusans. His role is to give intelligent advice and inspiring encouragement, especially at critical moments, and his calm wisdom is shown to have proved an invaluable asset to the Syracusan cause. Although Thucydides gives Gylippus credit for having saved Syracuse by breaking the Athenian blockade, he has chosen, rightly or wrongly, to represent Hermocrates rather than Gylippus as the principal architect of the ultimate Syracusan triumph.

[1] See above, 10.

CHAPTER XV

ASTYOCHUS

WHILE holding the office of *nauarchos* from 412 to 411, Astyochus exhibited defects of leadership similar to those of Cnemus and Alcidas, his predecessors in the Archidamian war. He lacked enterprise in conducting military operations as well as finesse in diplomacy; he also failed to win the confidence and loyalty of his subordinates and of the troops under his command. He might indeed be deemed to have earned greater discredit, even though he suffered no serious defeat, than either Cnemus or Alcidas: during his tenure of office the Peloponnesians and Athenians were far more evenly matched in naval power than they had been during the Archidamian war, so that his opportunities to benefit the Peloponnesian cause were correspondingly greater. On the other hand, it could be argued, in extenuation of his many failures, that his mission in Asia was an extraordinarily difficult one, demanding exceptional and diverse qualities of leadership. Such experience as he may have had in subordinate commands cannot have equipped him at all adequately for dealing with the problems with which he was confronted. He was responsible for a vast area, embracing the whole Asiatic coast with its adjacent islands. It was seldom possible for him to obtain information immediately concerning the whereabouts and the strength of Athenian naval forces, which were from time to time reinforced by squadrons from home. Nor could he always be certain when Peloponnesian reinforcements would arrive or how large they would be. The Greek cities in revolt from Athens were for the most part a liability, since few could provide military or financial resources on a considerable scale; but it was very desirable to win and retain their good will. It was even more important to remain on friendly terms with the

Persians, whose financial aid was indispensable. Astyochus was, however, like other Spartans except Lysander, totally unfitted to deal effectively with the oriental methods of diplomacy practised by the satraps. He was unlucky in that, when he arrived in Asia, he was unable to rely, as had been expected, on the services of Alcibiades, who was so well equipped both by innate talents and by experience to handle intricate negotiations but was now no longer even pretending to work for the Peloponnesians.

Thucydides is seldom disposed to excuse ineffective leadership, whatever mitigating circumstances there may have been. In this instance he evidently concluded from the evidence at his command that Astyochus was indeed incompetent, and while he includes no explicit assessment, his verdict is made abundantly clear.[1] It should, however, be observed that Astyochus, unlike Cnemus and Alcidas, is not presented merely as a typical Spartan, even though his defects are largely those associated with Spartan leadership. His personality leaves a very distinct imprint upon the parts of the eighth book describing the operations and negotiations in Asia while he was serving there. Thucydides has taken pains to convey to the reader what manner of man this Spartan admiral was: though not a very imposing figure, Astyochus occupied a position of great authority at a critical stage of the war, and his use of that authority deeply influenced the course of events. This picture takes shape mainly through the attention devoted to his relations with others, which were often uneasy and sometimes stormy. It is also noteworthy that, though Thucydides does not seem to have had much access to confidential information on the Peloponnesian side after the flight of Alcibiades to Tissaphernes, there are references to the motives of Astyochus (8. 40. 3–41. 1, cf. 23. 4). If his tenure of office had belonged to the period covered by the first half of the *History*, he would probably have remained little more than a name. Thucydides would, one

---

[1] It is reflected in the contemptuous comments of modern scholars, cf. K. J. Beloch, *Gr. Gesch.* II, 1 (1914), 393, 'die Unfähigkeit des lakedaemonischen Admirals'; B. W. Henderson, *Great War between Athens and Sparta* (1927), 412, 'a quarrelsome blunderer'.

imagines, have been content with a bare summary of his actions, in which attention might have been drawn to his typically Spartan lack of enterprise. The presentation of Astyochus illustrates how in the second half of the *History* Thucydides is much more inclined to accept the principle that the personality even of secondary figures may deserve, or indeed demand, close study.

After assuming office in the summer of 412 (8. 20. 1), Astyochus sailed with four ships to Chios, whence he found himself compelled to proceed at once to Lesbos to deal with a most unpromising situation there. At the instigation of the Chians, who provided most of a small expeditionary force sent to Lesbos under Spartan leadership, Methymna and Mytilene had revolted (22); but the rebels were in danger of being overwhelmed by a much superior Athenian fleet, which promptly recovered Mytilene (23. 1–3). On reaching Lesbos Astyochus did what he could to sustain and spread this revolt, but the inadequacy of his resources proved an insuperable handicap; he therefore withdrew to Chios, and the Lesbian revolt collapsed (23. 2–6). Although the narrative of this episode is somewhat confused, his motives at each stage are clearly defined, and in a situation which was not of his making his actions seem to have been, if not conspicuously daring, at least defensible in the circumstances.

Chios itself was now hard pressed by the Athenians (24. 2–3), and there was some danger of betrayal by democratic conspirators. Astyochus, who was visiting Erythrae on the mainland, was summoned back to Chios by the oligarchical government and remained there until the beginning of winter engaged on measures designed to suppress disaffection (24. 6; 31. 1).[1] While at Chios he learned that a large fleet under Therimenes, including a contingent from Sicily, had arrived at Miletus from the Peloponnese (31. 1–4). His reaction to this welcome news is surprising. He did

[1] These measures, which were not completed (31. 1), do not seem to have been wholly successful, since further disaffection, apparently of similar origin, occurred soon afterwards (38. 3).

not, as might have been expected, sail at once to Miletus to join Therimenes, who was charged with the duty of handing over the newly arrived fleet to him (26. 1), and to hold very necessary conferences with Tissaphernes on strategic and financial issues (29. 1). On the contrary, the general improvement of the Peloponnesian position encouraged him to sail in the opposite direction with a fleet of twenty ships[1] to Clazomenae and other cities on the mainland, where he conducted a series of minor operations which achieved nothing of value and evidently involved waste of time and effort (31. 1-4). The concentration of Athenian naval forces at Samos (30. 1), which caused a relaxation of the pressure on the Chians, doubtless led him to believe that he might win support for the Peloponnesians on the mainland opposite and north of Chios.[2] Thucydides implies in his account of these events that a bolder and more enlightened commander would have hastened to Miletus and sought to engage the Athenian fleet in a decisive battle.

At this point Thucydides reports very briefly the first of many conferences at which Astyochus failed to secure the willing acceptance of his views and was apparently too weak to impose his authority as admiral. When envoys arrived from Lesbos with plans for a second revolt there, he was prepared to support them. Some of his allies, however, including the Corinthians who provided half of his Peloponnesian squadron of ten ships, were unenthusiastic because the first revolt had failed. Accordingly he abandoned the project (32. 1). A similar incident occurred immediately afterwards (32. 3), when he was again requested to support a Lesbian revolt. He held a conference with the Spartan Pedaritus, who had recently arrived at Chios to take up the post of local commander, and with the Chians. Astyochus urged that aid should be sent to the Lesbians: if the revolt succeeded, the

---

[1] Ten were Peloponnesian (a squadron of six had reached him at Chios after his withdrawal from Lesbos, 23. 5) and ten Chian.

[2] His preoccupation with the strategy of trying to extend the area of revolt northwards will be discussed below.

Peloponnesians would gain more allies, while, if it failed, damage would at least be inflicted upon the Athenians. Pedaritus, with the concurrence of the Chians, would have nothing to do with this plan. Claiming that his command entitled him to complete control of all Chian forces, he refused to allow Astyochus to use Chian ships for the proposed expedition to Lesbos.[1] This stormy conference, which illustrates very clearly the inability of Astyochus to win the support of others, brought to a climax his increasingly strained relations with the Chians. After declaring that he would grant them no further help if they needed any, he sailed for Miletus to assume command of the main Peloponnesian fleet there (33. 1). Rather ignominiously he had a narrow escape from encountering a much superior Athenian fleet, which might well have annihilated his small squadron. At Erythrae he had a further meeting with Pedaritus on a minor issue, which does not appear to have caused further friction (33. 2–4).

The narrative of Thucydides does not contain any direct criticism of Astyochus during this stage of his command in Asia, but it does predispose readers to conclude that he possessed neither the intellectual talents nor the strength of character demanded of a leader occupying a position to which so much responsibility was attached. He was under a handicap because the Peloponnesians at home and their new allies in Asia gravely underestimated the recuperative powers of the Athenians and also because the Peloponnesian squadron which he commanded at Chios was so small. Yet, while he was constantly seeking means of benefiting the Peloponnesian cause, he was never in full control of the situation; he nowhere inspired confidence in others because he seemed content to let circumstances dictate his actions. His principal and indeed almost sole strategic aim was to impose a severe strain on the resources of Athens, military and financial, by

---

[1] H. W. Parke, *J.H.S.* L (1930), 45, regards this passage as evidence that 'a Spartan sent out on a separate command by the home authorities was not subject even to the navarch'. It may be, however, that Pedaritus was a stronger personality than Astyochus and was for this reason able to impose his will upon his superior.

inciting and sustaining as many revolts as possible on the Asiatic coast and the nearby islands. In adopting this policy he was doubtless carrying out with too much rigidity and too little imagination the orders issued by the Spartans at home, who were slow to grasp the needs of the situation in Asia. Very few Ionian cities possessed military forces of any value, and while revolts might deny the Athenians some useful bases, they also saddled the Peloponnesians with the responsibility of defending cities incapable of defending themselves. When the Athenians had built up considerable naval forces in Asia, the Peloponnesians might with advantage have modified their strategy, adapting it to meet the rapidly changing situation. In one respect especially Astyochus was very probably led into error by adhering too closely to his instructions. It has been suggested above that he was unwise to remain so long in the area around and north of Chios instead of sailing to Miletus. In making this decision he seems to have been influenced by the strategic plan adopted, after much negotiation, in the spring of 412 at Corinth, when it was agreed to send forces to support revolts first at Chios, then at Lesbos and lastly in the Hellespont (8. 2). This plan continued for a long time to serve as the basis of Peloponnesian strategy (cf. 39. 2; 80. 1), and it was doubtless responsible for the persistence of Astyochus in wishing to support insurrectionary movements at Lesbos despite the disapproval of his colleagues and allies. The Peloponnesian scheme to extend the area of revolt northwards from Chios was evidently designed to culminate in the closing of the Athenian shipping route through the Hellespont. When Lesbos was recovered by the Athenians, and the forces which had been on their way to the Hellespont (22. 1) were disbanded (23. 5), Astyochus was surely making a mistake in remaining so long at Chios. Like Nicias in Sicily and other weak but conscientious generals, he sought to avoid criticism by adhering very strictly to his instructions.[1]

---

[1] G. Fabrizio, *Contributo storiografico-storico allo studio della guerra deceleica* (1946), 227–8, defends Astyochus, arguing that to try to exhaust the Athenians was the best policy in the circumstances and that even his failures contributed to that

When he eventually arrived at Miletus about the middle of November,[1] the second of the agreements between the Peloponnesians and the Persians, which came to be known as the treaty of Therimenes (43. 3; 52), had, it seems, already been concluded (36. 1–38. 1).[2] The statement that Therimenes, because he was not supreme commander, showed lack of determination in his transactions with Tissaphernes on the provision of pay for the Peloponnesian crews (29. 2) implies some criticism of Astyochus for having delayed so long. Nevertheless, for some time after his arrival the Peloponnesians received satisfactory support from Tissaphernes and from the Milesians (36. 1). At Chios, however, the situation continued to deteriorate, and Astyochus received an urgent request for help. When he refused, Pedaritus sent a letter of complaint to Sparta against him ὡς ἀδικοῦντος (38. 4). The accusation of injustice is significant: he was not charged with cowardice or incompetence or faulty judgement but with maliciously withholding assistance from the Chians and Pedaritus because of their rejection of his proposals at an earlier stage (cf. 40. 3). The reaction of the Spartans to the complaint of Pedaritus was so prompt as to suggest that, even before they received it, they were already dissatisfied with Astyochus. Eleven commissioners were appointed to advise him and were sent out with a fleet under Antisthenes, which sailed in the second half of December. It was a commission of the same kind as those appointed to advise Cnemus (2. 85. 1) and Agis (5. 63. 4) when military operations were deemed to have been mishandled; but its members

end. If this view has any validity—and I believe that it has not—it certainly receives no support from Thucydides, who creates an unfavourable impression of Astyochus from the outset.   [1] Busolt, 1440 n. 4 and 1442.

[2] It is far more probable that Astyochus reached Miletus after the conclusion of this treaty (Schwartz, 73; Brunt, 83 with n. 1) than that it was negotiated by Therimenes but concluded by Astyochus (C. Meyer, *Die Urkunden im Geschichtswerk des Thukydides* [1955], 71–2). The passage in which Thucydides mentions the treaty and reproduces its text verbatim (36. 2–37) interrupts rather awkwardly his narrative describing the arrival of Astyochus (36. 1) and the handing over of the fleet by Therimenes (38. 1). The passage about the treaty appears to have been added after the narrative was completed; there was therefore difficulty in inserting it in its true chronological setting.

were charged with the exceptional duty of dismissing Astyochus from office if they thought fit (8. 39. 2). The Spartans were inclined to accept the accusation of Pedaritus that Astyochus was allowing himself to be influenced by personal animosity to the detriment of Peloponnesian interests.

While the fleet bringing the commission was on its way, Astyochus received an even more urgent appeal from the Chians and Pedaritus to come to their aid with his entire fleet before their desperate situation became irretrievable (40. 1–3).[1] Thucydides states that Astyochus καίπερ οὐ διανοούμενος διὰ τὴν τότε ἀπειλήν, ὡς ἑώρα καὶ τοὺς ξυμμάχους προθύμους ὄντας, ὥρμητο ἐς τὸ βοηθεῖν (40. 3). These words are carefully chosen in order to throw light upon the character of Astyochus. His first reaction was to reject the appeal for purely selfish reasons: the threat recalled here was that he would not grant aid to the Chians, if ever they asked for it, because they had refused to accept a proposal of his (33. 1). It might appear that, when he had second thoughts and yielded to pressure from the allies, he acted creditably in deciding that public interest must be given precedence over a personal grudge. There were, however, many occasions during his term of office when he lacked the strength of character to stand firm against opposition from subordinates, and it is natural to infer that here again he was guilty of the same weakness. The sequel is also revealing. Before he could start from Chios, news arrived that the Peloponnesian fleet with the commission aboard was at Caunus, and he promptly sailed thither, abandoning his expedition to Chios, in the belief that it was more important to establish contact with this substantial reinforcement and with the commissioners (41. 1). Thucydides, who could well have omitted any reference to the decision to sail to Chios, does not appear to have considered this further change of mind on the part of Astyochus to have been the outcome of sound reasoning. If the needs of the Chians were so urgent, the new fleet could surely have remained for a short time

---

[1] The somewhat emotional tone of this passage suggests that it closely reproduces the text of the dispatch.

at Caunus, where its leaders felt themselves to be out of danger (39. 4). The eagerness of Astyochus to meet the commissioners οἵ ἧκον κατάσκοποι αὐτοῦ suggests that he was not unwilling to pass on to them a share of his responsibilities (cf. 39. 2).[1]

While on his way to Caunus, he was prevailed upon by the people of Cnidus not to disembark his crews, as he had evidently intended, but to sail at once against an Athenian squadron sent from Samos to intercept the fleet bringing the commissioners (41. 3–4). The chief aim of Thucydides in giving details about this unimportant incident seems to be to show how Astyochus once again allowed others to make up his mind for him. He did succeed in engaging the Athenian squadron and gained an advantage in a confused skirmish in stormy weather, but this minor victory seems to have been mainly due to good fortune and the errors of the enemy (42. 1–4). He then returned to Cnidus, where he was joined by the fleet of Antisthenes from Caunus and also by Tissaphernes, who came to confer with the eleven commissioners on the vexed question of co-operation between the Peloponnesians and Persians in the prosecution of the war (42. 4; 43. 2).

This conference achieved nothing. Lichas, one of the eleven, bluntly demanded a new treaty on the ground that those negotiated by Chalcideus and Therimenes were unacceptable because they involved recognition of Persian suzerainty over all the territory occupied during the invasion of Xerxes. Tissaphernes was furious and broke up the conference by withdrawing abruptly (43. 2–4); his hostility towards the Peloponnesians may have been due as much to the influence of Alcibiades, who was already trying to persuade him to change sides (cf. 52), as to the provocative speech of Lichas. It is likely enough that Astyochus, who may well have presided, tried in vain to curb the outspokenness of Lichas and to mollify Tissaphernes, but he is not mentioned in the account of the conference. This silence on the

[1] Fabrizio, *Contributo storiografico-storico*, 15–16, again attempts to defend Astyochus; his defence is unconvincing and presupposes that Thucydides here gives a misleading account.

part of Thucydides is consistent with his normal method of presenting individuals. As soon as the commissioners arrive, Astyochus is no longer entirely alone in directing Peloponnesian strategy in Asia but has to take into account the views of the commissioners; he is accordingly allowed to recede into the background, emerging only when he is personally involved in some episode. Information could, however, with advantage, have been given about his relations with the commissioners, who did not exercise their right to dismiss him and apparently condoned his unenterprising policy. Their influence certainly did not produce a new sense of urgency: no attempt was made to aid Chios or to challenge the Athenian fleet at Samos. The Peloponnesians did, however, support the revolt of Rhodes, which was a most valuable acquisition because its financial resources relieved them of the need to beg Tissaphernes for money; but there seems no adequate reason why their fleet remained inactive there for eighty days until the winter was almost over (44. 1–4).

The intrigues of Alcibiades at the court of Tissaphernes, which have already been discussed,[1] had already been in progress for some months. Astyochus had received from Sparta an order to execute Alcibiades, who somehow became aware of his danger and fled from Miletus to Tissaphernes (45. 1). Thucydides does not state where Astyochus was when he received this order, but he was probably still at or near Chios; had he been at Miletus, Alcibiades might not have been able to escape in time.[2] It was while Astyochus was at Miletus and before he sailed for Cnidus that he went to Magnesia to confer with Tissaphernes and Alcibiades about the remarkable messages sent to him by the Athenian Phrynichus, who first disclosed to him the plan of Alcibiades to induce Tissaphernes to change sides and then offered to betray

[1] See above, 240–50.
[2] The view of some modern scholars that Astyochus warned Alcibiades of the Spartan order (cf. Busolt, 1437 n. 6 and 1469) has nothing to recommend it, though he may well have taken no action on receiving the order at Chios intending to investigate the charges when he reached Miletus (*J.H.S.* LXXVI [1956], 103 n. 25).

to him the Athenian base at Samos (50. 1–5). Thucydides appears to owe his knowledge of this puzzling episode to an informant or informants unacquainted with the motives of Astyochus, and he devotes much more attention to the parts played by Phrynichus and Alcibiades. Why Astyochus chose to go in person to Magnesia is not explained. His principal reason was surely to find out whether there was any truth in the report of Phrynichus that Alcibiades was intriguing with an oligarchical faction at Athens and was trying to induce Tissaphernes to transfer Persian support from the Peloponnesians to the Athenians; and if the report proved to be true, to do his best to scotch this plan.[1] Being no match for Alcibiades and Tissaphernes in diplomatic skill, he apparently allowed himself to be reassured that neither of them had any intention of harming the Peloponnesian cause, and he returned to Miletus satisfied on that score.[2] The report of this episode provides further evidence that he lacked both shrewdness and understanding of others.

At the end of the winter Tissaphernes, after the breakdown of his negotiations with an Athenian embassy led by Peisander (56. 4), decided to resume his subsidies to the Peloponnesians and concluded a third treaty with them, which included the promise of aid from a Phoenician fleet (57–9). Shortly afterwards the Peloponnesians left Rhodes in answer to an appeal from Chios, where the situation was becoming even more desperate, but they found themselves unable to relieve the pressure on the Chians without fighting a major sea battle against the Athenians, and so they put in at Miletus (55. 2; 60. 2–3). What part Astyochus played in these events cannot be determined, since his name is not mentioned. He cannot, however, have been wholly eclipsed by the eleven commissioners, since in the spring of 411 he was vainly considering how he could help the Chians (61. 1). During his absence at Rhodes a Spartan officer named Leon had been appointed to

[1] I have discussed the part played by Astyochus *ibid*. 102–3.
[2] The charge that Astyochus succumbed to bribes from Tissaphernes, which Thucydides reports with the caveat ὡς ἐλέγετο (50. 3), will be discussed below.

succeed Pedaritus, who had been killed in battle (55. 3). Leon
sailed with twelve allied ships to Chios, where with the assistance
of this squadron the Chians had slightly the better of a naval
engagement against the Athenians (61. 2–3). It is true that part of
the main Athenian fleet was absent from Samos at the time (44. 3;
55. 1), so that there was no need to keep Miletus heavily guarded;
but Leon demonstrated that, given the willingness to accept risks,
it was not by any means impossible to render aid to the Chians
from Miletus. Even Astyochus now plucked up courage (63. 1,
ἐθάρσησε), especially as most of the Athenian ships operating at
Chios had been sent to the Hellespont to deal with revolts there
(62. 2). He went in person to Chios and, after bringing back the
allied ships stationed there, sailed with his entire fleet against the
Athenians at Samos. The Athenians declined battle because their
confidence in one another was impaired by the suspicion and unrest which soon culminated in the overthrow of the democracy
(63. 1–2); they were also heavily outnumbered.[1] Astyochus at
last showed himself willing to fight a sea battle on a large scale
provided that the Peloponnesians enjoyed a substantial advantage;
and his action helped to relieve the pressure upon the Chians, who
were no longer in danger of being forced to capitulate.

Thucydides reports in greater detail a very similar episode in
which Astyochus was prominent (78–9) during the political crisis
at Athens leading to the establishment of the Four Hundred.[2]
Bitter feeling, amounting almost to mutiny, developed among the
Peloponnesian forces at Miletus against Astyochus and Tissaphernes, who were held jointly to blame for the unsatisfactory
lack of progress in the war. Astyochus was criticised for his

---

[1] They had 73 ships, whereas the Peloponnesians had 112 (cf. Fabrizio, *Contributo storiografico-storico*, 10–12).

[2] Some scholars, including Schwartz, 75–8, maintain that Thucydides has
inadvertently given two reports on the same episode (63. 1–2; 78–9). Since the
former passage is so brief, the problem is a very difficult one (more difficult
than that of the two reports on debates at Samos, considered above, 253 n.
3); it has little or no relevance to the presentation of Astyochus by Thucydides.

unwillingness to fight a decisive battle at sea either earlier when his forces were in the ascendant and the Athenian fleet was small or at the present moment when the Athenians were weakened by faction and their fleet divided (78).[1] The upshot of these complaints was that Astyochus held a conference with his officers at which it was decided to fight a decisive battle (79. 1). Once again he is seen to have allowed his hand to be forced, on this occasion, like Cleon at Amphipolis, by the clamour of his own rank and file whose knowledge of military strategy cannot have been profound. Once again the supreme commander is seen to have been not fully in command. Nor did the decision of the staff conference achieve the desired result: the Athenians refused to risk a battle, having only 82 ships against 112, and withdrew to Samos (78. 2). The Peloponnesians were prepared to press their attack on Samos from the promontory of Mycale, but when they learned that the squadron under Strombichides, which had been recalled from the Hellespont, had arrived to reinforce the Athenians, they promptly retired towards Miletus. Strengthened by this reinforcement, the Athenians were now ready to fight and sailed to Miletus with this intention, but the Peloponnesians in their turn declined battle, though they still enjoyed a slight superiority in numbers (79. 3–6). Many of the Peloponnesians and their allies disapproved of this decision (83. 3).

This series of events gave rise to profound depression among the Peloponnesian leaders at Miletus.[2] Even when their whole fleet was concentrated in the same place, they had not felt strong enough to engage the enemy; and because Tissaphernes was con-

---

[1] Schwartz, 76–7, rightly points out that, since Astyochus assumed command of the Peloponnesian fleet at Miletus, there had never been an occasion when the Athenian fleet had been small in relation to that of the Peloponnesians. Thucydides is, however, only recording the complaints of the troops and was doubtless fully aware that neither accuracy nor logic was to be expected from men on the verge of mutiny.

[2] They are defined only as οἱ Πελοποννήσιοι in 80. 1, but since they proceed to make a decision evidently reached as the result of a conference, the phrase must refer to those responsible for the direction of operations, including Astyochus, the commissioners and probably the leaders of allied contingents.

tinuing his policy of failing to pay the subsidy regularly or in full, the financial burden of maintaining very large forces was becoming unbearable (80. 1). Time was no longer on their side, and they could not now hope to break the Athenian capacity to resist by keeping their own forces intact and encouraging more revolts in Ionia. Accordingly it was decided to send forty ships under Clearchus to the Hellespont, where Pharnabazus had offered to pay for their upkeep (80. 1-2). When the commissioners left the Peloponnese in the previous winter, they were instructed to take this action if they thought fit (39. 2), and it is surprising that they delayed so long in view of their unsatisfactory relations with Tissaphernes. The attitude of Astyochus towards the decision is unknown. He perhaps welcomed it because it was authorised by the Spartans at home who could not blame him, and he may well have felt relieved that he was now unlikely to be in a position, before his term of office ended, to fight a decisive battle against the Athenian fleet at Samos.

The news that the Athenians at Samos had recalled Alcibiades increased Peloponnesian distrust of Tissaphernes, who had given him asylum for many months and was believed to have been deeply influenced by his advice (83. 1). The troops at Miletus, and even some men of higher rank, openly voiced their anger against Tissaphernes in conversations with one another, especially as he was now showing still greater reluctance to provide them with pay. They actually threatened desertion if their grievances were not met,[1] and they held Astyochus responsible for the present deplorable situation, charging him with toadying to Tissaphernes for the sake of personal profit (83. 2-3).[2] Such was the distrust

---

[1] The report on these complaints suggests that they at least began before the squadron under Clearchus was sent to Pharnabazus (80. 1-2); they are doubtless mentioned at this point because they form an apt prelude to the scene in which Astyochus was threatened by mutineers (84. 1-3).

[2] ἐπιφέροντα ὀργὰς Τισσαφέρνει (83. 3) means 'encouraging Tissaphernes to follow his own (Tissaphernes') inclinations'. Goodhart n. *ad loc.* has an excellent discussion of this phrase. The problem raised by the words διὰ ἴδια κέρδη will be considered below.

and hostility with which Astyochus was regarded that shortly before his term of office ended he was involved in a brush with some of his more turbulent critics. In this scene, which is graphically described by Thucydides, he played a most ignominious part. When a mob of Syracusan and Thurian sailors pressed upon him demanding pay, he answered them with disdain and threatened their spokesman with his staff. They retaliated by rushing angrily at him with stones in their hands, and he was compelled to take refuge at an altar to avoid injury (84. 1–3). Shortly afterwards the tension was ended by the arrival of Mindarus, who had been appointed to succeed him as *nauarchos*. He left for home accompanied by some Milesian envoys and Hermocrates, who were travelling to Sparta to denounce Tissaphernes (85. 1–4).

One last problem to which the career of Astyochus gives rise remains to be discussed, namely his alleged acceptance of bribes from Tissaphernes. Thucydides refers to this allegation in two passages, the first reporting the visit of Astyochus to Tissaphernes at Magnesia (50. 3, προσέθηκέ τε, ὡς ἐλέγετο, ἐπὶ ἰδίοις κέρδεσι Τισσαφέρνει ἑαυτὸν καὶ περὶ τούτων καὶ περὶ τῶν ἄλλων κοινοῦσθαι) and the second summarising the complaints directed by the troops at Miletus against Tissaphernes and Astyochus (83. 3, διὰ ἴδια κέρδη).[1] In neither passage does Thucydides express his opinion on the question whether Astyochus was guilty or innocent. He evidently felt impelled to mention the accusation of bribery because, whether true or false, it materially influenced the course of events by damaging the morale of the Peloponnesian forces at Miletus. He is not reporting gossip for its own sake. Clearly, however, he did not possess sufficiently reliable evidence to permit him to give a verdict with absolute confidence on the charges against Astyochus. He is always reluctant to commit himself

---

[1] See the previous note. In 45. 3 Alcibiades is stated to have advised Tissaphernes to bribe the trierarchs and the commanders of allied contingents, and this policy appears to have been successfully adopted except in the case of Hermocrates; but there is no mention of bribing the supreme commander.

where there is any shadow of doubt, and in such cases he is careful to use the caveat ὡς ἐλέγετο or some similar phrase.[1] On another vexed question, which belongs to the period immediately after Astyochus returned home—the question why Tissaphernes journeyed to Aspendus, where a large Phoenician fleet was assembled, and yet did not bring it back with him for service against the Athenians—Thucydides includes a long discussion (87. 1–5) and gives his own opinion (4, ἐμοὶ μέντοι δοκεῖ σαφέστ-ατον εἶναι). He might well have likewise debated whether Astyochus was guilty or not, but he has not chosen to do so. It may be that he did not feel himself to be in a position to produce any cogent arguments on this question and was therefore content to leave it entirely open. There is, however, a much more convincing explanation. To Thucydides the important point was that Astyochus by acting as he did brought upon himself charges of having succumbed to bribery; his guilt or innocence was a relatively insignificant matter, which might be deemed to be of mainly biographical interest.

Much attention has already been given to the practice of Thucydides of instilling his personal views into the mind of the reader without actually expressing them. In the eighth book, doubtless because it lacks a final revision,[2] this practice is less prominent than in other books. He does, however, give the reader at least some indication of his own judgement on the accusation against Astyochus. Suspicion is seen to have fallen on Astyochus because of his failure both to extract from Tissaphernes full and regular subsidies for the Peloponnesian forces (50. 3; 83. 3) and to bring about a decisive battle against the main fleet of the Athenians (83. 3). The narrative of Thucydides certainly suggests

---

[1] The closest parallel to ὡς ἐλέγετο in 50. 3 is 7. 86. 4; both refer to rumours, which could not be confirmed or denied, current at the time of the incident described. ὡς λέγεται is much commoner (cf. 1. 24. 4; 118. 3; 138. 1; 2. 48. 1; 3. 79. 3), and λέγεται is similarly used (cf. 2. 77. 6; 93. 4; 3. 113. 6; 4. 24. 5).

[2] Cf. Schwartz, 88–90, who cites (89) the absence of any verdict on the alleged acceptance of bribes by Astyochus as an example.

that these failures could have been due to the defects of Astyochus in character and in intellectual qualities and that there is no need to seek any more sinister explanation of them, as his exasperated troops did.[1] The feeble attitude of Astyochus towards Tissaphernes is sharply contrasted with the forthrightness of Hermocrates (29. 2; 45. 3; 85. 3) and Lichas (43. 3–4, cf. 52). This weakness has been seen to be a characteristic of Astyochus in other negotiations,[2] and he seems to have also lacked the ability to persuade even his subordinates to agree to his recommendations. His unwillingness to fight a decisive battle at sea unless he enjoyed a very substantial superiority in numbers—when the Athenians naturally refused his challenge[3]—is perhaps militarily defensible on the ground that the Peloponnesian fleet was still inferior in technical efficiency.[4] His caution is also to some extent vindicated by the disastrous experiences of his successors in the Hellespont,[5] though Mindarus was unlucky in having to engage Athenian fleets led by exceptionally able commanders. Yet readers of Thucydides are bound to feel that Brasidas or Gylippus would have found ways of being more aggressive without taking foolish risks, of handling Tissaphernes more satisfactorily, and of welding the oddly assorted Peloponnesian and allied forces in Asia into an effective weapon. Astyochus mishandled almost every situation with which he was confronted throughout his tenure of office. His conduct is very adequately accounted for by the defects

[1] The conclusions of modern scholars on this question reflect, as is usual, the impression created by Thucydides. No recent writer, so far as I am aware, accepts the validity of the accusation without some reservation or qualification, except Delebecque, 110, 129, 160 and 173. Hatzfeld, 234 and 253, seems inclined to find Astyochus guilty, cf. F. Taeger, *Alkibiades* 2nd ed. (1943), 174 and 181. Most scholars, however, maintain that he was innocent, including Busolt, 1445 n. 5, Fabrizio, *Contributo storiografico-storico*, 253–4, cf. 5–17 and 30–4 (whose detailed arguments are not all equally convincing), and apparently E. Meyer, *G.d.A.* IV, 2 (1956), 306.

[2] See above, 293–4 and 301–2.

[3] Cf. W. S. Ferguson, *C.A.H.* V (1927), 333: 'the Spartan admiral had adopted the policy of fighting only for a certainty.'

[4] Fabrizio, *Contributo storiografico-storico*, 5–17.

[5] Fabrizio, *ibid.* 254; Meyer, *G.d.A.* IV, 2, 306.

plainly exposed in the narrative of Thucydides. It is most unlikely that Thucydides believed him to have been guilty of accepting bribes.[1]

[1] According to Xenophon (*Hell.* 1. 1. 31) Astyochus spoke in support of Hermo-crates when the latter complained at Sparta about the behaviour of Tissa-phernes. This evidence does not help to establish the innocence of Astyochus, who could not have acted otherwise without appearing to confirm the charges made against him by his troops and was doubtless eager to find excuses for his own lack of success in Asia.

CHAPTER XVI

CONCLUSION

T HE foregoing chapters would appear to have established the general principle that there are differences between the two halves of the *History* in the treatment of leading individuals. Thucydides devotes more attention in the second half to examining the personality of such individuals and their relations with others, not because he has become more interested in biography but because he is more convinced that their general qualities constitute a vital factor in determining the course of history. Leaders in the first half of the *History* tend to be idealised, like portraits by Greek sculptors before the close of the fourth century, or to be presented as representatives of a species. Pericles is the ideal statesman, Brasidas the ideal man of action; Archidamus, Cnemus and Alcidas typify the defects of conventional Spartan leadership, while Phormio represents the dash and skill of the Athenian navy. Thucydides shows relatively little interest in their personal feelings or aspirations, nor does he study the motives leading them to take important decisions which affected, for good or ill, the fortunes of their cities. His treatment of them as individuals is less subtle and penetrating than his treatment of leading personalities in the second half of his *History*, notably Nicias and Alcibiades.

These differences should not be exaggerated. It would be unwarranted to maintain that all the major figures in the first half are presented in one way and all the major figures in the second half in another way. A case might be made for believing that Thucydides began to change his attitude towards leading individuals before he reached the end of the first half, since he records the exploits of Brasidas and Demosthenes so fully, especially in the fourth book. This wealth of detail, however, is more probably the result of having access to unusually good and reliable sources: as has been pointed out in earlier chapters, he leaves unanswered some important questions about Brasidas,[1] and he seems reluctant to commit himself to a verdict on the ability of Demosthenes.[2] The case of Cleon is an exceptional one because the feelings of Thucydides about him were exceptionally emotional and personal. That Thucydides developed a different attitude towards individuals in the second half of the *History* receives less support from his treatment of Spartans than from his treatment of Athenians.[3] If, however, his presentation of Cnemus and Alcidas in the first half is compared with his presentation of Astyochus in the second, it will be seen that more light is thrown upon the personality of Astyochus, though he was neither more competent nor more interesting than his two predecessors. Admittedly Gylippus, though he belongs to the second half, is a somewhat colourless figure, but there are, as has been pointed out,[4] good reasons why he is allowed to fade into the background during the later stages of his mission to Sicily.

The events recorded in the first half of the *History* differ somewhat in general character from those recorded in the second half, and these differences have to a certain extent influenced the treatment of leading individuals. In the Archidamian war most military operations were modest in scale, took place on or near the Greek mainland, and were completed within a few months. Together with diplomatic activities connected with them, they could normally be supervised from Athens or Sparta, where major decisions were taken. Consequently, military commanders, though tactically in control and free to a limited degree to use their own initiative, had little scope for developing their ideas about major strategy, on which they normally had to accept orders from home. Brasidas in the north-east was exceptionally independent, since communication between him and Sparta was so difficult, but he was severely hampered in the later stages of his

---

[1] See above, 164–5. [2] See above, 120–1.
[3] This point, which is a perfectly legitimate one, has been made to me by D. M. MacDowell. [4] See above, 286–9.

309

mission when, because of disagreements about its aims, he was in conflict with the Spartan government. During much of the period covered by the second half of the *History* the situation was different. The commanders of the Athenian expedition to Sicily were given special powers because they were to conduct a campaign in a distant theatre of war, so that even Nicias, in spite of his reluctance to take any action not specifically authorised by the assembly, could not wholly avoid making, or at least sharing in, major strategic decisions. During the Ionian war, although neither the Peloponnesians at Miletus nor the Athenians at Samos were enormously far removed from their home bases, the slowness of communications, combined with special circumstances including the negotiations with Tissaphernes and the oligarchical revolution at Athens, gave Spartan *nauarchoi* and Athenian generals an unusual measure of independence. The greater isolation of the leaders on both sides in the period covered by the second half of the *History* may be regarded as a contributory cause of the closer attention paid to their personal qualities. In itself, however, this factor accounts only to a small extent for the divergences of treatment noted in foregoing chapters.

There is no justification for believing that these divergences are due to fundamental differences in the sources available to Thucydides. It is true that, when writing about Nicias and Alcibiades, the two most prominent figures in the second half of the *History*, he evidently had the good fortune to be able to obtain very full, and in many instances secret, information from persons whom he considered to be trustworthy. On the other hand, though he seems to have regarded the evidence of his own eyes and ears as his best possible source (1. 22. 1–3), it is very improbable indeed that he witnessed any of the events recorded in the second half of the *History* in which Nicias or Alcibiades played a part, whereas before his banishment he must have had abundant opportunities for personal observation of leading individuals on the Athenian side. He doubtless heard speeches delivered by them in the assembly; he certainly had close contacts with several of them when he was strategos, and probably earlier; he may well have served in military forces commanded by some of them. Except perhaps in the case of Demosthenes, and there only to a limited degree, he has not chosen to take full advantage of these opportunities to elucidate their personal qualities.

A striking difference between the two halves of the *History*, and one relevant to the treatment of individuals, is that in the first half debates are mostly public, in the second mostly private. It is true that in the sixth book there are full and admirable reports on public debates at Athens, Syracuse and Camarina, including speeches in *oratio recta*; that the eighth book contains shorter accounts, without speeches in *oratio recta*, of public meetings at Athens and Samos at the time of the oligarchical revolution. A feature of the second half, however, is the abundance of reports, some of them detailed, on conferences between a few leading individuals. In many cases it was undesirable that what was said should be widely known, so that, while some subordinates were doubtless present, the attendance was limited for reasons of security. Thucydides is content in some instances to state only the outcome of the conference, but often he reports proposals rejected as well as those accepted. He sometimes contrasts with one another the leading individuals attending the conference and occasionally studies their motives.

In the first half of the *History* reports on conferences of this kind are few and brief. One of them records the discussions held by Alcidas at Embatum in 427 with his Peloponnesian officers and some representatives of his Asiatic Greek allies as soon as he received confirmation of the news that Mytilene had capitulated (3. 29. 2–31. 2). This passage has been considered in an earlier chapter;[1] its purpose is to underline the typically Spartan lack of enterprise displayed by Alcidas. An interesting feature of it is that it includes a speech by an Elean officer in *oratio recta*, which is not used elsewhere in reports on small conferences. Thucydides probably wrote it at an early stage in the composition of his *History*

---

[1] See above, 143–4.

before he adopted the practice of confining himself to *oratio obliqua* in such cases. In the fourth book he refers to consultations held in 425 when Eurymedon and Sophocles rejected proposals by Demosthenes first to land at Pylos and later, when bad weather had made a landing unavoidable, to build fortifications there (4. 3. 1–4. 1). As has been suggested in an earlier chapter,[1] Thucydides probably mentions these discussions in order to stress his point that the occupation of Pylos was largely fortuitous. During the mission of Brasidas relations between him and Perdiccas were uneasy because their interests were irreconcilable, and two stormy interviews, while they were on active service together, are mentioned (4. 83. 2–6; 124. 4).[2] Yet Thucydides, though exceptionally well-informed about Brasidas, provides hardly any detail on the many private consultations in which he took part. A passage describing the antecedents of the Boeotian victory at Delium illustrates how public speeches are preferred to private in the first half of the *History*. Ten of the eleven Boeotarchs were opposed to committing their forces to battle because the Athenians had already left Boeotian territory; Pagondas, who was at the time in command in accordance with a system of rotation, disagreed with his colleagues (4. 91). A conference must have been held at which Pagondas explained why he favoured offensive action, but Thucydides does not expressly mention it. He prefers to include a speech in *oratio recta* giving the substance of what Pagondas said to successive bodies of troops as they were brought before him (4. 92). This speech consists mainly of arguments in favour of taking the offensive which must already have been expressed at the meeting of the Boeotarchs and would indeed have been more appropriate to that occasion.

To take a negative case which is concerned with the same series of events viewed from the Athenian side, Thucydides is very well informed about Athenian plans for the operations in the Megarid and in Boeotia in 424;[3] he probably attended meetings when the

---

[1] See above, 107–8.

[2] Cf. 78. 2–5 on his negotiations with the Thessalians.   [3] See above, 111.

board of strategoi considered these plans, which must have been kept secret through fear of betrayal to the enemy. Nowhere does he refer to any discussion of them by the strategoi. To have learned whether there was any opposition would certainly have been valuable to the reader; the scheme to gain control of Boeotia was so complicated and so dependent upon synchronising action at widely separated points that Nicias, who was a member of the board, might have been expected to oppose it. Light might also have been shed upon the relations between Demosthenes and Cleon, which are obscure. It is indeed remarkable that Thucydides nowhere records the substance of discussions by boards of strategoi at Athens, which could, one imagines, have been among his most valuable sources of information about Athenian war policy in the years before his banishment. He may not himself have attended many meetings of the board, but his election as strategos suggests that he enjoyed sufficient standing at Athens to have been in close touch with prominent men, such as Nicias, who had long experience of service on the board. If he had chosen to include information about some of its most important meetings, the rivalries and associations between Athenian leaders, which undoubtedly influenced the course of the war, would have been much clearer to posterity.

The tendency of Thucydides in the first half of the *History* to prefer public debate to private is also illustrated by his treatment of embassies. Some meetings of public assemblies at which embassies from other states were present are reported fully, with speeches in *oratio recta* by their spokesmen. The account of the debate at Athens in 433, when unnamed envoys from Corcyra and Corinth addressed the assembly, is a notable example (1. 31–44). Thucydides makes much of such great occasions, using the speeches as a means of providing his readers with instruction. Often, however, the Greeks conducted inter-state diplomacy through negotiations, which might be held in secret, between small bodies of delegates, and sometimes negotiations of this kind produced important results. In the first half of the *History* Thucydides normally refers very briefly to diplomatic exchanges, mentioning only the bare results,[1] so that there is doubt whether or not they involved public debate. Nowhere, however, does he give details about negotiations which were undoubtedly conducted in private,[2] as is his practice in the second half, especially in the fifth[3] and eighth books. Nor does he often name any of the persons who played a part in inter-state negotiations.[4] His treatment of the diplomatic activity leading to the Peace of Nicias is remarkable. He explains at some length why public opinion at Athens and Sparta was in favour of peace (5. 14–15); he analyses the personal feelings of Nicias and Pleistoanax (16–17. 1); he summarises the terms on which peace was concluded (17. 2) and then reproduces verbatim the text of the treaty with its list of signatories (18–19). He provides, however, no details whatever about the course of the negotiations to which an event of major importance owed its origin, apart from a bare statement that they continued throughout the winter and that each side put forward many claims (17. 2). One consequence arising from this dearth of information is that nothing is known about the part played by Nicias in the discussions leading to the Peace which was to bear his name.

Reports in the second half of the *History* on consultations of various kinds between a few individuals have been discussed in foregoing chapters, some of them in detail. Many such reports are brief, but some are lengthy amounting to miniature antilogies. Among the most striking are those on conferences between the Athenian generals in Sicily; on deliberations about granting Peloponnesian support to revolts by Asiatic Greeks; on the advice

---

[1] Examples are: 1. 58. 1; 126. 1–2; 139. 1; 2. 59. 2; 67. 1–2; 3. 3. 1; 86. 3; 4. 41. 3.

[2] 1. 28 (on exchanges between Corcyra and Corinth) is a possible exception. The negotiations between Archidamus and the Plataeans (2. 71–4), which Thucydides reports in the form of a dialogue, were not really private, since both sides certainly wished their views to be publicly known. Nor was the congress at Gela (4. 58), at which Hermocrates spoke (59–64), a private meeting.

[3] I.e. the latter part, 25–116.

[4] He does so occasionally, cf. 1. 139. 3; 2. 12. 1–2; 67. 1–2; 95. 3; 3. 5. 2; 92. 2.

given to Alcibiades to Tissaphernes; on the reception of Peisander and his embassy at the court of Tissaphernes. Examples of discussions reported briefly are those between Gylippus and Pythen at Locri (7. 1. 1–2) and between Astyochus and Pedaritus at Chios (8. 32. 3–33. 1). Some of the consultations recorded by Thucydides were not attended by any leader of outstanding importance. In his long account of the complicated intrigues in the Peloponnese after the Peace of Nicias he summarises negotiations between persons of whom some are left nameless and others, though named, do not play a significant part elsewhere in the *History*.[1] Phrynichus, whose views expressed at two conferences are recorded in some detail (8. 27. 1–5; 48. 3–49), was prominent as an enemy of Alcibiades and a leader of the Four Hundred but hardly merits a place among the greatest figures of the Peloponnesian war. Nevertheless, the prevalence of reports in the second half of the *History* on discussions between small numbers of individuals has the effect of throwing light upon the personal qualities of great men. There is every reason to believe that Thucydides adopted the practice of including such reports largely because he had this object in view.

A significant contrast may be drawn between the treatment of two individuals much involved in negotiations: the Macedonian king Perdiccas, who belongs almost wholly to the first half of the *History*,[2] and the Persian satrap Tissaphernes, who is not mentioned before the eighth book.[3] Both exerted some influence upon the course of the Peloponnesian war from the fringes of the Greek world, and they, and their policies, have affinities which are not purely superficial. Each sought to promote his own interests and those of his country by seizing opportunities offered by

[1] The only Peloponnesians named more than once are the ephors Cleobulus and Xenares (5. 36. 1; 37. 1; 38. 3; 46. 4). The former is not mentioned elsewhere in the *History*, the latter only as governor of Heraclea (51. 2).

[2] There are four brief references to him in the second half: 5. 80. 2 and 83. 4; 6. 7. 3–4; 7. 9.

[3] L. Pearson, *T.A.P.A.* LXXVIII (1947), 54–5, refers briefly to the fact that they are differently treated.

the conflict in which so many Greek states were involved. In their relations with the Greeks both were compelled by deficiencies in the military resources available to them to rely largely upon diplomacy and intrigue, to which they applied themselves with zest and pertinacity. Thucydides was evidently unable to obtain much reliable information about their aims and plans, partly because these were for the most part deliberately concealed and partly because he seems to have been exclusively dependent upon what he could learn through Greeks who had had contacts with them. Despite these similarities he presents Perdiccas and Tissaphernes very differently. The account of the former is little more than a bare factual summary, except where he was associated with Brasidas, and even passages describing their uneasy relations reflect only the viewpoint of Brasidas. The numerous occasions on which Perdiccas changed sides are for the most part mentioned,[1] but hardly any effort is made to account for these shifts of policy. Consequently, since the *History* is the principal source on his reign, there have been very wide divergences of opinion among modern scholars who have tried to assess his ability.[2] On the other hand, though Tissaphernes is perhaps an even more mysterious figure, Thucydides makes every endeavour to analyse his aims and motives,[3] using inference and logical argument to explain why he acted as he did in cases where satisfactory evidence was unobtainable.[4] Readers of the *History* are left in no doubt that Tissaphernes was a remarkably shrewd schemer, whose subtlety made him a match even for Alcibiades. The picture of him, though inevitably somewhat incomplete and blurred, is much more carefully drawn than that of Perdiccas. Each of these pictures is characteristic of the half of the *History* to which it belongs.

[1] Cf. the table compiled by Grundy, I, 371–2.

[2] He is rated much higher by F. Geyer, *Makedonien bis zur Thronbesteigung Philipps II* (1930), 77 and J. Papastavrou, Ἑλληνικά, xv (1957), 256–65, than by Grundy, I, 371–2 and S. Casson, *Macedonia, Thrace and Illyria* (1926), 181.

[3] See above, 4 n. 1.

[4] The fullest and most interesting passage is 8. 87. 1–5, which has been discussed above, 254–6.

There are also appreciable differences, which are relevant to the present investigation, between the general character of the speeches in the first half of the *History* and those in the second. Many of the former are attributed to 'the Corinthians' or 'the Mytileneans' or 'the Thebans' and are evidently based upon what was said by a spokesman, or possibly in some instances more than one spokesman. The second half contains hardly any speeches of this type,[1] though it is true that Athenagoras (6. 35-40) and Euphemus (6. 81-7) have some affinity with unnamed spokesmen because neither plays any part in the *History* except as a speaker on a single occasion.[2] Speeches in the first half by eminent men, including even Pericles, provide the reader with relatively little enlightenment on their personalities, as has been pointed out in earlier chapters. It is upon the policy of the speaker that attention is mainly centred, though his capacity to convince his audience is naturally an important factor. Sometimes in general tone and occasionally in substance these speeches are not altogether well-suited to the speaker. In the second half, on the other hand, the speeches are more revealing and instructive in regard to personality, the most striking example of all being the speech of Alcibiades at Sparta (6. 89-92). The general content of speeches in the first half differs significantly from that of speeches in the second half. The former are concerned to a very considerable degree with broad issues relevant outside the immediate context of the speech in space and time, with human behaviour in politics and war, with the legal and moral problems of inter-state relations. Because Thucydides was so much influenced by the intellectual movement of Periclean Athens, he was himself profoundly interested in such questions, and it is mainly in the speeches in the first half

[1] The Melian Dialogue, which is to be ranked among the speeches, is conducted by unnamed Athenians and Melians (5. 84-113). It is, however, unique in many ways. A case might be made for believing that it was not originally written for its present context but was intended to be a separate minor work, an experiment in a new medium which was beginning to supplant the antilogy. The speech of the Syracusan generals and Gylippus (7. 66-8) has been considered above, 283.

[2] Athenagoras, it may be noted, is by no means an impersonal mouthpiece.

that he has given them prominence. He has sought to evoke interest in them from his readers, including readers of future ages, and he has indeed been successful in his aim. It is this element of universality in the speeches that has attracted more attention and given rise to more discussion than any other feature of his work. The speeches in the second half are written in the same language and style as those of the first; arguments of a similar character are used, and there are still plenty of generalisations. Speakers tend, however, to apply themselves more directly to the practical problems of the moment, to the immediate occasion of the speech, and are less inclined to visualise it as an exemplification of broader, more universal issues. It is partly for this reason that their personalities are more sharply portrayed.[1]

It is natural to believe, though impossible to prove, that during the long exile of Thucydides the influence of the Athenian intellectual movement upon him gradually faded. Skapte Hyle in Thrace, where he is said to have written his *History*,[2] was an obscure place in a remote area. Opportunities of associating with other Athenians, except perhaps fellow exiles, must have been very few, and especially with Athenians whose background was similar to his own.[3] On the other hand, he was free to travel anywhere outside territory under Athenian control, even in time of war, and he expressly claims that his banishment gave him the advantage of plentiful contacts with the Peloponnesians (5. 26. 5), from whom he undoubtedly gleaned a substantial amount of information. Such contacts with other Greeks, which must have been illuminating to an Athenian brought up in the intellectual coterie of Periclean Athens, may well have contributed to a

---

[1] It may be observed that in a recent discussion of the speeches by Adcock, 27-42, there are far more references to those in the first half than to those in the second; and that of the references to the latter two are to passages where the wording reflects the personality of the speaker (34), while another is to a speech which 'is part of the characterization of Nicias' (41).

[2] The evidence of Plutarch, *Mor.* (*De exilio*) 605c, has some value, that of Marcellinus, *Vit. Thuc.* 25, 47, hardly any.

[3] There was doubtless greater freedom of movement during the years of nominal peace after 421.

gradual change of outlook affecting his interpretation of his function as a historian. In the first half of the *History*, written probably during the early years of his exile, he is often seen to visualise historical events as raw material for the establishment of general principles about human behaviour, usually the collective behaviour of whole communities under stress of war. This interest in general lessons is maintained to a limited degree to the end of his *History*, though there is little trace of it in the eighth book which is so manifestly no more than a draft. It seems, however, that in the course of his long exile, while he studied the progress of the war at his leisure as a spectator (5. 26. 5), a new concept evolved in his mind. The events of the war which he recorded began to assume in themselves a significance transcending the lessons about human society which might be extracted from them—a step, it may be thought, in the development of history as an independent subject. His study of events in the light of this new concept appears to have altered somewhat his attitude towards causation, which was always of absorbing interest to him. Hitherto the paramount element in determining the course of events, especially in the political sphere, has been found mainly in the collective feelings and decisions of large bodies of men, often public assemblies; the influence of leading individuals has been seen largely in their ability or inability to steer public opinion. In the second half of the *History*, while Thucydides continues to attach importance to the reactions of the masses, he seems to have come to believe that the personality of leading individuals was a much more influential factor than he had been prepared to acknowledge; that their aspirations and rivalries, their general qualities of leadership, their success or failure in imposing their will on other leaders might, and often did, determine the course of history. It may be that the principal reason for this shift of attitude should be sought in the impression made upon him by the career of one man—Alcibiades.

INDEX

(Persons mentioned once in the appendix to chapter II are not included)

320